T0386255

UNTOLD
LONDON

Praise for *Untold London*:

It's sometimes important to see the things you love through other's eyes, and in Untold London Dan Carrier has whetted my appetite for my city, just as I was beginning to take it for granted. He's the perfect on-street companion: insatiably curious, generous, good humoured, scurrillous where necessary, pointing out the fine detail that makes London the most interesting city in the world.

Just pick up a copy and set off. You'll be amazed at what you've missed.

Sir Michael Palin

I have this image of Dan doing everything on the *Camden Journal* - which of course is an award winning local newspaper, regularly voted the best in the country,if not the planet. Dan seems to write most of it - and I am sure gets up at six in the morning to deliver it,door to door,before he starts a day's work. He is the most enterprising journalist I know,and the most committed,with a strong social conscience. I admire everything he writes.

Hunter Davies, OBE

While the rest of us were locked away in our flats and houses during lockdown - Dan Carrier was touring the city. In his imagination. These extraordinarily fascinating essays take us on a personal, historical, biographical ghost-ride around the crevices and crannies of the capital city - a place that Dan knows better than anyone else. His curiosity and knowledge are evident on every page - as is his deft skill as a writer. He's a 'Boz' for our age - and these his loving sketches of a city situated somewhere between sleep and waking.

Kevin MacDonald

Untold London is a good read - wide-ranging, lively, entertaining, surprising, and written with a lifelong journalist's skill and curiosity.

David Gentleman

UNTOLD LONDON

Stories From Time-Trodden Streets

DAN CARRIER

First published 2022

The History Press
97 St George's Place, Cheltenham,
Gloucestershire, GL50 3QB
www.thehistorypress.co.uk

British Library Cataloguing in Publication Data.
A catalogue record for this book is available from the British Library.

ISBN 978 1 8039 9049 1

Typesetting and origination by The History Press
Printed and bound in Great Britain by TJ Books Limited, Padstow, Cornwall.

MIX
Paper from
responsible sources
FSC® C013056

Trees for Life

PREFACE

E very Thursday morning, the drill would be the same.

I would sit down at my desk, roll up my sleeves, twiddle and stretch my fingers like a concert pianist about to embark on a marathon bit of Scott Joplin, and get started, rustling up 1,500 words for a column in the *Westminster Extra*.

The content was based on whatever had tickled me over the past seven days. It was fun to do – a way of decompressing after working for a weekly newspaper that goes to print on a Wednesday night. Interviews and gossip, quirky news, opinion and observation, review and preview, historical bits, the odd urban myth, and honourable mentions for anything else that had piqued my interest over the previous seven days.

On 23 March 2020 the coronavirus pandemic had crept in our direction, starting as a sparsely covered news item in January about something happening a long, long way away, to the virus reaching Italy in February, and then moving with frightening speed through our nation, just as the first crocuses appeared.

Certainly interesting times to be a newspaper reporter, and having found myself in the midst of the biggest story myself or my colleagues had ever covered, my gentle musings for the *Westminster Extra* Diary page had been shoved to the dustiest reaches of my mind in the week we went into lockdown.

But there it was, the regular Thursday deadline, virus or no virus and there I was, with a blank page to be filled and more fear than joy in my heart after what had been a week of frightening news from uncharted territories.

There were no gigs or exhibitions I could now preview. My attempt at light-hearted jape-y tales were redundant, and felt disrespectful and flippant. Other papers had already done the 'Top 10 Lockdown Books', the 'Shows that have Gone Online', and other hastily scrabbled together cultural features for the non-news sections. I didn't feel much like reading lifestyle in virus times pieces elsewhere, so the idea of bodging together something similar from listings on the internet for my page was an unattractive morning's work.

I sat back at home, still getting used to the new non-office-based idea of work, and thought about those empty streets just beyond the front door.

I felt wistful, pining, and wondered why slow walkers along Oxford Street or packed Tube carriages, the Chuggers and litter and garish lights and expensive food, and all those other irritants, had ever given me the grumps.

To see it all now, I thought, and decided I felt homesick, despite lying back on my sofa at the time.

There are writers who make you feel nostalgic for a city that one may never have known personally, that ceased to exist long before you were born, but was created by our ancestors and whose foibles and characteristics we have inherited. HV Morton's gently slanted insights through his *In Search of ...* series, JB Priestley's more honest and considered *English Journey*, and then all those wonderful London writers: Norman Lewis, Patrick Hamilton, Dickens, and Pepys.

Without being able to walk down streets we take for granted, and thinking of descriptions of what we were missing, I had a topic for the next edition. I would write a soppy but heartfelt message to my city, and ask the reader to take my hand on a journey through time and place, and remember, discover, investigate.

As I cast my eye over the streets I knew well and had therefore taken for granted, the reasons behind telling their stories also struck me.

'It is a curious characteristic of our modern civilisation that, whereas we are prepared to devote untold physical and mental resources to reaching out into the further recesses of the galaxy or delving into the mysteries of the atom – in an attempt, as we like to think, to plumb every last secret of the universe – one of the greatest and most important mysteries is lying so close beneath our noses that we scarcely even recognise it to be a mystery at all,' author Christopher Booker once wrote.

He was considering why we tell each other stories.

'At any given moment, all over the world, 100s of millions of people will be engaged in what is one of the most familiar forms of all of human activity,' adds Booker. 'In one way or another they will have their attention focused on one of those strange sequences of mental images which we call a story. We spend a phenomenal amount of our lives following stories: telling them; listening to them; reading them, watching them being acted out on the television screen or in films or on a stage. They are far and away one of the most important features of our everyday existence.'

Bearing this in mind, recalling the tales heard, read, imagined between the covers of this book felt a good way to remember what had gone before us, and remember that such things would happen again.

It wasn't planned this way. After finishing the first instalment, I wanted to carry on a virtual exploration, so I did. And so it continued throughout the pandemic, and, with a few tweaks here and there, that is what you will find in this book – a lockdown love letter to our city.

I'd like to send many thank yous to Joyce Arnold for all her help over the years, not least with the text you are about to read.

The following yarns are for my dad, who loves to tell a story, and for Juliet, Luc and Laurie, who listen patiently to mine.

DOGS, DOLPHINS, DANCERS AND DINERS

We had been due to go to Manchester Square and visit the Wallace Collection but our vague plan to take in an exhibition with a peculiar subject matter was scuppered. Central London was out of bounds, unless on urgent business, and looking at art inspired by dogs did not fall into the relevant category.

When you live in London (and I imagine it is the same for other dyed-in-the-wool city dwellers who have a cradle-to-grave relationship with the urban neighbourhood of their choosing), you feel like you are on the doorstep of the world.

To be told this vast, rich, inspiring cornucopia is off limits and out of bounds for the foreseeable is a lot to take in, so we decided to look into the future, a future when this horrible airborne virus no longer seeped through our streets. Perhaps, we thought, a period of enforced absence would make the heart grow fonder, would remind us why we lived here in the first place. To feel cut off while pretty close to living in the bull's eye, one of the most vibrant and connected places in the world, was a strange contradiction. We asked ourselves what was it that we cherished, and what it was we were missing. We cast our mind's eye over rooftops and recalled the stories of the streets.

London is the greenest capital city in the world, with one-third of its land allocated to public open space, and 48 per cent turned over to green spaces of all kinds – knocking New York's 27 per cent and Paris's 9 per cent literally out of the park. Ah, to be strolling in one of our parks with an eager dog pulling on a lead. Instead, let us find satisfaction in the thought that the Wallace Collection in Manchester Square, then closed for the duration, has more than 800 depictions of hounds in its possession, ranging from paintings to porcelain, furniture and even firearms.

A gallery in the afternoon, and then on to the theatre, where the range of shows waiting to once more entertain is bettered nowhere else in the world. Such diverse delights once included a performance at the Peacock Theatre in Soho, owned by porn baron Paul Raymond. In the 1970s, a popular afternoon pastime was to watch a show that included a tank with two dolphins being raised up on the stage, where they would perform tricks, culminating in removing the bra from 'Miss Nude International' with their teeth. Later, the theatre would become home to the TV programme *This Is Your Life*. The dolphins' tank still remains beneath the stage.

After such theatrical delights, join members of the Beefsteak Club, an after-show dining society formed to discuss a heady mix of intellectual titbits focusing on theatre, liberty ... and beef. Established in 1705 and still meeting at 9 Irving Street, just off Leicester Square, you can't rock up wearing just anything. The strict dress code is blue coats and buff waistcoats with buttons proclaiming 'Beef and Liberty'. To avoid having to remember the names of your fellow diners, once you are inebriated on a good crusted Madeira, the custom is to simply call everybody – even the waiting staff – Charles.

And while we're ruminating on the performances currently postponed, oh to stroll down to the stalls of the lovely Savoy. When the late Charlton Heston appeared in *A Man for all Seasons* in 1987, he was told by the make-up team he would need to wear a wig. Chuck already sported a toupee – but was too shy to tell the person making him up. He therefore appeared on stage wearing a wig, on top of a wig.

'Brizo, A Shepherd's Dog' by Rosa Bonheur, 1864. (© The Wallace Collection, London)

Ede & Ravenscroft, originally wig makers to the judiciary.

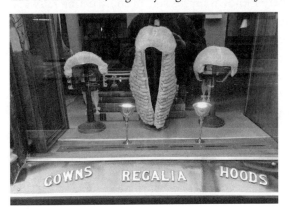

And while we are thinking of the Savoy Theatre and hairpieces, head eastwards a little along The Strand to the Royal Courts of Justice, and check out the scalp-warmers on display. The horsehair wigs the legal beaks perch atop their heads are based on a patent filed by Humphrey Ravenscroft in 1822. And they're not cheap – the going rate for one is £700 upwards. Ede & Ravenscroft still have a wig shop around the corner from the grand court house, and as well as wigs they specialise in that particularly swanky and silky type of smart tailoring those on a legal professional's salary like to indulge in.

Joseph Bazalgette.

From here, how about heading over the road and south for an amble along that most London of landmarks, the Embankment. It was warmly welcomed by Londoners when work finished in the 1860s, bringing some order amidst the chaos of the Thames banks.

Charles Dickens wrote to his friend William de Cerjat, who lived in Switzerland and had not had the pleasure of gazing along the new riverside, saying, 'The Thames embankment is (faults of ugliness in detail apart) the finest public work yet done. From Westminster Bridge near Waterloo it is now lighted up at night and has a fine effect …'

Designed by the famous Sir Joseph Bazalgette, he of sewers fame, it was actually built by an engineer called Thomas Brassey. Brassey is better known for his role in constructing railways, and so prolific was he that it is estimated that by the time of his death in 1870 he had built one mile of every twenty railway tracks around the entire world.

And finally, while we're thinking about trains and tracks, let us not forget how incredible it is that we can descend down a moving staircase to hop on a metal cylinder that will whoosh us to another bit of our home town – although should it actually be called the Underground, when 55 per cent of its 249-mile network has sky above it?

THE TUBE MAP MAESTRO

We embark on this marvel of late Victorian and early twentieth-century engineering, and pause for a moment on the platform, with its ox-red tiles, improve-your-life-you-miserable-commuter adverts and LT info-graphics, dusty dot-matrix schedule signs and Mind the Gap strips of yellow, to remember Harry Beck and his Tube map.

It is a story worth retelling, and doing so with the help of the late Ken Garland. Ken is one of that generation that came of age in the aftermath of 1945, born of an era where a war-forged sense of communal responsibility gave us a generation of highly educated, highly motivated people who greatly enhanced our creative economy.

He died in 2021, leaving a studio packed with original work that has become an unconscious motif in the public mind: from early posters for CND that helped popularise the famous peace sign, to designs for the toy maker Galt that every child in the 1960s and '70s would recognise, he spent a life creating graphic iconography that was pleasing to the eye.

When Ken moved to London from his native Devon via National Service in the Parachute Regiment to study art at the Central School of Arts and Crafts he was, at first, slightly overwhelmed by the size of the city and felt a little lost in the bustle. Travelling from his coin-slot gas meter and soggy-mattress digs in the lodger-land of Earl's Court, London's sprawl was at first disconcerting.

That was until he got on the Tube and studied the Beck map.

Never before had he seen such striking graphic design, making easy to understand and frankly beautiful logic from the swirling mass of streets and buildings above ground. The map announced a new London, and inspired cities around the world to follow our capital's lead.

Ken decided he had to meet the man behind this simple and effective piece of genius. He learned Beck was teaching at the London College, so he headed there and one lunchtime and found Mr Tube Map in the college canteen. Ken explained why he had come, and the pair struck up a lifelong friendship. Ken would sit in on Beck's lectures and write a biography of him.

'I turned up unannounced and asked around for him,' Ken told your correspondent. 'He was in the canteen and so I introduced myself. He said pull up a chair and got me a coffee. We became firm friends. The Tube diagram is one of the greatest pieces of graphic design produced, instantly recognisable and copied across the world.'

Harry Beck died in 1974, but not before he had told Mr Garland the story behind the diagram. He was 29 and had been working for the Underground as an engineering draughtsman since 1925, travelling to an office in Victoria from his home in Highgate Village. 'I must have lived a very energetic life in those days,' he told Ken. 'Rarely missed my daily dip in Highgate Pond before breakfast and I was in the rowing club and the Train, Omnibus and Tram Staff Philharmonic Society.'

Harry Beck.

When the cold winds of the Great Depression swept across the Atlantic, grandiose plans to expand the Tube network were mothballed. This included a deep, fast-track line to zoom passengers from north to south, stopping at just the main stations. As well as projects iced, employees were laid off – and Harry was one of them.

His time out of work did not last too long, thankfully. The London Underground bosses came knocking – work piled up in his old office and because he had been playing in the transport orchestra, his former colleagues decided he really was the most irreplaceable of those laid off. So in 1933, Beck was re-employed – a decision that would lead to the creation of the greatest transit system map ever committed to paper.

Before being given his cards in 1931, Harry had often looked at the Tube map and felt there was room for improvement. Although geographically correct, the swirling lines and bunched up stations in what is now Zone One were, he felt, confusing. It was a map made using Victorian design principles and aesthetics, not a neat, eye-catching, easy to understand piece of graphic design. In Harry's eyes, it did not do this futuristic transport network justice.

'Looking at the old map of the railways, it occurred to me that it might be possible to tidy it up by straightening the lines, experimenting with diagonals and evening out the distances between stations,' he told Ken. His colleagues in the engineering department thought he'd hit on a good wheeze when he showed them his plan for a neater Tube map – but the Underground's publicity team were not convinced.

While unemployed, Harry continued to lobby them and in 1932 they relented, printing an initial run of 750,000 of his Tube maps, and then gave him his old job back. Beck would constantly update and improve the map – not least because this was an era of Tube expansion – but his hard work did not bring him the rewards that surely the creator of such an icon deserved.

The Underground paid him 5 guineas in total – and nothing more, at all, ever … despite his invention becoming as ubiquitous when talking about the Tube as the roundels used for station names. This meagre sum, considering the map's eventual worth as a marketing tool, would rile Beck in the years to come, as did the occasional clumsy changes made to his original design, which would see him fire off a letter offering better ways to improve his work.

Your correspondent got to know Ken and once heard the following story. It comes with a disclaimer that it may be just a nice, slightly twisted, anecdote. However, the outcome is certainly what happened.

When Beck died, he left no children or a wife. His niece was tasked with clearing out his home, and as the story goes, she spent hours carrying heavy sacks of books, sketches, papers and manuscripts downstairs and into the street. Ken came to lend a hand, and noticed, in a skip the niece had hired, sketch books that contained Beck's first ever drafts of the map we know. He rescued them and, being of a civic-minded nature, donated the electrical circuit diagram-like sketches to the Victoria and Albert Museum, where they remain today.

'I had a secret admiration for him – I admit it was a bit of hero worship,' recalled Ken. 'His map was groundbreaking – it was only about connections and not geographical. This meant he could use only horizontal, vertical and diagonal lines. It was not to scale – the central area, which was congested with stops, is enlarged compared to the outlying areas.'

And as we conclude the story of Ken and Harry and the Tube map, here comes a train. Let us hop on board and head north, back into the heart of our town, and see where our noses take us.

PICCADILLY PECCADILLOES

From Embankment Station – which first opened for trains in 1870 and was built using the cut-and-cover method, and then had deeper Tube lines added in 1898 – we can catch a train on the Circle, District, Northern or Bakerloo lines. Let's hop on the Bakerloo line and alight at Piccadilly Circus, normally a byword for London's throbbing throngs, now eerily empty.

Deserted of its usual pedestrians, we can stop to admire the statue of Eros in all its glory. The statue of the Greek God was erected in honour of Anthony Cooper, the 7th Earl of Shaftesbury, for all his work looking out for the poor of London in the nineteenth century.

Ah-ha – but here's the thing: it isn't a statue of Eros at all. Instead, sculptor Alfred Gilbert, who cast it in 1885, modelled the figure on Eros's brother, Anteros. We've been muddling him up with his bro all this time, but despite the general ignorance over who he actually is, Anteros is very much loved by Londoners. During the Second World War, the statue was removed for safekeeping – and put back in time for VE Day so that jubilant revellers could clamber all over the misnamed sibling.

Londoners have long treated the statue as something more than a piece of public art. Unlike similar installations, which very much have a 'keep off' vibe about them, Anteros has a more embracing relationship with the people who swirl around its base. When it was first unveiled, the West End flower girls set up stations around its base, using its fountain to keep their blooms looking fresh. A set of copper taps had been installed, to provide fresh drinking water to thirsty pedestrians. They didn't last long – the taps were pinched within a week, and when their replacements were also quickly filched, it was deemed too expensive to keep replacing them.

It is incredible to think that Piccadilly Circus as we know it today – and apart from the types of vehicles clogging up the thoroughfare, would also be recognisable to a time traveller from the Georgian period – was under threat of wholesale redevelopment in the 1960s. That decade, where car was truly king, planners envisaged high-speed dual carriageways whisking the pampered commuter into the centre of the city. The remnants of these frankly awful schemes – fought off by grassroots campaigns – are the Westway and Park Lane.

Piccadilly Circus.

Our internal combustion engine champions at Westminster Town Hall could not resist the urge, suffered by every generation, to undo and fix up, make good and alter what has come before, pasting their tastes like layers over every building and every street. As the 1960s progressed, planners cast unforgiving eyes over the ragtag mixture of buildings and organically evolved streets snaking off Piccadilly with apparently no rhyme nor reason. Ideas were floated. Opportunities discussed. One such scheme, which remarkably gained traction, envisaged a row of thirty-storey office blocks around Piccadilly Circus, linked to Leicester Square, Shaftesbury Avenue, the Haymarket, Brewer Street and Regent Street by raised walkway, 60ft up.

At ground level, a six-lane dual carriageway would whisk traffic west to east, signalling the ultimate triumph of the car over the city. Perhaps planners backed down due to the pressure applied by a coalition of residents, activists, councillors and civic groups. Perhaps the 1973 oil crisis put paid to it. Regardless of the reasons, the scheme was shelved, but not before it had caused one unpleasant side effect. Speculators, knowing that something was a foot, bought up as much property as they could – and of course wanted a return. The project, which never got further than sketches on a drawing board, pushed up the costs of living in central London, and added to the long-term trend of small businesses declining in numbers in the surrounding side streets.

PELICANS, PARAKEETS AND SIR HUMPHREY'S NUTS

From Piccadilly, let's potter south down Waterloo Place to saunter through St James's Park. As well as being rather pleasant sculptured gardens, there are the pelicans to look out for: the park has five in situ, and they are the direct descendants of a pair given to Charles II in 1664 by the Russian ambassador (great present – remember readers, a pelican is for centuries, not just Christmas, etc). Park keepers keep them topped up with 12lb of fish each day.

Diarist John Evelyn wrote in 1665 of his fascination with the pelicans he came across. While not so well known as his contemporary Pepys, Evelyn witnessed and wrote about the execution of Charles I, the death of Cromwell, and both the Great Plague and the Great Fire of London in the 1660s.

Evelyn wrote about politics and culture – but he was also a gardener, and was drawn to St James's Park to see what latest wheeze the king had come up with. He wasn't disappointed: 'I saw various animals and examined the throat of the Onocrotylus, or Pelican, a fowl between a stork and a swan; it was diverting to see how he would toss up and turn a flat fish, plaice or flounder, to get it right into his gullet at its lowest beak, which, being flimsy, stretches to prodigious wideness when it devours a great fish.' He also encountered 'deer of several countries, white, spotted like leopards, antelopes, an elk, red deer, roebucks, stages, Guinea goats and Arabian sheep'.

As we will discuss shortly, Trafalgar Square is no longer a prime spot to feed city scavengers and come up close to the feral wildlife that has as much a sense of ownership of this city as we do. Instead, if the urge to break bread with smaller creatures takes you, St James's Park is the place. The descendants of James II's pleasure garden menagerie today include the well-entrenched populations of parakeets and squirrels. They no doubt enjoy a lazier and more fruitful life than their forebears, who had to keep an eye out for the two crocodiles James I had installed in the lake after being gifted them by the Egyptian envoy.

Despite signs pleading with visitors to cut it out – apparently it encourages the rats – a grand magnolia tree on the banks of the lake by a footbridge with lovely views is a spot where human, bird and rodent know to gather to feed and be fed. It is an undoubted thrill to have the bright green birds swoop down and sit calmly on your arm while they peck at whatever you have to offer.

Likewise, kneeling down and offering a little something to a nose-twitching, bushy-tailed little fellow is a pastime full of charm. There are regulars – those who idle away the time they have to spend in our green spaces, and strike up a relationship with the animals they see each day. They display a sense of ownership over the patch. Woe betide any occasional visitor who offers up a piece of their park cafe flapjack (amateurs!), and entices a parakeet or squirrel away from one of the serious feeders, who come equipped with high-grade healthy muesli for their furry and feathered chums.

There is, however, one parakeet and squirrel charmer who enjoys nothing more than showing off quite how tame his dependants are. He has something of a legendary status in the park, and your correspondent can vouch for this at first hand, having met him on the many occasions a parakeet feeding trip has been under taken by yours truly and child.

This human snack dispenser is in his 50s, and a very senior civil servant working in a stressful and high-powered job in Whitehall. He makes his way through St James's every evening at 5.35 p.m., heading from a day of important government business, decked out in the requisite suit, mac and brolly. His Whitehall mandarin look has one important addition: in the deep pockets of his trench coat, he stores a seemingly bottomless supply of monkey nuts.

He interrupts his saunter home to his loving wife, children, dog, meat and two veg – and no doubt a pudding followed by slippers and crossword – to spend a pleasant forty-five minutes feeding families of squirrels. Generations of the bushy-tailed blighters have known and loved him, and are tame enough to clamber on his person as they feast on the supper he provides.

As he moves from London plane tree to London plane tree, he isn't averse to sharing his squirrel-whispering skills with any wide-eyed child in the vicinity. He happily hands over a fistful of nuts and allows youngsters the thrill of having Nutkin clambering across them to gently feast.

St James's Park.

LANDSEER'S LIONS
AND LIVINGSTONE'S
POST-PIGEON PLAZA

From St James's, let's head up The Mall, where urban myth says the road is designed to be an emergency runway for the RAF to land on and whisk Her Maj and hangers-on out of the city should we ever get round to revolting … and then on to Trafalgar Square, lying beautifully quiet, perhaps the first time in centuries that humans and pigeons have not run the place.

Ah, the pigeons of Trafalgar Square – no longer do they run the show, no longer do their sheer weight of numbers tip the urban balance from human to creature.

The Mall.

Trafalgar Square.

Pigeons and Trafalgar Square appear to have become a thing from the 1840s, about a decade after the square was laid out. The birds (*Columba livia var*) seemed to like the tall buildings around the square to roost on, and pigeons have a tendency to stay close to the nests they sprung from. They also form family units, with the cock and hen offering each other love and fidelity, through sickness and in health, no matter how gammy their legs may become. It meant the population of pigeons grew and grew – and that in turn attracted traders specialising in bird seed to take up residence. It wasn't unusual – bird seed sellers were to be found across the city in any public space or pleasure park.

In 2001, it was estimated that 35,000 feral pigeons lived around and about the square, enjoying the lunches in return for a picture with a tourist. The then-mayor, Ken Livingstone, was livid at the fact it cost £140,000 a year to stop Nelson's Column from being damaged by the birds' acidic poo. He called them flying rats, cited research about the public health risk, and decided to withdraw the street trader licences issued to the stalls that sold bird food. It was a decision that caused huge controversy and nearly reached the High Court.

The anti-pigeon policy meant licences for street traders to sell seeds and grains were going to be withdrawn – prompting one of those David versus Goliath, Little Man versus the State-type stories that newspapers lighten a gloomy news day with. Seed seller Bernard Rayner, whose family had been happily selling seeds for nearly half a century, was joined by animal welfare activists to try and reverse the decision. Some feared the birds would starve to death, and brought sack loads of grain to scatter. It meant war, and the pigeons and their fanciers were not going to go quietly.

Westminster Council counter-attacked by moving a brigade of street cleaners in with giant vacuums to suck up stray bird food and employed pimply faced youths in oddly branded civic uniforms to shout at the birds – and those feeding them – through grating loudhailers.

On being told his licence, held since 1956, was not going to be renewed, Mr Rayner sought legal advice. The fate of the pigeons' free lunch was in the balance. A showdown beckoned in front of a judge. Before the beaks could rule on feeding beaks, the GLA blinked and offered the Rayners an undisclosed amount of money in an out-of-court settlement. Whatever, the sum, it clearly wasn't chicken (or pigeon) feed.

Today, there are still the remnants of the huge pigeon community – but naturalists say there are no more pigeons in the square per square foot than any place else in central London.

Still, there is a tooth and claw deterrent in situ. Hawks have become the go-to for councils hoping to keep feral pigeons away from civic centres, and if you're lucky, you may well see one on patrol, winging its way past Nelson. If you're squeamish, look away now. The hawks are trained and well fed, so they don't need to hunt pigeons because they are hungry. Instead, if one gets to close, the hawk dives in and whips the poor thing's head off, letting it tumble to the ground. It is said one unfortunate janitor each month draws the short straw and has to clamber out on to a fifth-storey ledge of a well-known block facing the square, and using a broom pole, dislodge a couple of headless carcasses.

The story of the friezes around the base of Nelson's Column being made from the melted-down cannon of captured French ships during Napoleonic wars is well known. However, it isn't such common knowledge that sculptor Edwin Landseer, who was commissioned to cast the four lions around the plinth, made sure his depiction was accurate when he'd never seen one on the flesh. He managed to source a dead lion from London Zoo and crated it back to his studio. From there, he knocked up the cast, racing against time as the poor creature's cadaver began to decay and stink the place out.

Now on to St Martin's Lane, first built by Robert Cecil, the 1st Earl of Salisbury, in 1610 and then added to by Sir Thomas Slaughter in the 1690s. It was known for two things: it was the centre of London's horse tack industry, with shops selling bridles, saddles, reins, stirrups and assorted horsey bits and pieces, and the upper floors became a favoured residence for struggling artists, who could walk to the National Gallery for inspiration.

Later, furniture maker Thomas Chippendale was based there – and then the artist Hogarth set up an academy in the street.

HOGARTH AND THE
ANGEL OF THE ROOKERIES

And with Hogarth in mind, it's time we swing north-eastwards a little bit and head past Covent Garden to the Rookeries in St Giles, the scene of Hogarth's seminal London illustrations, 'Beer Street' and 'Gin Lane'. Drawn in 1751, 'Beer Street' depicted hearty Londoners supping good-for-you ales and being generally happy and well behaved, while 'Gin Lane' – based on what he had seen in the tenements of St Giles – depicted a society rotten through the imbibing of spirits.

St Giles was always seen as something of an unsavoury haunt, and fifty years after Hogarth had shone a revealing light (and Hawksmoor's St George's Church, built to oversee the St Giles parish and to offer some spiritual nourishment, had made little headway,) it was still a place of wanton debauchery.

It was in St Giles that the famous Billy Waters could be found. Billy, who had one leg, was a disabled busker and performer who was celebrated for his shows on the streets around Seven Dials. He was a former slave who had escaped captivity and joined the Royal Navy.

Billy served during the Napoleonic wars on HMS *Ganymede*, a well-armed frigate. The ship had been captured from the French by the Royal Navy (it was originally a 40-gun, 450-ton ship called the *Hebe*) in 1809. They intercepted the ship as it headed to the Caribbean with 600 barrels of flour on board. The Royal Navy renamed the ship HMS *Ganymede* and it went off to war under the Royal Ensign.

It was while Waters was serving on the ship that his life would be changed irrevocably: he had climbed to the top of the rigging before losing his grip and falling

Billy Waters.

to the deck below. He was badly injured and had his leg amputated on the spot by the ship's doctor. Somewhat remarkably, he survived the operation and returned to dry land. Down on his luck, he found lodgings in St Giles and found fame among Londoners, who liked his war hero story, his freed slave story and his agility and humour in performing a role. He was feted enough for Staffordshire potters to cast figurines in his likeness, and to be referenced in numerous books and plays.

But poor Billy was fated to have a trying end. Despite his talent, his hard work and his undoubtedly good relationship with his London crowd, Billy never made enough money from busking to be comfortable. As age-induced decrepitude crept in, he fell foul of the Poor Laws and ended his days in the St Giles Workhouse.

And on that note, we shall head into The Angel pub in St Giles High Street for well-earned refreshment. Or rather, we would if it was open!

The Angel pub.

The Angel has been there for centuries, and while the years have, of course, meant multiple refits and repairs, it retains a genuine sense of its longevity. A side passage, once used for horses to access the back stables, now leads you into a beer garden. Inside, it still has the moulded plaster ceilings, the old light fittings and the frosted windows and etched mirrors. The pressure on housing and the cost of living in central London has had a knock-on effect on pubs like The Angel. Sixty years ago, its regulars would have been people who lived or worked nearby – certainly, a sizeable proportion from within a 400m radius. Now West End pubs make up the trade lost from the changes in land use around them by hosting people from much further afield.

The Angel pub.

The Angel was in the midst of the infamous rookeries, the slums of St Giles, and no doubt saw life in all its glory. It was once the haunt of an infamous criminal, whose exploits gripped the working classes and to many was a folk hero. The Angel was cited in a 1741 Old Bailey trial of serial house-breaker and general rapscallion Thomas Ruby, whose exploits were the stuff Penny Dreadfuls loved at the time. Publican John Tucker of The Angel gave evidence to the court, explaining how Ruby had broken into the tavern and pilfered cash and stock. He was arrested in an advanced state of inebriation, snoring in the passageway for horses we first walked up, ending a long and prolific career as a burglar.

GOD GAVE ROCK
AND ROLL TO YOU

Right, we've drained a pint in The Angel in St Giles High Street, a handy resting place on our stay-at-home stroll through the centre of town. Let us resume our locked-down ramblings, and walk off a couple of lunchtime beers.

Our first stop is Denmark Street, aka Tin Pan Alley, where your correspondent, aged 13, bought his first axe from Andy's Guitar Shop on the corner.

The street is the original home of London's live music scene and is the place musicians would gather to be hired for jobs, where recording studios churned out hits, where music publishers and composers plotted ear worms for all, where instruments were bought, sold and traded, and where *Melody Maker* and *NME* started their lives.

Regent Sounds Studio, Denmark Street, aka Tin Pan Alley.

We shall pause for a moment outside the former offices of *Melody Maker*, and spare a moment's thought for one of the heaviest days at work surely any postman has ever endured.

In 1932, Louis Armstrong had travelled to London and done a two-week show at the Palladium that had knocked everyone for six. 'His technical virtuosity and his rich, red hot personality gained many new converts to jazz music,' wrote David Boulton in his 1959 book, *Jazz in Britain*.

Every one of his concerts was given national press coverage. When, a few months after his return to America, the *Daily Express* headlined on its front page an account of his death, it led to vanloads of hysterical letters from distressed and distraught fans to the *Maker*'s HQ. In those halcyon days of a nationalised and pre-email postal service, letters were delivered up to ten times a day. It left the magazine staff, along with the hard-working postie, in no doubt of the affection in which Armstrong was held.

Thankfully, the *Express* had made a critical error in their reportage. Armstrong was, of course, alive and kicking. He had simply been nipped in the leg by a depressed dog, 'and rumour had magnified the event out of all proportion,' wrote Boulton. Quite so.

Melody Maker focused on the type of music young intellectual types enjoyed: this was a period when the great historian Eric Hobsbawm wrote a jazz column for the *New Statesman* under the name Frances Newton, after the communist trumpeter who played with Billie Holiday, and the political cartoonist Wally 'Trog' Fawkes tried to balance his absolute genius at a draughtsman's board with his equally world-class skill at blowing the clarinet. Trad Jazz was linked with polo neck-clad arty types whose duffel coats in the 100 Club cloakroom would have pockets stuffed with Lacan, Sartre, De Beauvoir and whatever else was cool on Bloomsbury campuses that term.

Perhaps because *Melody Maker* was seen as a more serious magazine than the *New Musical Express*, a more learned and intellectual tome as opposed to one happy to cover skiffle, it was through its pages that one of the country's first artistic, anti-racist movements was born.

In the aftermath of the 1958 Notting Hill riots, in which Black Londoners were attacked by racists, *Melody Maker*'s editorial team were not going to stand idly by. In early September, just a week after the frightening disturbances, *Melody Maker* put on the front page a heartfelt letter signed by twenty-seven big names, ranging from Humphrey Lyttelton, Eric Sykes and Tommy Steele to Lonnie Donegan, Chris Barber, Peter Sellers, Harry Secombe, Tubby Hayes and Cleo Laine: 'At a time when reason has given way to violence in parts of

Britain, we, the people of all races in the world of entertainment, appeal to the public to reject racial discrimination in any shape or form ...'

The Denmark Street publication would, a week later, print a two-page article by Frank Sinatra no less. His message to music fans was 'you can't hate and be happy', and he threw his weight behind an anti-racist campaign prompted by the *Melody Maker* letter. It was a cause close to the magazine's heart: years later, in 1975, they would print furious reactions to guitarist Eric Clapton's nasty speech on stage in Birmingham, where he drunkenly spouted racist nonsense at the audience.

The stretch was known in 1930s and '40s as a meeting point for big bands, the skiffle boom of the '50s, the British blues explosion of the 1960s, '70s punk and onwards – but today the browser can go even further back in time by stepping through the doors of the Early Music Shop. This wonderful establishment has a collection of traditional instruments, including the UKs biggest collection of recorders. Among the harps and harpsichords, the tabor drums and Baroque oboes, you can find hurdy-gurdies and the brilliantly bizarre-sounding 'long-scale Medieval drum', a cross between a finger piano, lute and tambourine. How much trade such a specialist shop does on a daily basis is one of those window shopper's conundrums of time immemorial – who buys these things, we ask – but it is yet another reason to love and cherish city-dwelling alongside others who clearly have a need for such things.

While in Denmark Street, it would be churlish to miss the chance to name drop horrendously – after all, this is a thoroughfare that has borne witness to the musical development of the Sex Pistols (a possible oxymoron, you may say), David Bowie, The Stones, The Kinks, Led Zep and countless others in a host of dimly lit basement studios. It was where Elton John and Bernie Taupin wrote their early hits, where Lionel Bart of *Oliver!* fame had an office, and where Paul Simon was told by a music publisher that his songs 'Homeward Bound' and 'The Sound of Silence' were nice but not marketable.

But while these guys are comfortable bestsellers, let us spare a thought for a man who has carried the torch for this musical Mecca, ensured the street remained relevant and added greatly to its reputation over the years.

Andy Preston spent his youth working in Cumbria as an engineer and a musical instrument restorer. In the late 1960s, he headed to London to seek work repairing and restoring guitars. He headed down Tin Pan Alley to see what opportunities there might be to fix, mend and spruce up axes in need of TLC.

Walking along Denmark Street, he found a corner shop owned by a Greek family, selling groceries and whatnot. 'I went in to buy an apple, and there was a husband and wife working behind the counter,' he recalled. 'I asked them if they knew anywhere round here I could set up a guitar workshop. "A-ha", they said.'

The couple showed him the cellar beneath the thin, four-storey terrace. When Andy first went down the narrow, winding staircase, he had to stoop because the ceiling was so low. Buried in the floor was a pickaxe. The owners had decided to deepen the cellar and set up a club for other Greek Cypriot émigrés, and made a half-hearted attempt to get the place useable and ship-shape by digging out a couple of feet and lowering the floor. Instead, Andy set up his workbench and a Tin Pan Alley institution was born.

As his reputation spread, he employed other guitar makers and technicians. 'I soon had a team of five of us working in the basement,' he recalls.

But when the smell of glue, polish, paint and resin began to take over the ground-floor store, the shopkeeper said he didn't believe the two businesses were compatible and offered Andy his lease for the whole building.

Andy's had a shop on the ground and upper floors, and in the nooks and crannies you would find wood being worked, electrics being fixed, necks varnished, strings strung. Andy's was painted in an ad hoc yet striking manner – a colour scheme of bright yellow and red, slopped on by staff and possibly from a mix and match selection of half-used pots. It all added to the charm.

Performers at Andy's Guitar Shop and the 12 Bar Club.

But there was more to come – it was from this humble workshop that a legendary music venue was born. Andy's team of craftsman were all, unsurprisingly, rather handy at playing the instruments they were fixing.

'When we shut up the shop each night, we would go to this place called the Diamond Dive Bar, on the corner of Tottenham Court Road,' Andy remembered. 'We used to go there for a jam and drink. Lots of customers would come into hear us play. We were all jamming there and then one day the landlord said, out the blue: "I am fed up with you all!" and kicked us out. We were stunned – he'd made good money out of us.'

A grumpy landlord meant they were looking for somewhere else to play. Next door to Andy's was a blacksmith's forge. Its bellows had long stopped huffing, its anvil no longer clanged and its furnace had not known warmth for decades. It had been used by the Covent Garden health food restaurant Food for Thought as a store room, and a kip house for the owner's daughter and her friend.

When they moved out, Andy's amp repair department moved in – and soon a small stage had been built along a wall, a PA set up and the jams began again.

'It attracted customers – they'd come in to hear it,' recalls Andy. 'It was like hey, this is like a little club, so why not open the doors. People started coming in – not one or two, but lots and lots.'

The official opening night of the 12 Bar Club saw Andy rustle up ten buskers he knew who worked pitches in the West End. Andy and buskers had a long-term relationship. Andy would save strings he had taken off guitars, clean them, sort them out and then give them away to skint street performers for free. He arranged for all ten to meet on Charing Cross Road and all launch into 'Hey Mr Tambourine Man' as they led a parade to the new 12 Bar.

At first, food and drink came in an unconventional way. Staff would take an order, and then nip out of a back door and across the alleyway to the kitchens of a Greek restaurant. They'd return with a tray and charge a little on top for the hassle of popping across an alley.

'It really took off,' recalls Andy. 'Eventually we had to move the amps we were repairing out and make it in to a proper club.'

Its draw was such that when successful Swedish businessman Lars Ericsson found himself inside, he sought Andy out and offered to back him.

'This guy came in and said I love the blues,' recalls Andy.

The pair formed a partnership, and the club expanded, taking space from a comic book shop next door, a Chinese restaurant, and running music studios above the venue.

'It was a whole colony of music,' Andy states.

Awards followed, and big names made a point of turning up. When headliners would be at the Astoria, their road crew would make a point of bringing musicians over to the 12 Bar to unwind.

'We would get really famous people turning up and they'd get on stage on play – they'd do an unplugged number. You'd get this great atmosphere – ordinary, amateur players sitting in and playing alongside very famous musicians. It was quite an oddball place.'

Among those who entertained were Adele, The Libertines and Bert Jensch. But it wasn't about the names who came in through the door – or the unknowns who cut their teeth in the eighty-capacity gig room.

'I had a policy, and this is what people really liked. If you are just starting and play at a pub or club, people can heckle, be rude, shout you off. The 12 Bar just allowed people to come and play. You have to have courage to play in public, but we felt because we were in a guitar repair shop, and we were repairing ordinary people's guitars, we wanted them to be playing here, too. We didn't let anyone take the piss out of anyone who had the courage to play. If that happened, we'd throw them out. That was the magic of it. It was a natural place. It really didn't matter how good they were.'

Today, a time-travelling blacksmith would struggle to locate the forge – as would a 1970s axe man looking for a new set of strings. Andy's and the 12 Bar were shut when permission was granted in 2015 to redevelop the stretch. A new 12 Bar is said to be opening – but it's incomparable to what was there before, spread over a number of floors and with a greatly increased capacity. Andy, now in his 80s, still owns the rights to the 12 Bar name and is involved in negotiations with the developers over what the new venue will be called, and whether the 12 Bar will rise once more.

CROSSRAIL, CENTREPOINT AND THE LOST FOUNTAINS OF JUPP

Now, just around the corner from the feedback-soaked air of Tin Pan Alley, we come to Tottenham Court Road Tube Station and Centrepoint.

As with the Denmark Street block, huge amounts of rebuilding have been undertaken in the last two decades. Building Cross Rail, or the Elizabeth Line as it's now been branded, has been a colossal job. They poured more tons of concrete into the ground than the chief engineer said he'd used when building a nuclear power station. Hidden beneath the ground, it's hard to quite get the scope of the size of what they have been ferreting away doing down there.

The figures are pretty hard to quantify on paper. They used more than 3 million cubic metres of concrete building the line. Added to this immense amount of material were 26,000 concrete rings, with each station – how many Olympic swimming pools is that, you ask? I'll tell you. A lot. An Olympic swimming pool is about 2,500 cubic metres, so more than 3 million is a lot of swimming pools.

Centrepoint.

As well as the immense civil engineering feat going on below, the same corner has had another building project going on, as high in the sky as they are deep underground. This was the scheme by upmarket property developer types Almacantar, who turned Centrepoint from a white elephant office block to exclusive apartments (the top-floor flat, once a night club, was originally on the market for £50 million).

A new entrance for the Tube was dug out at the foot of Richard Seifert's stunning 1960s tower, and led to the loss of one of those wonderful, quirky landmarks that has a story worth preserving, even if planners did not protect the subject of the following yarn physically.

Now, of course, trends come and go. What we consider cutting edge in one decade will inevitably fall from grace, only to be fondly remembered and fêted further down the line. London is full of such things – lost pointers to trends and the needs of our forebears that have been unceremoniously hoiked into skips and erased in the name of progress.

And when plans were unveiled to dig out a massive new station for Cross Rail at Tottenham Court Road designers went for something of a nuclear option. It meant buildings such as The Astoria were deemed surplus to requirements, as were a set of modernist fountains at the foot of Centrepoint. The abstract pieces, shaped like giant Ys with water coming

Jupp's fountains.

out of jets where the arms met, sat in a tiled pool, cut off from being truly appreciated by the swirling traffic around its base.

Designed in 1963 and Grade II listed, they were in the way of a new sloping glass atrium leading to a wide and shiny new subterranean concourse. To a small group of modernists, members of the Twentieth Century Society or students of post-war urban design and place making, removing the fountains was like taking our old friend Anteros away from Piccadilly Circus. To others, they were brutal reminders of the creep of concrete, and their destruction a worthwhile sacrifice for the incredible civil engineering project to bring a new, super-fast cross-London underground rail link.

The fountains were the work of Jupp Dernbach-Mayen, an émigré artist born in Germany in 1908, the son of a stonemason. Aged 12, he became a decorator's apprentice. Jupp spent his lunchtimes painting and his boss was so impressed with his talent that he paid for his tuition at the Cologne School of Art. He went on to work as a set designer for the State Theatre in Berlin.

As for so many of his generation, the rise of the Nazis brought despair; a Roman Catholic, he worked to help Jewish people escape persecution until he was tipped off that the Gestapo planned to arrest him. He fled to Ibiza, where he spent two years as a decorator while working on his own studies.

With war on the horizon, he returned briefly to Berlin in 1938 to close up his studio, and by the summer of 1939 had arrived in Eton Road, Belsize Park. He was interned as an enemy alien and then did a stretch in the Pioneer Corps before being hospitalised. In 1942, struggling under the strain of war, he had a nervous breakdown.

Once recovered, Jupp had to find work. With no connections in the art world, he got a job coating watch faces with luminous paint. Then in 1946 he found a job working with potter Lucie Rie. Setting up shop in Albion Mews, St John's Wood, Jupp showed his wide range of talents by designing and building a larger kiln for the studio. 'He had an ability to turn his hand to anything,' recalls his daughter, Mireille Burton, whose Kentish Town home is full of her father's work. 'He was an experimenter. He liked to be able to work in all sorts of mediums. He was multi-talented and it means it is hard to focus on just one aspect of his work. But the fountains were typical of what he wanted to achieve.'

Dernbach-Mayen's art ranges from watercolour scenes to abstract oils. He built furniture and his sculptures include a mosaic that graced the 1951 Festival of Britain. The courtyard of the five-star Sanderson Hotel includes his friezes and water features. He worked with Basil Spence on Coventry Cathedral and designed wallpaper for Heals. Then he was asked by Centrepoint architect Richard Seifert to produce public art for the base of the tower block.'He was inspired by designs he had seen in Grenada, Spain,' recalls Mireille. 'He envisaged the fountains running at different heights. He crafted them in fibre glass in his studio and they were then taken to the site, where he filled them with concrete.'

They did not survive. At the time, architect Richard Hawkins, who was responsible for the new entrance, said, 'They were designed at a time when people were thinking of things like elevated pedestrian walkways above our streets. We have to look at the potential of this space. It is going to completely and radically change. It is simply not relevant to put something back that does not function.'

The 'dozers came in and Jupp's fountains, for a time, disappeared from view. Investigations by your correspondent discovered half of them were in a lock-up on an industrial estate in Wembley, the others in a barn in Norfolk.

After some persuasion and with the help of conservationists, the Architectural Association – for whom Jupp had worked – took the fountains from their dusty corners and installed them at their country base in Devon.

THE BROLLY BREWER

Moving on from the radically changed face of the St Giles area, we shall keep going westwards, across Oxford Street and towards Fitzrovia.

On route, let's duck down Hanway Street, one of those narrow, and empty cut throughs whose silence contrasts sharply with the noise and bustle in its connecting roads.

Hanway Street is named after the son-in-law of brewer Joe Girtle, who ran a pub here in the 1660s called The Harp. His daughter married an engineer, Major John Hanway, and the major would develop the street that bears his name. His nephew, Jonas, happens to be the man who popularised the umbrella, an item that saw him roundly ridiculed when he first popped one up to shield off the London drizzle, but soon persuaded others that the odd looks were worth being the dry person beneath the contraption.

Behind Hanway Street was Hanways Yard, and it was here in the 1700s you could find Broughton's Amphitheatre, home to champion fighter Jack Broughton. This bare-knuckle bruiser formed a code for the ring that was adhered to for the next 100 years. His innovations included a thirty-second time out for anyone on the receiving end of his upper cuts, and he also invented 'mufflers', a precursor to the boxing glove, which he wore to prolong the bouts he fought against weaker opposition, thereby ensuring his paying attendees got their money's worth.

Hanways Yard was typical of the layout of this patch. A mixture of well-to-do homes and workers' accommodation, light industry and the need for stables meant there was a sense of living cheek by jowl. The mews and yards of Fitzrovia, now swanky real estate, were the engine rooms of central London's economy.

Despite the age of the buildings lining these time-trodden streets, its name is comparatively new. It began to be referred to as Fitzrovia in the late 1930s, inspired, it is said, by the Fitzroy Tavern in Charlotte Street, the drinking den of all manner of bohemian authors and artists including Dylan Thomas, George Bernard Shaw and George Orwell.

FITZROVIAN THOUGHT
AND BOHO SOHO

While we think of how and why Fitzrovia and Soho earned a Bohemian reputation, it's worth us considering quite how far back and well entrenched this reputation is. More than 100 years ago, it had already been identified. The word Bohemian entered the English lexicon from mid-nineteenth-century France. There, it was at first used to describe Romani people, who had travelled through Bohemia. But it was soon tagged on to anyone living a non-traditional lifestyle and morphed to mean in particular artists, writers, musicians and actors who became part of cultural communities in cheap neighbourhoods across European cities.

Firstly, let us note the area's restaurant culture with a unique flavour that stretches back through centuries, giving a certain cosmopolitan and anti-establishment air to the surroundings. It was known for the Italian, French and German names above the shop fronts. Old Compton Street, for example, built a deserved reputation for its European range and affordable prices, catering for both Soho-ites during the day and then an influx from a jolly post-theatre crowd later.

It was this range of all human life to be found that has been the fuel in London's engine, the global flagstones that provide the base and superstructure to a capital city.

In 1919, 'The inhabitant of London,' wrote economist and philosopher John Maynard Keynes, 'could order by telephone, while sipping his morning tea in bed, the various products of the whole of the earth, in such quantity as he might see fit, and reasonably expect their early delivery upon his doorstep; he could at the same moment and by the same means adventure his wealth in the natural resources and new enterprises of any quarter of the world, and share, without exertion or even trouble, in their prospective fruits and advantages.' Keynes's well-stocked Londoner could ignore 'the projects and politics of militarism and imperialism, of racial and cultural rivalries, of monopolies, restrictions and exclusion, which were to play the serpent to this paradise, were little more than the amusements of his daily newspaper and appeared to exercise almost no influence at all on the ordinary course of social

The French House, Soho.

and economic life, the internationalisation of which was nearly complete in practice …'

These abundant Anglo–Euro–Global cultural ingredients were stirred and mixed and baked to produce something that smelt and tasted fresh. A gluttonous and honest description of such Soho food joints at the turn of the 1900s can be found in Arthur Ransome's *Bohemia in London*, a mix of fiction and memoir.

Ransome's life reads like an adventure in its own right. He travelled to Russia in 1913 with the aim of studying the country's folklore. He worked as a foreign correspondent, covered the Russian Revolution, and passed information to the British Secret Service – although later it was suspected he may have also worked for the Russians. He is best known, of course, for his bucolic adventure stories that began with *Swallows and Amazons* and led to an entire series set on unspoilt waterways around the UK, featuring the Walker children.

His Soho book told the story of the young artists' travails, setting scenes against backdrops of steamed-up cafe windows, and finding something youthful, inspirational, romantic and exciting in the melee, an experience similar to that described by the American writers in Paris during the 1920s.

Ransome decided he must take lodgings in the West End after missing his last train home too many times, having spent an evening gossiping in taverns from Fleet Street to Marble Arch.

His book begins with a very *Swallows and Amazons*-like description of having to head back to suburbs west of London after a night out: 'then on, along the Embankment, past the grey mass of the Tate Gallery, past the bridges, looking out over the broad river, now silver-specked in the moonlight, now dark, with bright shafts of light across the water and sparks of red and green from the lanterns on the boats. When a tug, with a train of barges, swept from under a bridge and brought me the invariable, unaccountable shiver with the cold noise of the waters parted by her bows, I would lean on the parapet and watch, and catch a sight of a dark figure upon her, and wonder what it would be like to spend all my days eternally passing up and down the river, seeing ships and men and knowing no hours but the tides, until her light would vanish round a bend and leave the river as before, moving on past the still lamps on either side.'

When he made the jump from the bosom of well-meaning older relatives to strike out as a penniless and aspiring writer, he began his journey in a style he felt was fitting. As book reviewer Lloyd Williams wrote in the *Weekly Sun* newspaper on 12 October 1907, Ransome 'ordered a grocer's van to call after lunch. The van drew up before the door. He packed his books into it, a railway rug, a bundle of clothes, and his one large chair, said good-bye to his relations, and lighting his clay pipe seated himself complacently on the tail-board. Here we have the typical incursion into Bohemia – the tail-board of a grocer's cart and a clay pipe, with some few books and no furniture.'

The book was his first success – and came to be written after he was approached by an employee at the publishers Curtis Brown. Her name was Stefana Stevens, and later she would become a world-renowned anthropologist. The story goes that Ransome was having tea with the journalist Cecil Chesterton, younger brother of GK. She had heard Ransome talking about life in London as an aspiring writer, and legend has it she interrupted him mid-pour as he topped up Cecil's tea cup and said, 'There's a book that ought to be written, and you are the one that ought to write it, a book on Bohemia in London, an essayistical sort of book, putting Bohemia of today against a background of the past. Think it over, I've got a publisher waiting for it.'

While this patch may have been recognised as the haunt of London Bohemia, for other literary types the fact this neighbourhood was full of wannabe writers, pretend painters and failed artists of both great and little talent made it both enticing and horrifying. They were drawn to it like a moth to a flame – conscious of a sense of danger as they explored Soho streets.

None more so than the writer Patrick Hamilton, who based his novel *20,000 Streets Under the Sky* on the patch. He haunted the pubs of the locality, drinking himself into stupors as he pined for a prostitute he had met in Fitzrovia's backstreets and fallen passionately in love with. She gave him the inspiration for the love-rat character of Nettie in the brilliant tragedy *Hangover Square*.

Patrick Hamilton.

It was the success of *20,000 Streets* – which for the curious today offers a splendid window on London past – that allowed Hamilton to set up home in New Cavendish Street and concentrate on getting the stories in his head on to paper. And it was from his New Cavendish Street lodgings that he hit upon the wheeze for his play *Rope*, which would be adapted for screen by Alfred Hitchcock twenty years later and stars James Stewart.

It was said by critics – who loved it and were not trying to disparage his work – that Hamilton based the story of the two murderers who hide the body of their friend in a trunk and then calmly host a dinner party on a real case in Chicago a few years previously. He denied the link between the two, but the similarities are such that it is hard to believe he wasn't influenced, either consciously or otherwise. Nathan Leopold and Richard Loeb were friends and lovers who came from privileged backgrounds, the spoiled scions of wealthy families. They considered themselves Nietzsche's Supermen, and decided they would prove this by pulling off a perfect murder. However, things did not go the way their arrogance had told them it would. A plan to strangle their victim, a cousin of Loeb's, failed and they instead beat him to death in the back of their car. They left a trail of clues and were soon caught.

Hamilton set *Rope* in a Mayfair flat and showed his flair for the macabre, which is all too apparent in his books *The Gorse Trilogy* and *Hangover Square*. The work was read by the Repertory Players on a Sunday night at The Strand Theatre – and its brilliance saw it quickly transferred to The Ambassadors, where it enjoyed a long run. Later, Hamilton would follow up its success with the play *Gaslight*, from which we get the phrase 'to gaslight', meaning in modern parlance to persuade someone that what they know to be true is otherwise.

SHERLOCK HOLMES AND THE MYSTERY OF THE HEAD-TURNING HOTEL

From Fitzrovia, we're promenading along Euston Road, that thoroughfare that until two weeks ago was a busy fume-choked highway and now lies silent and its fresh-tasting air feels mournful for a bustling world temporarily lost.

When Ken Livingstone was Mayor of London, he commissioned architect Sir Terry Farrell to look at how Euston Road could be improved. He employed architectural students to monitor traffic flow. They could not understand why some sets of lights caused tailbacks, while at others the cars flowed freely. The lights' timings were all the same – until Sir Terry realised that each set where traffic built up happened to be opposite one of the road's listed buildings, such as the St Pancras Hotel – and drivers were each pausing a little longer to gaze out at them.

Baker Street.

And as we head west down Euston Road, we soon find ourselves at Baker Street. Let us pause outside 221b, the fictional home of Sherlock Holmes. And while the tourists who gather outside can sometimes mistake Holmes for a real person and the address as genuinely where he mused upon the great mysteries of the human psyche, it is true his creator, Arthur Conan Doyle, was partial to a bit of sleuthing himself.

As Holmes's fame grew, Doyle found himself asked to consider interesting cases. Fans would send him letters asking for his help, and occasionally his interest would be piqued, as if he were donning the famous deerstalker himself. Where he suspected someone had caught a blow off the heavy hand of injustice, he threw himself in.

One such a case that was brought to his attention via the morning post involved a Sherlockian tale of a mutilated pit pony found in a field in a Midlands mining village in 1903. It was the latest of a spate of nasty such happenings, going back a good few years, and had baffled and appalled the rustic country folk of thereabouts, leading to sour vibes and unpleasant innuendo in a tight-knit community.

The village rozzers, acting under increasing pressure and fear of ridicule when off duty in the local pubs, eventually pointed the finger at a chap called George Edalji, an Anglo-Indian considered to be something of an outsider. The officers charged with bringing this murky tale to a conclusion were egged on by others and decided that because they found George 'a bit odd', he was probably guilty of stomping across muddy fields at night armed with sharp tools and enjoyed a weird kink harming quadrupeds. The keen country Bobbies raided his humble home, and finding what looked like blood and horsehair on a coat, and muddy boots, they banged him up.

After Doyle read about the case, he was convinced that poor George was innocent, and threw himself into proving so. Doyle arranged to meet George and his first impression was pure Holmes.

As he approached, he saw a young man reading a newspaper – and struggling to do so as he was staring at the newsprint through extremely thick glasses. It was clear he was partially blind – making the idea that he could sneak into a field in the dead of night, overpower a large animal and make the extremely precise, deadly incisions impossible.

Doyle investigated further and eventually found the real culprit – a man called Rodney Sharp, who worked in a butcher's shop and on a cattle boat, and had a long-standing grudge against George and his family. Eventually, after Doyle's investigations caused a national outcry, George was released after three years of porridge.

Chiltern Court.

Opposite Holmes's fictional address is the home of another active imagination – the Baker Street flat of HG Wells. He lived in the grand Chiltern Court, which is just up on the right from the Marylebone Road.

It's an imposing block that towers over Baker Street, with its original double front doors still in place, complete with polished brass fittings. It gives off a pre-war serviced apartments vibe, and if Wells had managed to time travel as his hero in his 1895 novel *The Time Machine* did, he'd certainly recognise it.

While Wells is, of course, known for his science fiction tomes, his Fabian politics, his advocation of free love and vegetarianism, he had a perhaps surprising penchant for playing with toy soldiers, considering his avowed pacifism. He wrote two books based on the games he had invented for his children on the carpets of the sitting room of his Chiltern Court home – *Floor Games* (1912) and *Little Wars* (1913). The second volume was packed full of rules to follow, making him the father of modern war gaming and thus even more beloved by geeks and nerds who have enjoyed his marvellous novels.

An aside, and an esoteric link as we plough forwards: he can also been spotted on the cover of the Beatles' seminal 1967 album, *Sgt Pepper's Lonely Hearts Club Band*.

BEATLEMANIA AND GUILD-Y SECRETS

While we are in this general area, both physically and figuratively, let us swerve north-east and head to St John's Wood, and Cavendish Avenue, to be precise. It is here Paul McCartney bought a house in 1965 for £40,000 from Dr Desmond O'Neill. How McCartney, aged 23, must have felt the first time he closed the heavy front door behind him and considered his journey from a two-storey terrace in Liverpool to this white stuccoed detached mansion! It was close enough to Abbey Road for him to be able stroll to work each day, and he was also partial to walking the neighbourhood's leafy streets late at night with his big shaggy Old English sheepdog Martha, for whom he wrote the song 'Martha My Dear'.

And it was while out walking Martha, accompanied by Beatles' biographer Hunter Davies, one spring morning that Paul revealed how they had penned the *Sgt Pepper* song 'Getting Better'. It was a phrase used by a stand-in drummer Jimmie Nicholl, while the Beatles toured Australia in 1964. When asked how he was getting on, standing in for a sick Ringo, he'd always reply: 'It's getting better.'

Abbey Road.

Now – while considering the Beatles and St John's Wood, we must swing west to Abbey Road, where 'Getting Better' was recorded. We know that the lockdown has given Westminster Council the chance to repaint the famous zebra crossing outside the studio, but let us step through the doors and recall an incident that occurred with John Lennon while the Beatles were making *Sgt Pepper*.

Producer George Martin was in the process of adding a piano lick to the song 'Lovely Rita' – about the parking attendant who would book the Beatles when they parked illegally outside the studio – when John complained of feeling a bit rough. Martin took him upstairs to a large,open window to get some fresh air, unaware that John had taken what he thought was an 'upper' – but in fact it was a tab of acid.

Paul, realising what had happened, rushed upstairs to rescue his friend before any accidents could occur. The story goes that Paul found John perched precariously on the window frame, admiring the view, and carefully began to entice him away – at which point John said, 'Stop bloody fussing. I know I can't fucking fly, Paul – you know I'm fucking scared of fucking heights.'

Let us finish today's walk by heading back east to another centre of counter-culture London – this time along Wellington Road, a ten-minute saunter from the Beatles' studio. It was here that the Cambodian government's embassy was based – and when the Khmer Rouge took power in 1975, its staff left their Wellington Road base in rather a hurry.

And what would become of such a magnificent, abandoned building in a desirous neighbourhood? Why, it became the headquarters for the Guild of Transcultural Studies, a squat set up by counter-culture poet, writer artist and general happenings organiser Dave Tomlin.

Tomlin was a cog in the counter-culture machine of the period. His adventures ranged from travelling England with a horse and cart to getting stranded on an island off the African coast. He played the saxophone for far-out free jazz groups, including experimental music ensemble The Third Ear Band, and the Giant Sun Trolley at the infamous UFO Club. He also wrote for the far-out hippie paper, *International Times*. Such occupations will not get one rich, and Dave made the derelict Victorian houses of north London his home – a seasoned squatter who lived a peripatetic life until that stroll along Wellington Road.

In 1975, he had noticed the large number of telephone directories building up on the doorstep of the house on his daily constitutional – a sure-fire sign that a house was not occupied. He crept around the side, clambered in – and it became his and many others' home for nearly two decades.

Dave Tomlin and the Guild for Transcendental Studies. (Picture courtesy of Dave Tomlin)

We'll let him take up the story.

'Ready to board with a crow bar up his sleeve, Jubal Smith contemplates an empty house,' he wrote in his memoirs. 'The basement door is nailed up fast with timber struts ... he opens a gap large enough to slip through. Inside it is devastation: the house has burned and gutted from within, floorboards and ceilings fallen, the joists charred beyond redemption.'

Dave and his friend were on the hunt for a new squat, having been served ten days' notice from their place in Belsize Park. But this Regent's Park home was 'way too fucked', as he put it, to be of use. Despondently, they started the long trudge back up to Belsize Park – and it was while on Wellington Road that Dave spotted the telltale phone books.

Once inside and after tackling the to-do list of getting the leccy on, dragging a mattress upstairs and putting a new lock on the front door, Dave made a brass plaque proclaiming it was home to the Guild of Transcultural Studies to give it some sense of respectability. Artists, musicians and philosophers took rooms, while the ground floor, the Grand Salon, once the haunt of ambassadors, politicians, business people and other such hobnobbers, played host to far-out events.

CHIPS WITH EVERYTHING

We'll head now on to Avenue Road, past the home of heavyweight champion boxer Anthony Joshua, and stop by another notable landmark – the former home of property developer Harry Hyams.

Hyams was the man who built Centrepoint, which we have already considered – and despite the 1960s skyscraper's teething problems, Harry obviously liked it enough to employ the same bloke, Richard Seifert, to build him a London residence.

Hyams hated the limelight and did all he could to avoid publicity. He held his firm's AGM when few would show up – 4.15p.m. on New Year's Eve. He once appeared wearing a Mickey Mouse mask to avoid the scrutiny of photographers outside. He loved spending his fortune on art, which he would then loan anonymously to galleries: Turner's 'Bridgewater Sea Piece' has been on display at the National Gallery for more than thirty years in this way.

But such a collection attracted unwanted attention, too – Hyams became the victim of what coppers believe is the biggest domestic burglary ever recorded in Britain: a booty of art and antiques valued at £80 million, only half of which was recovered.

Right – off we go, this time to the bottom of Avenue Road, and right along Prince Albert Road. At its western end you can find St John's Wood Church – a beautiful building constructed in 1814 by Thomas Hardwick. It has been the venue for some illustrious weddings and funerals: your correspondent remembers attending a service for poet and author Ursula Vaughan Williams – widow of composer Ralph – in 2007 for the *Camden New Journal*. Happier moments the pews have witnessed include the 1953 wedding of Peggy Cripps – daughter of politician Sir Stafford – and the Ghanian lawyer and campaigner Joe Appiah.

St John's Wood Church.

The Seashell of Lisson Grove.

Appiah, whose family were members of the Ashanti aristocracy, was heavily involved in the liberation of his home country. He was mates with Ghana's first president, Kwame Nkrumah, before politics drove a wedge between them. Nkrumah was his first choice to be his best man (he lived nearby in Tufnell Park). But Nkrumah couldn't make it – so communist and African revolutionary George Padmore stepped in to hand the ring over and make the speech.

All this walking is making one peckish – so let's head south-west and buy lunch from the Queen Mum's favourite chippy, The Seashell of Lisson Grove. It opened at the end of the First World War and is still going strong. She was such a regular that when her driver pulled up outside, owner John Faulkner knew what to get ready – crispy battered cod, chips with plenty of vinegar, and sides of mushy peas, pickled eggs and a wally.

Now on to Edgware Road – the home to some of London's best Middle-Eastern restaurants. It also has its fair share of casinos, and we will stop outside The Grosvenor for one of those rare stories of punters beating the house.

Such gambling palaces like to keep the high rollers at the table for as long as possible, so they offer free sandwiches and drinks. This piece of common knowledge prompted a rather nice scam, established by a group of older ladies who lived in the area.

This ten-strong group signed up for free membership and then would meet twice a week for lunch at one of the casinos. They'd exchange £25 for poker chips and then sit at various tables as if they were going to have a flutter. Along would come waiters and they'd politely request a platter to keep them nourished as the cards were turned over and the roulette tables spun.

Once the fare was devoured, they would pick up their £25 worth of tokens, swap them back, bellies full and purses untouched. It was an unofficial pensioners' lunch club that ran for years.

One of these ladies' uncles was the great Sammy Cohen, an East End tailor who was also the British draughts champion. He could play a dozen games at once and win them all – and it was watching him being plied with sandwiches and drinks to keep him at tables in social and working men's clubs that gave his niece the idea to start with.

A RIGHT ROYAL RAMBLE

Leaving the rattle of poker chips behind us, we're stretching our legs south for a decent potato chip-burning stroll. We shall return to the Edgware Road later, but right now let us snake through backstreets in a southerly direction. We shall get our footsteps bearing down on Park Street, the longest road in the Grosvenor Estate, which takes us in a straight, Roman-esque southerly direction.

This road is so packed with notables that its inhabitants boasted not double but triple-barrelled surnames, such was the family pedigree they felt they had to honour. It was home to Edward Charles Stewart Robert Vane-Tempest-Stewart, the 8th Marquess of Londonderry, who would then go on to inherit the more manageable title of Viscount Castlereagh.

He came from a family of mine owners, and had a frosty relationship with his dad – they took opposing views during the General Strike of 1926. He also had a love of football, the working man's game, and would become a director of Arsenal. Vane-Tempest-Stewart (let's use it in full as it's a cracker) was renowned for the joyful parties he would throw. One Christmas, he decorated his tree with condoms, aware that his vicar was due to pop over on his annual visit.

Once, after a heavy session, he had retired to his bedroom. It was announced that Ruth Graham, the wife of Evangelical Christian TV pastor Billy, had come to see him. When told he was otherwise engaged, she would not take no for an answer, and so was shown into the Lord's chambers. She entered to the invitation, as Vane-Tempest-Stewart pulled back the covers, to 'hop on in'.

OF PUBIC INTEREST

Less keen on such bodily contact was Park Street resident John Ruskin, and it was from this address that one of those enduring Victorian scandals took place.

In 1848, Ruskin, aged 29 and with a blooming reputation as writer, critic and art historian, married 19-year-old beauty Euphemia Gray. The pair set up home in Park Street, and it was here, on their wedding night, that things are said to have gone wrong. The couple were to separate six years later – Euphemia, known as Effie, fell in love with Ruskin's protégé, the artist John Everett Millais. She asked for the marriage to be annulled, on the rather embarrassing grounds for a Victorian gentleman that he had failed to consummate their betrothal.

Effie explained what had happened on the night Ruskin first saw a woman in the nud. She said it struck her that he had 'imagined women were quite different to what he saw I was, and that the reason he did not make me his Wife was because he was disgusted with my person the first evening.'

Ruskin, whose only exposure to the female nude was through the well-sanded marbles of classical sculpture, was apparently horrified that Effie

had pubic hair – and was so turned off by it he refused to have sex with her. However, he tried to explain it away by suggesting there was something about her character that was a bucket of cold water in the bedroom. 'It may be thought strange that I could abstain from a woman who to most people was so attractive. But though her face was beautiful, her person was not formed to excite passion. On the contrary, there were certain circumstances in her person which completely checked it.'

Still, his Park Street home was productive in other ways: in the three years he lived there, he completed his work *The Seven Lamps of Architecture* and the first volume of *The Stones of Venice*.

Euphemia Gray painted by
Thomas Richmond.

A few doors down from Ruskin's pad we come to the address of Sir Robert Vansittart, diplomat, politician and arch opponent of appeasement in the 1930s. As well as his role in national affairs – he had the unenviable task of serving in the Foreign Office through the 1930s and, like Davy's lamp, was very much a canary in the mine when it came to Hitler – he was an accomplished novelist, poet and playwright. Had he been born in less trying times, his temperament no doubt would have seen him idle away his days by a lake with a pen in hand and a sonnet in his head. He was suited to the romantics, both in literature and painting. Known as Van to his friends, this remarkable man shouted from the rooftops his fears over German aggression, and was a respected figure in parliament and Whitehall.

Sir Robert Vansittart.

But the serious politician could not keep the sprightly artist under wraps. Van was a friend of the film director Alexander Korda, and he helped finance his films. He turned his hand to writing screenplays in the 1930s, perhaps escaping from the pressures of his role at the Foreign Office, and, extraordinarily considering the circumstances, during the war he penned the lyrics for Korda's musicals *The Thief of Baghdad* and *Jungle Book*. Quite the polymath.

Van would often stroll from his Park Street house to Green Park, where he occasionally met Winston Churchill to discuss the state of play away from the noise of the Commons.

Churchill was notorious for demanding a good night's sleep – and during the war, he told his staff not to wake him unless Britain was actually being invaded. In the map room in Whitehall, in Churchill's bunker where the Prime Minister rested up, Royal Navy reservist Captain Richard Pim heard on 7 May 1945 that the war was over.

The captain faced a dilemma: should he wake the chief, or let him sleep through? He waited until Churchill stirred, and then stood by the Churchillian scratcher and shared the fact the Germans had surrendered.

'For five years you have brought me bad news, sometimes worse than others, Pim,' said the stirring Winnie. 'Now you have redeemed yourself.'

He was clearly one for an instantly snappy response when roused from slumbers, which takes us nicely on to a favourite Churchill anecdote. During his second stint as PM from 1951, he was woken one Sunday morning by his aide carrying the papers: the aide's ashen face instantly put Winnie ill at ease.

'What is it?' hurrumphed the PM. 'Is it war with Russia?'

'No,' replied the aide, and proceeded to explain that one of the tabloids had wind of a backbencher easing their stresses and strains with a Grenadier Guardsman in a Green Park bush the night before.

Churchill paused and said to his aide, 'It was rather cold last night, wasn't it?,' to which the aide replied, 'Yes sir, only 2 degrees, very chilly indeed.'

Another brief silence, before Churchill said, 'Makes you proud to be British.'

Saucy.

GOOD FOR YOUR CONSTITUTION

Right – heading to the south-western end of Green Park, we find Constitution Hill. It is a road with an important, political-sounding name, isn't it? Some kind of symbol of nationhood and the civic state, like the grand-sounding avenues they do really well in France.

But no, it has nothing to do with Bills of Rights or our lack of a written one. Instead, it earned its name simply because Charles II liked to use it for a daily walk.

There is a story that he was once kicking the leaves through Green Park with just a couple of attendants, when his brother James rolled past in a grand carriage with full-on escort. When James leaned out of the window in a fury, and remonstrated with his brother for travelling without guards, Charles replied something along the following lines:

'I have no fear, James. I am perfectly safe. No man in England would ever do me in, because it would put you on the throne.'

Constitution Hill.

It seems his judge of his brother's character was accurate – James II was shoved off the throne in the Glorious Revolution of 1688.

James's reputation has, as with so many monarchs whose names are learned by rote, been solely remembered in our popular imagination as the Catholic king booted out by William of Orange. When William landed in Brixham in 1688, his 15,000 troops scared the life out of James and his followers. James turned tail for France, where he remained in exile for the rest of his life.

Pity poor James (to some degree): second son of Charles I, he'd seen his dad's head cut off and what he'd been told was his family's by Divine Right become a republic. He was given the title the Duke of York, and fought alongside his father at the Civil War dust-up, the Battle of Edgehill. When Cromwell's New Model Army surrounded Oxford in 1646, James II was taken by the Parliamentary troops to be held prisoner at St James's Palace. But from here, he masterminded a daring escape by dressing up as a wizened old washer woman and sneaking past guards. He made his way safely to Holland and then to France.

When his brother, Charles II, returned, York was given swathes of land in the American colonies – his title was bequeathed to New York – but he was not held in high regard.

Firstly, there was the smell in many nostrils of popery about him, and as Charles II lacked male heirs, James' religious leanings mattered politically. This monkey on his back was not made any lighter by his personal life.

James met and then promptly fell in love with Anne Hyde, a commoner and the daughter of one of his ministers, Edward Hyde. Such a match was scorned by gossiping gentry, and raised questions about his character. James didn't care – he was smitten.

They had eight children, but lost six before they'd reached toddlerhood. This seemingly continuous and punishing set of tragedies must have knocked the poor couple for six. It got worse for poor James. In 1671, his lodestone, Anne, died.

Such personal pain may have been a reason for James looking for solace in the bosom of a religion that had pronounced rituals concerning the living and the dead, and a long-standing, cast-iron belief in the afterlife. Just as spiritualism gained a public foothold following the deaths of so many in the Great War, perhaps James found his personal solace in the Catholic Church.

He was certainly exposed to Catholicism while exiled in France, and when asked to renounce the faith in 1673 when the anti-Catholic test act was introduced, it was too much for him to bear. Instead, he resigned his commission as the Lord High Admiral and made his loyalty to Rome public.

When Charles II died in 1685, leaving no heir to take on the family business, a groundswell of horrible anti-Catholic terror filled public discourse. James was clearly the rightful king, and in April 1685 he was handed the crown at Westminster Abbey. He didn't last long. Rebellions were afoot, and when William of Orange landed in 1688, James got as far as Salisbury before he lost his bottle and his army disappeared, leaving the route open to London for William with minimum fuss and a thankfully bloodless coup.

Now, back to Green Park, the haunt of these two brothers who were kings. It is known, unsurprisingly, for its expanse of general greenness. This deck-chaired pleasure garden has an interesting design feature. Gaze about you and you may note the lack of ornamental flower beds that are usually standard to these remaining tributes to the once-unsullied lands that lie beneath our species' impact on this patch by a river. It is said that flowers have never thrived in Green Park because of a huge communal grave holding the bodies of leprosy sufferers beneath the topsoil – which is also why it lacks a pond or lake.

Before we dive back into town, a quick word about the Wellington Arch, which is at one end of Constitution Hill. In the 1830s, committees were formed to create national monuments to celebrate Wellington and Nelson. Nelson's cheerleaders gave us the Column – but the Wellington lot were less successful.

Wellington's statue.

An eighty-strong committee was appointed, and it was envisaged no doubt that over a few brandies and a cigar or pipe these fine gentlemen would come up with a suitably imposing wheeze to commemorate the hook-nosed conqueror of Napoleonic France. But it panned out somewhat differently. The forceful Duke of Rutland managed to form a clique that hoodwinked their fellow committee members. They suggested plonking a statue on top of an arch already built as a northern entrance to Buckingham Palace, positioned as it was across the way from Wellington's home.

But what should have been an easy enough task soon turned into a bit of a stink: the job was given to the sculptor Matthew Coates Wyatt, a mate of Rutland's, and then he proceeded to forge something completely out of proportion to the arch itself.

It was huge, and ridiculed by Londoners, many of whom thought Wellington was no hero but the public face of an oppressive army that had conspired to discourage the population from following the French Revolution. It was eventually removed.

Onwards! Along Piccadilly a little way and then north a bit to pause for a moment outside Dartmouth House, the home of the English-Speaking Union since 1926. The Union was established in 1918 by Sir Evelyn Wrench as an inclusive, non-partisan, non-sectarian club open to both men and women (not usual then) with its stated aims fostering 'international fellowship and peace'. It organised cultural exchanges, literary projects and much more. During the Second World War, it became an aid hub – and singer Gracie Fields donated every penny she earned from a British and American tour to it.

After some Mayfair window shopping at outlets selling stuff for a lot of money to people who like that sort of thing, we find ourselves in Albemarle Street, one-time home to Edward Hyde, Earl of Clarendon (1609–74) ... which brings us nicely back again to the time of Charles II, as it was this chap whose daughter the unfortunate king went kooky for. He was Chaz's Lord Chancellor for a while and the monarch gave him land in Mayfair, where he splurged £40,000 on building a magnificent mansion. He didn't spend much time enjoying it: soon after the last brick was laid, he was accused of treason and fled abroad.

His son had to sell the house for less than it cost to build to pay off debts. It was bought by Christopher Moncke, the 2nd Duke of Albemarle, who was a well-known fritterer of inherited wealth. Creditors came calling and once again the house was sold to pay debts. When new owner Thomas Bond (of Bond Street fame) decided to demolish the pile, he named the street Albemarle to mark what once lay in situ.

Bond Street.

The unfortunate Earl of Clarendon has no such lasting mark in the neighbourhood, but he does hold a unique claim. His daughter Anne, who as mentioned married James II before he was crowned, had two daughters who went on to take the throne – Mary II, who reigned jointly with her husband William III, and Queen Anne. He is therefore only the second man who can claim to be grandfather to two English queens, the other being Mary I's and Elizabeth's old gramps, Henry VII.

PICK UP A PICASSO

Ah, goodbye, Albemarle Street and on north a couple of blocks to stop in Bruton Street, the former home of the celebrated Lefevre Gallery.

Set up in the 1920s by well-connected dealers Alex Reid and Ernest Lefevre, it was the place to go for Impressionism and modern art during those heady times. Reid had lodged with Van Gogh during a spell in Paris, and the list of those who displayed shows his impressive contacts: Matisse, Renoir, Cezanne, Dali, Bacon, Degas – and Picasso.

And it was from the Bruton Street Gallery that one of the many, many paintings by Picasso called 'Tête de Femme' was pinched in 1997 and led the famous cat burglar Peter Scott to have a day in the Snaresbrook Crown Court dock. Scott's career was impressive: he was known for his athletic daring and his penchant for pilfering the jewellery boxes of the wealthy. He once stole a £200,000 necklace from Sophia Loren as she worked on the Peter Sellers film *The Millionairess*; Lauren Bacall, Zsa Zsa Gabor and the Shah of Iran were also victims. He said those who he stole from were the 'real meaty jugular vein of society', but he also sometimes came away empty-handed. After raiding the homes of Bette Davis, Elizabeth Taylor and Shirley Bassey, he complained they 'didn't own anything worth stealing'.

He'd been straight for years when his collar was felt for the Picasso heist, having worked as a gardener at a King's Cross church. At his trial, he claimed he was just a go-between for the real culprits and a buyer, before changing his plea after being caught in a sting operation where he was found with a carrier bag full of cash.

The Lefevre closed its doors in 2002, citing too much competition from auction houses, signalling an end to one of those places where things seemed to happen.

Now, to Curzon Street, which reminds us of another old 'un on the wrong side of the law – Charles Curzon. A conman who earned 579 convictions, he was nicked for armed robbery aged 72. He lifted £271,000 over a ten-year period

Sophia Loren.

A Take on 'Tete de Femme', After Picasso.

and became known as 'Bang Bang Charlie'. With a love for well-cut suits, he was described as an old rogue by the press – a moniker he hated. 'I am a successful fucking bank robber,' he retorted.

In 2000, he was asked by a reporter if he had any remorse for the scare he had given those he waved a gun at. He replied, 'Some may have been mentally harmed, but there you go. Plenty of quacks around to sort them out.'

Stroll to the bottom of Curzon Street, swing right and you'll soon find yourself in Marble Arch. It is a regularly repeated urban myth that this is London's smallest police station – although it was used by the Old Bill as 'accommodation for six single men' in the 1800s. It was during this time the phrase 'if you ever want to know the time, ask a policeman' was coined. It has nothing to do with coppers being reliable – in fact, exactly the opposite. In the mid-Victorian period they were renowned for hassling street drunks, and as they did so, skilfully filching their pocket or wrist watches.

MAGIC HORSES
TALKING FRENCH

We've not headed westward much on our journeys so far, so let's go along the Bayswater Road. Its name dates from at least the 1300s, and was originally called Bayard's Watering Place – which suggests thirst-slaking ponds for horses.

Bayard is the name of a nag that stars in an ancient French *chansons de geste* (folkish songs that tell of derring-do). According to the songs, Bayard could speak French and would change size to suit the number of riders it wished to carry. Owned by the four sons of Duke Aymon, it could take the siblings about the place, and was a present from their magic cousin, Maugris.

The poor brothers are forced to hand the horse over to Charlemagne, who then weighed it down with rocks and bunged it in a river. But Bayard was having none of it. He smashed the stones with his hooves and escaped into the woods to live happily ever after.

Let us look, from Bayard's road, into Kensington Gardens and admire the Victorian-built Italian gardens, complete with fountains. It is here that JM Barrie would stroll and create amusing tales, one of which was *Peter Pan*.

While the story of the flying, perennial child, his battles with Captain Hook and a hungry crocodile have charmed pantomime lovers for decades, there is an element of sadness about the story, a sense of a lost innocence that Barrie felt acutely.

Peter Pan was first staged in 1904, and set against an Edwardian backdrop of lost innocence, war and a society emerging, painfully, from its Victorian cocoon into a modern century.

Barrie was inspired to write the story after meeting the Llewelyn Davies family in 1897. The writer had taken to walking through Kensington Gardens and Hyde Park to ease his personal torment: he was caught in a marriage he described as a 'horrid nightmare', and was suffering the grief of losing his mother and sister

Peter Pan.

the year before. As he walked slowly through the park, staring at his shoes and wondering how he could endure the pain, he gradually found some comfort in watching children play – and it prompted a conversation between himself and the Llewelyn Davies.

It was his relationship with the children, Peter, Wendy and their siblings, that prompted *Peter Pan*. The tale is laced with tragedy: the children had lost their father, Arthur, who had cancer of the jaw. When the mother, Sylvia, died in 1910, Barrie became guardian of the family and used their characters and experiences as a basis for his extraordinary story. His kindness extended to him passing all royalties and ownership from his work to the Great Ormond Street Hospital for children in 1929 – and it remains a good money-spinner for the renowned paediatric centre today.

NONE-THE-LESSING,
WE ARE SCHMEISSING

Back to Kensington Gardens, and our statue of Peter. You cannot, I am afraid, jump into their cooling waters (unlike Colin Firth and Hugh Grant, who use it for a punch-up in the film of *Bridget Jones's Diary*), but to refresh ourselves and feel like kids again, we can spin a short skip northwards to Porchester Baths in Porchester Road.

Here, we shall involve in a touch of *schmeissing*, a lovely Yiddish word that describes stripping off and getting thwacked about the torso in a steamy room with a raffia *besom*. The ornate Turkish Baths were built in 1923 by the architect Herbert Shepherd. *Schmeissing* was introduced to Londoners by East End Jewish immigrants in the 1880s and continues there today.

It makes the skin tingle and the pores sweat – a great way to live a long and happy life, according to regulars. It is also good for the libido as you get older, they claim – although one frequenter, when telling friends that sex now lasted an hour and twenty minutes, admitted under cross-examination that it included nineteen minutes of prep work and an hour to sleep afterwards.

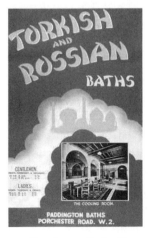

Porchester Baths.(Images courtesy of Malcom Shifrin.)

After completing a bout of rigorous *schmeissing*, now dried and togged up, let us head to Chepstow Villas, a quick mooch westwards from Porchester Road.

It was at No. 24 that 'Angry Young Man' novelist Colin Wilson, whose books so brilliantly captured the spirit of London in the late 1950s and early '60s, lived for a time – and recounted the Beatnik Bohemian goings on behind its front door in his book *Adrift in Soho*. The lead character, based on the author, hangs out at No. 24 and watches various arty types mope around and achieve little.

When he wrote about how he researched the bestseller for the *Sunday Dispatch*, he spoke of getting stoned at the Villas. The article caused a stir among the squares, with questions raised in the House of Lords as to whether Wilson's article might incite the innocent to dabble in drugs.

The Director of Public Prosecutions decided, on reflection, there were no grounds for charges to be brought. Wilson was himself no advocate of turning on, tuning in and dropping out: he writes of the Villas' inhabitants with a detachment that sees through their attempts to be 'cool', and when his protagonist gets passed a reefer, he decides 'the kind of muzzy happiness it created was the enemy of incisive thought or feeling'.

While Wilson flips and flops from his shared digs further west to central London for some action, in *Adrift in Soho: Beatniks, Bums and Bohemians*, he offers an insightful chronicle of the West One area in the 1950s, he casts an outsider's scornful yet somehow admiring eye on its inhabitants, and the morals and philosophies to which they adhere.

And while he may not have approved of tripping the light fantastic, he finds his own form of escapism in the windows of shops who advertised their wares in this pre-internet age with glorious ways to implore the browser to step in and buy something.

As he wanders down Tottenham Court Road, Soho bound, he writes: 'I finally stopped by the lighted window of a bookshop, and stood looking at the expensive volumes on art. The centre of the window was occupied by a display designed to sell some new set of art books. An automatic device turned over pages set in a metal frame, and each page contained an illustration. As I stood there, a reproduction of two Egyptian statues appeared; they were, I think, Mycerinus and his Queen. Something about their mechanical perfection excited me, and I stood there staring. The page turned again. This time it was a photograph of a black basalt statue of a seated man; its form was so abstract it was almost cubical in shape. The knees and pedestal were covered in hyroglyphics. Again the excitement made me tremble; I stared at it as if I could eat it. Then the page turned once more. I walked away, possessed by a vision of mathematical perfection that was nevertheless wrought from living material. I understood now what I detested about London. The life people lived in this city was designed to interpose between man and that image of perfection.'

From the Villas and Wilson, it seems fitting to now head to nearby Portobello Road, where a cornerstone of London's counter-cultural publications was once based, and although a generation on from Wilson, something of a kindred spirit to the Kitchen Sinkers and Angry Young Men of 1950s literature, theatre and film.

Frendz magazine was the spiritual sibling to such publications as *Oz* and *International Times*, and had originally been the London edition of the California magazine *Rolling Stone* – but when they had differences of editorial opinion, *Frendz* editor Alan Marcuson had enough advertisers to break out alone. True to all good counter-culture magazines, the editor would be charged under the Obscene Publications Act, for, as he put it, 'a picture of Otto Muhl sh***ing on stage and something by Malcolm Livingstone about the secretary on the way to work that gets knobbed by everyone'.

Portobello Road.

WAY OUT WEST

Along from the broom cupboard offices of *Frendz* you will find the Westway, worthy of a begrudging eye glanced in its direction.

In purely engineering terms, that dank monstrosity is special. At its completion in 1970, it was the longest continual elevated structure in Europe and boasted heated slopes so ice did not form on its gradients.

Urban myths surrounding the road include rumours that the concrete contains various bodies of unfortunates who crossed the Krays. Apparently, the thousands of tons of hardcore became a discreet resting place for those they didn't want to have around.

One of the many houses demolished to make way for the A40 was the childhood home of world middleweight champion boxer Terry 'The Paddington Express' Downes. Much loved in the neighbourhood, he was generous with his time and his wit.

Westway.

Westway.

Once, after being knocked down rather too quickly by another boxer, he was asked in a post-match interview who he'd like to fight next. Still bloodied and groggy, he replied, 'Whoever it was who arranged my last one.' He was also known, as a young man, for sticking up for his mates against anti-Semitic street bullies. A tough guy with a warm spirit.

CANAL KNOWLEDGE

From the Westway, we cross the Grand Union Canal, the 137-mile-long route from London to Birmingham, at the junction of Harrow Road.

Let us pause for a moment to consider how (usually) today the canal bristles with walkers, cyclists and people living on boats. Not so, of course, in the 1970s when London's canals were symbolic of our industrial decline. Because the canals were seen as places to dump stolen safes, used firearms and other unwanted detritus, not many wanted to wander along them.

Change came almost unintentionally. The GLC, which managed the waterways, struck a deal with the Electricity Board. They needed to lay new high-powered cables across London, which would mean digging up miles of roads and sinking cooling shafts to keep them from overheating. Instead, they hit on the wheeze of laying them along towpaths – and using the canal water to make sure the cables did not get too warm.

But by doing so, workers had to clear the towpaths of obstacles, bushes and the like, thus making them accessible. It helped kickstart the canals' renaissance.

Before we sign off for another week, let us bask in this early May sunshine in the gardens at Edbrooke Road, just north of the Union Canal. While it looks like a traditional west London Victorian square, its creation is marked with tragedy. Two high-explosive bombs landed on the street on the night of 7 October 1940, partially demolishing a row of houses and leading to multiple casualties.

After the war, instead of rebuilding on the bomb sites, a campaign by neighbours turned them into a public space. They are a little patch of green remembering the dark nights of the Blitz, complete with a memorial to those who lost their lives. Today, as we mark the seventy-fifth anniversary of Victory in Europe, we will rest a while, eat our sandwich and raise a glass as we remember the sacrifices made by the generation who beat the Nazis.

Edbrooke Road plane tree.

BEYOND THE VALE

From Edbrooke Road Gardens, we now continue our tramp in a westwards direction, joining Elgin Avenue just beyond Paddington Rec, where Sir Roger Bannister ran lap after lap of a cinder track as he trained to beat a four-minute mile in the early 1950s. He was a medical student at nearby St Marys, an unknown at the time, but those who watched him clock up ever faster laps, his medical books and packed lunch left by the finish line, knew they were watching a young man destined for greatness.

He is not the only champion of the Paddington Rec track. Built around the sides was a concrete bowl, and it was here that champion cycler, the Leeds-born Beryl Burton, also trained regularly when in London to keep up to speed using pedal power. She would zip around the outside of Bannister's track.

The Paddington Recreation Ground's running track, home to record breakers.

Beryl Burton. (Public domain)

What an extraordinary champ she was: she absolutely dominated the sport, winning over ninety UK championships, seven world titles and smashing records at will. Her mastery of the twelve-hour time trial was such that she held a world record faster than any male cyclist achieved at the time, one that stood for two years. Burton remained an amateur throughout her life, choosing instead to earn a living working on a rhubarb farm and not accepting the numerous offers from sponsors who beat a path to her door.

Sadly, Burton died aged just 58, of heart failure – fittingly, while out on a bicycle ride. She was delivering invitations to her 59th birthday party.

Other speedsters who honed their craft on the Rec's cycle track include Sir Bradley Wiggins, Tour de France winner in 2012, a year when he also scooped an Olympic gold, which isn't bad work. He went to nearby St Augustine's comprehensive school in Kilburn and would work out at the Rec.

From such dashing feats of athletic prowess, we shall move from the physical to the aesthetic. Artist Edward Ardizzone made Elgin Avenue his home in the 1920s, and when not illustrating children's books, he could be found sketching the interiors of the area's pubs on anything that came to hand. These jottings would eventually become the subject of a book, *The Local*, published in 1939, a celebration of the great Victorian gin palaces of London.

One such boozer was the Chippenham Hotel in Shirland Road, where Ardizzone would find a chair in the saloon bar. Over a pint of mild, he would get down the characters slinking in for refreshment.

Its first licensee was William Pullen, who had his name above the door in 1881, and the place did a good trade until the 2010s. Its interior was admired by Ardizzone – period mirrors and tiling were uncovered after a refurb in the 1970s.

And around this time, Clash frontman Joe Strummer was living in a squat round the corner in Walterton Road. He was in a band called the 101ers, named after the house number of the squat where they resided, and they had a weekly gig at 'The Chip'.

But neither Joe nor Edward would recognise it today. The Chippenham was sold by Punch Taverns to a firm based in an offshore tax haven around six years ago. It was closed down, its interior stripped out, and threatened with demolition in 2018.

CREATING THE CARNIVAL

On this sad note, let us stroll past Strummer's squat until we hit Harrow Road, and take note of another one of Strummer's haunts, the Windsor Castle pub: it is said The Clash's song 'Protex Blue' is named after the type of condoms in the gents' vending machine. The Castle also played host to the likes of Madness and Dexys Midnight Runners, while Iron Maiden showed up and refused to play as the pub was empty – leading to a furious row with the landlord and the heavy metal rockers being banned for life.

From screeching guitars and feedback-saturated amps, we're moving into warmer, bass line territory as we leave Harrow Road behind us and hit Ladbroke Grove – original Carnival territory.

While Carnival legend Claudia Jones, the civil rights-battling, USA-baiting writer, philosopher and seasoned communist firebrand, is rightfully given dues for establishing the event at the end of the 1950s, it was the work of others that laid the foundations for the biggest street party in Europe. Jones had organised

Claudia Jones.

the first carnivals indoors at St Pancras Town Hall – but in 1964, Ladbroke Grove-based social worker Rhuanne Laslett put on a street party for children whose parents could not afford to take them on holiday. It had nothing to do with Caribbean culture, merely something for the neighbourhood's youngsters to do. Attractions included a donkey and cart lent by a trader at Portobello Market and a box of false moustaches.

And also there that day was the Russell Henderson Steel Band, a trio led by Henderson, a Trinidadian musician. Their pans hung around their necks and as the day wore on, they decided to remove the barriers at one end of the street and take the children for a walk as they played.

'Although this was only a children's fete, it still had quite a carnival flavour, so I'm thinking like a carnival in Trinidad, we should have a road march,' Russell told author Lloyd Bradley in an interview more than forty years later. Off they went – and on, and on, gaining followers … they ended up looping through the entire neighbourhood in what would be the longest carnival route in the history of the annual pavement rave-up.

Cambridge Gardens.

Norman Jay of the Good Times Sound System.

Let us follow the ghosts of these pioneers, until we reach Cambridge Gardens – and here we shall pause for another brief consideration of a key moment in Carnival history. As with much of the area in the 1970s, the white stucco housing had been split up into flats: the vast majority were run down, and many were still occupied by squatters.

It was outside No. 37 that the Jay brothers turned up in 1980, knocked on the door and told the occupiers they would be setting up their home-made sound system – then called Great Tribulation – in the garden for Carnival. They offered the yawning, dressing gown-wearing, stoned hippies on the doorstep £10 for electricity and said they could make a few bob by selling beers, too.

Norman and Joey Jay played a mixture of reggae, soul, disco and funk – and it was the beginning of the Notting Hill institution, the Good Times Sound System.

And it is here we will pause for another week, to sit on the garden wall of No. 37, sup a Red Stripe and gather our thoughts.

NOTHING LIKE A DAME,
BLACK STAR LINERS
AND HERO RAILWAYMEN

We have now strayed briefly in to Kensington and Chelsea, unable to resist following the beat of the Carnival. But let us get back on track, so we will head back up Ladbroke Grove until we reach the famous Kensal Green Cemetery.

While Westminster is famous for the three cemeteries its council under Dame Shirley Porter sold for a grand total of 15p – just one of a number of scandals that engulfed the Tory council in the 1980s – Kensal Green was thankfully not under their jurisdiction. It is the resting place of plenty of famous people, ranging from black activist Marcus Garvey, who was buried there in 1940 before his body was repatriated to Jamaica, to Victorian tightrope walker Emile Blondin, who traversed the Niagara Falls on a flimsy rope.

Kensal Green Cemetery.

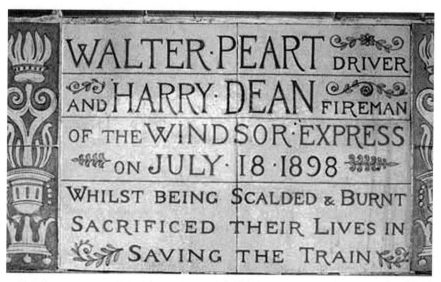

Dean and Peart Memorial, Kensal Rise Cemetery.

Let us pause by the graves of two lesser-known men, who deserve utmost respect. Train driver Walter Peart and his fireman Henry Dean died in 1898, and their graves were built by the Amalgamated Society of Railway Servants. They lost their lives as they saved passengers on the Paddington to Windsor express. Their train's boiler exploded and the pair were seriously injured, but they did all they could to get the runaway engine to a standstill before they sought help for themselves, saving the lives of hundreds. Their graves include a plaque marking their heroism, and a relief sculpture of a train.

DROOPY DRAINS AND
THE HUMAN SCARECROWS

N ext up, we'll head along nearby Droop Street, partly because it has an excellent name, and partly to mark the person who built it.

Victorian developer William Austin started his working life being paid 1p a day as a scarecrow on a farm. He worked his way up to running a firm that built drains – and then spent his fortune on building homes for workers. He created the 2,000 Gothic-style cottages around Queen's Park – and Droop Street was one of the roads he built. It took the name from a Mr Droop, who was a director of Mr Austin's Artisans', Labourers' and General Dwellings Company. Mr Austin gave all his Queen's Park streets such tributes to those who had dug out the foundations.

From here, let's head back along the Harrow Road, and pause outside the All Stars Boxing Gym. Established by Ghana-born Isola Akay MBE, it has become a stable for champs – but more importantly, a magnet for young people who want to work out and learn the discipline. In 1974, Mr Akay's son, Tee Jay, wanted to box but he and his friends were banned from other gyms in the area because they were considered to be disruptive. Mr Akay took it on himself to give them training sessions on Paddington Rec – eventually earning rightful respect and finding a permanent home. Aware of the poor relationship between young people and the police, he had the brainwave of inviting coppers in to train.

Mr Akay's dedication and brilliance has become a beacon in the neighbourhood – and produced a few winners at the Police Boxing Championships, too.

Leaving behind the atmosphere of the ring, we will schlep up to the BBC Maida Vale studios, Delaware Road. Dating from 1909, it was originally an ice-skating rink before Auntie moved in. In 1934, it became home to the BBC Symphony Orchestra (in which your correspondent's uncle played lead flute) and then became the centre for news broadcasting throughout the Second World War.

It has a glorious back story in terms of artists who have recorded there. The John Peel Sessions ran from one of its studios between 1967 and 2004. Led Zeppelin and the Beatles, Jimi Hendrix and David Bowie all sang and

BBC Maida Vale.

strummed into the Maida Vale microphones – although The Clash only completed half a session, after saying the recording equipment wasn't up to scratch, a complaint that Peel said was 'unbelievably pretentious of them'.

Nearby, we'll admire the cream facades of Warrington Crescent – where computer genius and posthumous war hero Alan Turing was born in 1924. The rooms from which he leapt forth started their lives as a boarding school and then became the Warrington Lodge Medical and Surgery Home for Ladies. Converted into a hotel in the mid-1930s, Sigmund Freud enjoyed an extended stay in its upper floors while he did up his Hampstead home.

Sigmund Freud.

At the end of the road is another hotel, named The Warrington. Its interior is amazing – stained glass windows and mosaic floors, mahogany throughout and marble fireplaces. In the bar is a series of art nouveau-style murals, featuring scantily clad ladies – apparently a nod to the fact it was once a brothel that enjoyed the patronage of many a peer.

It is said that Randolph Avenue, on whose corner it sits, gave the English language the term 'randy' to signify someone keen to enjoy time between the sheets with another.

The Warrington Hotel.

BOWLING ALONG

Now, at one end of Randolph Avenue, we meet the stretch of canal dubbed Little Venice. There has been some discussion as to why it has earned such a grand moniker. It is undoubtedly pretty, its homes mimicking the Nash terraces further east.

Some say poet and playwright Robert Browning, who lived there, coined the term back in the 1860s. Not so, argued Lord Kinross in 1966, who reckons it had something to do with Lord Byron. However, further research suggests there was no reference to Little Venice until after the Second World War, kiboshing both attractive theories.

Whatever the reason, its barge spots are much sought after: Richard Branson had a boat on this stretch for years and apparently still pays his mooring fees.

Little Venice.

Crocker's Folly.

Let's cross the upper ends of Edgware Road and seek out one of the best-looking pubs in London: the former Crown Hotel in Aberdeen Place.

Designed by architect Charles Worley in 1898, no expense was spared by the developer, Frank Crocker. They really went to town: using fifty different types of marble, chiselling out playful cherubs, shipping in stacks of wooden panelling, commissioning yards and yards of stained glass – it was a gin palace on acid.

Crocker's investment turned on a tip he got that said a new terminus of a major railway station was about to be carved through north-west London and end right on its doorstep – so it seemed worth a punt. But disaster struck when the board of the Great Central Railway changed their minds and no carriage-loads of guests appeared. It suffered a chequered history for decades.

Dubbed 'at risk' by English Heritage by the 2000s, it has recently become a Lebanese restaurant – and changed its name to Crocker's Folly.

Worley also designed Wimpole House in Wimpole Street, a Flemish renaissance block that architecture expert Nikolaus Pevsner described as a 'somewhat ridiculous pink terracotta pile', suggesting he wasn't overly discouraged by his earlier experience.

A few steps away, we shall pause to gaze upon Lord's Cricket Ground: built by Yorkshireman, groundsman and journeyman bowler Thomas Lord, it was his third attempt at creating a home for the game. His first was in Dorset Square, but it did not last as the land was too valuable as housing. His second fell foul of the Regent's Canal, which was built right through the wicket. The current site also nearly succumbed to London's sprawl – he was offered a good whack by developers, but thankfully for cricket's heritage, he did not succumb.

And so we find ourselves back in Boscom Prioris Sancti Johannis, as St John's Wood was named in the 1200s, when it was the property of the Order of the Hospital of St John of Jerusalem. Let us walk down that chi-chi St John's Wood high street, where people in expensive cars seem to revel in double parking as they pop out for something caffeine-fuelled and topped off with skinny milk, and where the Queen buys her Rigby and Peller underwear.

It is said the street's Oxfam is the best place in London to buy a cheap second-hand designer suit – but we shall ignore the one-owner Armanis in the window and head to the Harry Morgan deli for a nosh-up. *Nosh*, of course, being Yiddish for grub, and fitting to use in this case, as Morgan's specialises in the type of food Jewish immigrants brought from their *shetels* in the east to London and New York. Morgan's has been peddling such delights since 1948. It has become famous, not just for its take on borscht – the beetroot soup in which floats one lonely potato – nor its excellent latkes or salt beef, but for its waiting staff and clientele. Everyone there seems to have a tale to tell and such a fact formed the basis of a play by writer Nick Grosso, which had a Royal Court run twenty years ago.

THE WORLD'S MOST DANGEROUS ANIMAL

From here, we pop into Regent's Park and wander through London Zoo. Home to the Royal Zoological Society, it's a place packed with history. We could recall the tale of Jumbo the Elephant, or the affair of Charles Darwin and Jenny the Orangutan. Instead, let us consider the yarn of John Slater, a curious fish worth toasting.

Slater was a Royal Marine commando and is believed to be the only person to have walked from John o'Groats to Land's End wearing his pyjamas and in his bare feet (his labrador, Guinness, was kitted out in doggie walking boots). Interested in panda conservation, he offered to spend six months in a cage in London Zoo as a human exhibit, an offer they 'foolishly declined', he said.

And on that note, we shall have a cup of tea and gaze at the giraffes, who are still in the home the Victorians built for them.

London Zoo.

'Regents Canal' by Algernon Newton, the Regent's Canaletto.

Regents Park's Castlehaven football team.

Let us follow the giraffes' gaze over the fence and on towards the Outer Circle, a 4.45km-long gyratory around Regent's Park, once the favoured promenade of Georgian dandies and today appreciated by the urban cyclist keen to burn off wobbly bits caused by the ageing process.

As we follow the curve of Regent's Canal, a camber mimicking the shape of the Outer Circle, we will recall the 'Regent's Canaletto' – Hampstead-born painter Algernon Newton (1880–1968), who earned the nickname for his various studies of the canal in the early twentieth century. His devotion to the canal network, whose terminal decline as a means of moving goods was by then well entrenched, saw him become the vice president of the Inland Waterways Association, a post he held for more than half his life.

We now look incredulously at John Nash's preposterous villas on the western side of the park – home to ambassadors, billionaires and princes – before we duck into the park proper and tread upon ancient ground.

Henry VIII hunted here, while Oliver Cromwell confiscated the land that now constitutes the park and turned it into smallholdings for the foot soldiers who made up his New Model Army. They cut down 16,000 trees to raise crops before their plots were snatched back by Charles II. The Prince Regent commissioned the current layout, while the fields became an accessible playground for Londoners from the Victorians onwards.

Boasting scores of football pitches, they had a well-earned reputation for being virtually unusable after autumn's first rains. The reason for their pools, ruts and puddles dated back to the Second World War. Nearby homes and railway lines were heavily bombed, as was the canal. The park had all manner of debris tipped on it and then grassed over. Just beneath many a goalmouth are the bricks and mortar of the lost homes of pre-war Camden Town.

The park's lakes also have tragedies hidden beneath their surface: forty youngsters drowned when ice collapsed beneath them during a winter skate in 1867. The lake was over 4m in depth and following the incident, the basins were made shallower.

THE JACKANORY
OF ROGER FRY

We now move to the southern end of the park, and as we reach Albany Street, let us all pull our most 'stop messing about' faces we can muster and prepare to squeak out an impression of the late, great comedian Kenneth Williams. It is here, on the corner of Osnaburgh Street, that the master of camp comedy lived for decades in the now-demolished Marlborough House flats.

Williams' screen-ography is immense, his unique voice being heard on everything from the twenty-six *Carry On* films he starred in through to the sixty-nine episodes of *Jackanory* he presented. It is said his tone of voice was caused by being whacked on the nose by a football as a child, which irretrievably squashed one of his nasal passages and gave him a lifelong dislike of the Beautiful Game.

Now we cross the car-fugged mess of the Marylebone Road, and turn for a moment to see the empty plinth that once hosted a bust of the assassinated US prez John F Kennedy. It was moved in 2017 to a spot around the corner after vandals allegedly fired a gun at it. The piece was by sculptor Jacques Lipchitz, a Lithuanian-born Jewish artist who was to become a key twentieth-century figure in Cubism and was good friends with Pablo Picasso. He had settled in France in the 1920s but when the Nazis invaded, he knew his life was at risk: he got himself south to Marseille, where he met the American journalist Varian Fry.

The JFK bust.

Fry had set up the Emergency Rescue Committee, a group that worked both in the open and clandestinely in occupied Europe to save people from the Nazis. Working from a shortlist of people wanted by the Gestapo, he raised £3,000 and helped writers, artists, musicians, dissidents and hundreds of others flee. He hid Lipchitz in a villa in Marseille despite constantly being watched by the Vichy regime, before helping him and others get over the Pyrenees to Spain. Among the 2,200 Fry rescued were Marc Chagall and Arthur Koestler, and of course the man behind the JFK piece, Lipchitz.

Now we head back towards town, and stroll down Great Portland Street, home to fashion house sample stores, swanky neo-British restaurants and the Portland private hospital for women and children. Has there ever been a fee-paying maternity unit to see such well-heeled baby booties emerge from their private rooms? Those who have pushed out sprogs from this postcode include everyone from royals to A–Z-lister celebrities such as Victoria Beckham, the Duchesses of Sussex and York, Kate Winslet, Liz Hurley, Trudie Styler, Jemima Goldsmith, Anneka Rice, Victoria Wood and Pamela Stephenson.

The hospital, which opened in the early 1980s, is on the site of a famous car showroom that was synonymous with the area for much of the twentieth century. Second-hand car sales was the bread and butter of the businesses along the stretch. Ralph Gorse, the criminal protagonist in author Patrick Hamilton's *The Gorse Trilogy*, buys a red open-top sports car from a dealer there. Hamilton lived in the vicinity and had seen young men from whom he drew his rat-like character browsing the showrooms, and heard the salesmen drinking after work in the pubs he frequented.

HG Wells also drew on Great Portland Street's slightly seedy, spivvy reputation when he gave *The Invisible Man* a slum there to lodge in.

Now dipping eastwards for a moment, let us admire the Robert Adam-designed Fitzroy Square (OK, he did the east and south sides). Fittingly, the Georgian Group are located here.

The square is neat and tidy, its private garden so immaculate it looks like it is permanently out of bounds to absolutely everyone but its fastidious gardeners. That made the events one Saturday afternoon in the 1990s more incongruous when it bore witness to a more bizarre complaint made to the Boys in Blue. A heavy rock band called Slow Boat were booked to play at a community festival in the square. Cranking their amps up to 11 at a summer street party made up predominantly of children and older people was a brave move. The strange atmosphere was added to when a group of rock enthusiasts appeared from nowhere and started 'dancing' in the loosest possible sense of the word.

Later, a statue of Venezuelan revolutionary General Francisco de Miranda, who had lived in nearby Grafton Way between 1802 and 1810, was covered in half-eaten slices of pizzas and beer bottles, the suspects being the group of gate-crashing revellers. Two rookie PCs on duty that day, reacting to complaints from more strait-laced attendees, began questioning possible suspects but to no avail. Eventually, under pressure from partygoers, the coppers scaled a fence and cleaned the general up themselves, and never lived it down back at the station, we're told.

THEATRICAL MARIONETTES AND MENUS

From uneaten pizzas to plates of crocodile: off we trot down Cleveland Street, to pause briefly outside the famous Archipelago restaurant. Much fun can be gleaned from this eaterie's à la carte offerings of exotic meat. Starters include crocodile wrapped in vine leaves served with honey-poached plums and pickled samphire. If that sounds a bit chewy, how about pan-fried crickets with quinoa and spinach, or a crispy zebra jerky? Make sure you save room for the mains, where you'll find more crocodile, ostrich, kangaroo and something called Durban Bunny Chow.

From here, we'll nip along Fitzroy Street – pausing briefly to scowl at the home of scientology founder L Ron Hubbard. He lived there in the 1950s, and the building houses objects relating to his world. At No. 19, artist Walter Sickert rented a studio along with some other arty friends, thus founding the Fitzroy Group of painters, who would later morph into the Camden Town Group.

If you wiggle your way southwards through the backstreets of Fitzrovia, you may stumble across Scala Street, home to Pollock's Toy Museum. This charming private collection has a nice back story. It started life in 1851 in a printer's shop in Hoxton, and remained there until a high explosive dropped by a Luftwaffe pilot in 1940 put paid to nearly 100 years of continuous trading.

It was taken over in the 1950s by Marguerite Fawdry, daughter of a French dad and English mum. She graduated from the University of Lille and then became a journalist, working for the French section of the BBC and then as General de Gaulle's press officer.

Her husband Ken was a school teacher. The pair held radical political beliefs allied to a love of the arts, they were also toy theatre enthusiasts. They used to buy stock from the famous Benjamin Pollock's store – and when the business went bust in 1954, Marg was upset she could no longer buy sliders to move characters about the miniature stages at 2p a time.

She spoke with the receiver, who was pricing up the stock when she arrived, and was told, 'I believe there are hundreds of thousands in the warehouse, madam, but there's no one who could look them out for you. Of course, you could, I suppose, buy the whole lot if you wanted them.'

Pollock's Toy Museum.

She did – and turned Pollocks into a much-loved celebration of all things connected to our innate desire to play.

An aside: this area was developed in dribs and drabs from the 1760s, and the land has been used by residents as an ash tip for decades. The detritus of hearths was used by builders to make bricks with: mixed with mud, they piled this low-quality material high. Marg discovered this when, in 1975, Pollocks' basement showed signs of weariness: the ash bricks had come very much to the end of their working life, and the museum had to be underpinned.

Onwards we go, now heading to rest once more in Colville Place and Crab Tree Fields. The latter recalls the name of the land that carpenter John Goodge gained when he married a wealthy young woman in 1718. His sons developed the land around – but German bombs altered its original face. Crab Tree Fields, a tiny splash of green and shade, was actually created in 1985 by the GLC: it is on the spot where a high-explosive bomb landed, the site being used as a car park for many years afterwards.

The delightful terrace of Colville Place, a set of modest workers' cottages dating from the 1760s, was also fairly knocked about by the bomb. At No. 1, designer Max Neufeld built a modernist masterpiece, which is now listed. He lived in Colville Place for more than forty years, and helped found the Charlotte Street Association.

THIS IS A STICK-UP

Here we are now in Tottenham Street, where we will pause for a moment to remember the late Alec de Antiquis, a man who in life was unknown but whose death prompted an outpouring of grief and a tabloid campaign to make sure his widow never had to work again.

Jays Jewellers was a small business that sold trinkets and repaired keepsakes. On Tuesday, 29 April 1947, three men entered and drew pistols. They grabbed what they could and scarpered to their getaway car, a four-door Vauxhall saloon. A delivery van had pulled into the road and was now blocking their route. The three men, long coats flapping and hats lost in the milieu, set off on foot.

Just as the trio reached the corner, a motorbike ridden by mechanic de Antiquis came zooming towards them. He had clocked on to what was happening. He cut his engine and guided the bike into a skid, aiming at the closest stick-up kid. As he leapt off, a gun was drawn, and the sound of a shot echoed through the streets …

Poor Alec did not survive, and catching his murderers became one of the biggest manhunts of the post-war period.

While we are back in the 1940s, let us look at what neighboured Jay's Jewellers. Opposite was Tora and Sons, Barbers and the New Scala Restaurant. Further along you would find Wilson Fish and Chips, Handy's Cafe, Lawrence Treble Boot Repairs and Simon Kaufman's Leather Goods. All were owned by families of the Jewish faith, and Fitzrovia had a large Jewish community for at least three decades after the war: its proximity to the theatres and the hotels provided those in the rag trade employment.

While we linger on the fringes of Soho proper and consider past occupations and industries, let us head down Rathbone Place and pause outside The Wheatsheaf, which dates from the early 1800s and today serves beer in a mock-Tudor building. Its saloon bar was the haunt of that famous Bohemian who cared little for hard graft, Julian Maclaren Ross. His book, *Memoirs of the Forties*, captured the area's louche extravagances, all of which were performed on a shoestring. JMR was always chronically skint and in the 1930s found himself in Bognor Regis trying to flog vacuum cleaners door to door.

Julian told Graham Greene about it – which in itself is interesting as Greene would later use a vacuum salesman who pretended the parts of a Hoover were top secret Soviet nuclear plans in his novel *Our Man in Havana*, perhaps inspired by JMR. Greene's interest was piqued, and he asked him if he was doing the job as research for a book. 'No,' replied JMR. 'I'm doing it because otherwise I wouldn't have any money.'

Others fond of this pine-panelled hostelry include George Orwell, Quentin Crisp and the film maker Humphrey Jennings, whose work for the Post Office film arm revolutionised non-fiction film. He would make movies that played in cinemas before the main feature – and his work considering what it meant to be a Briton during the Second World War played a key role in girding the loins and rolling up the sleeves of the population.

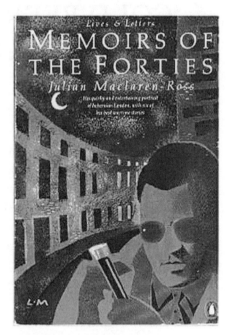

Julian Maclaren Ross.

Jennings' films included *Fires Were Started*, his documentary about how auxiliary firefighters tackled the Blitz. His films were thoughtful and insightful reminders of what that generation were fighting for. We raise a glass in his memory, a life tragically cut short when he met his end while scouting for film locations just after the war. He was visiting the Greek island of Poros, and toppled off a cliff.

'COLD BEER IS
BOTTLED GOD'

We can't pop into The Wheatsheaf and not mention Dylan Thomas – although the same could, plausibly, be said about every other pub in the immediate district. However, The Wheatsheaf does have a little bit of extra Thomas oomph to it, for it was here on 12 April 1936 that the Welsh poet met his love Caitlin Macnamara for the first time, introduced by the painter, Augustus John.

Thomas was living with the American writer Emily Holmes Coleman, who was fifteen years older than the poet, and her daughter. Coleman recalled entering the pub to find Thomas on a stool with Caitlin's head in his lap. He was pouring sugary sweet words of everlasting love on to her, stroking her face and saying quite how incredibly enchanting she was, and that they would be married. Emily noted they had met each other not an hour before. Friends say Thomas lost his virginity that night – and for the next five days and nights the pair went on a booze and culture bender, failing to eat one morsel as they swayed from pub to pub to pub to pub, travelling through an alcohol-warped kaleidoscope of writers, artists, muses and benefactors.

Opposite The Wheatsheaf you can find The Marquis of Granby, another of Thomas's haunts and one with a reputation back in the 1930s. It was just over the borough boundary from Marylebone, and in the Borough of St Pancras, which allowed pubs an extra half an hour drinking time. As a result, the place would become full before the bell rang, much to Thomas's displeasure. He enjoyed picking fights with gay Guardsmen who came in looking for other willing men to enjoy a tryst with.

Now let us head back to the Wheatsheaf – we shall not be following a Dylan Thomas pub crawl, for while our time is plentiful, it remains that there are not enough hours in the day to trace the Welsh poet's journeys via where he sunk pints.

ON YOUR MARX

A t the side of The Wheatsheaf, and no doubt handy for slipping away from the bar stool preachers and literary bores the place could be relied upon to host, is Percy Mews. It's one of those dead ends built when the workers who made the West End wake up and get on with it had to live close by, but out of sight. A small row of artisan cottages hold a revolutionary story from the 1880s. One of these little two ups, two downs was the home to the International Working Men's Club.

An offspring of the First International and founded 154 years ago, it was one of a number of such organisations that made late nineteenth-century Fitzrovia its home. The nearby Grafton Arms in Fitzroy Square was home to the Social Democratic Club, which would later move to Rose Street, Soho, now occupied by Foyles bookshop.

Our Percy Street group had once been close comrades with the Grafton Arms politicos, but they split from their Social Democratic friends as they veered towards anarchist thought rather than socialism or communism. They pitched up in the Mews and it was here the police caused a riot on 9 May 1885. The Boys in Blue came down mob-handed to deal with these potential insurrectionists, and got carried away by the opportunity to smash some Red heads.

The arrested anarchists filed charges for assault and questions were asked in Parliament, leading to an unlikely show of solidarity from a Peer of the Realm towards those who no doubt saw him as a sworn class enemy. The Earl of Wemyss called for legal aid to be provided for the injured so they could pursue the case, stating in Parliament, 'The International Club, though it might be a Socialistic body, was, as long as its members obeyed the law, as much entitled to the protection of the law as Brooks's, the Carlton, the Reform, or any other club frequented by the rich'.

'I make this appeal on two grounds. One was the confidence which the public had in the police. It was well known how admirably they did their duty, and how seldom one heard of any charge being brought against them. But the public ought to know that there was no divinity which hedged round the policeman if he misconducted himself. The other is the justice of the case. This club stood on the same footing as the Carlton or the Reform, and there should be equal justice for the poor man and the rich.'

Later, these clubs would become a mix of talking shops with good food for hand-wringing, middle-class activists and philosophers, but still attracted the thinkers of the age.

After moving to nearby Tottenham Street, the International Working Men's Club hosted the likes of Friedrich Engels, George Bernard Shaw, Keir Hardie and William Morris. After another move, this time to Charlotte Street in 1902, Stalin and Lenin both spoke to its members.

For those who like completely unrelated links, let us note that the venue for Lenin and Stalin to bring news of revolutionary thought from the Continent would later be the childhood home of actress Anna Wing, who played Albert Square matriarch Lou Beale in Eastenders. Perhaps slightly more in keeping with its political roots, between 1963 and 1984, it housed the Anti-Apartheid movement, too. Next door, in the 1810s, it was home to the opera singer Angelica Catalani. A notorious diva, she demanded big wages to strut her stuff and became the highest-paid opera singer of her time. But her love of the lucre, which became famous, was said to be behind a series of riots by disgruntled, pleasure-seeking theatre-goers. To be able to afford this star, prices went up – and the audiences did not take kindly to it, causing damage to box offices and foyers in protest.

Later, the Working Men's Club premises in Percy Mews would become the 1930s home to Charles Forte, who ran a milk depot from the address to stock his Regent's Street milk bar and would go on to build the Trust House Forte Hotel and catering business from this humble address.

Now let us shake off the beery fog of a Welsh poet's boozer and on leaving The Wheatsheaf cut through the alley alongside Rathbone Square and come out into Newman Street. This road is on land once owned by Josias Berners, who purchased a swathe of land in 1654. He had an interest in the New River Company, held radical Republican politics and was a supporter of the Cromwellian Commonwealth. His grandson, William, struck a deal with the nicely named Thomas Huddle in 1738 to develop a garden and cow yard: it was 665ft long and is the precursor to what is now Oxford Street.

As the Berners estate was developed, it became fashionable with musicians and instrument makers (Bach lived in Newman Street in 1773) and artists of both the aesthetic and the confidence varieties.

INDECENTLY EARLY
FOR VERSE

B erners Street was home to sculptors John Moore and John Bacon in the 1770s, while glass-painter Joseph Backler enjoyed visits from royalty to see his stained glass windows being made.

DG Rossetti had a base in Newman Street, and would paint well into the night. Artist Ford Madox Brown borrowed studio space there, where he stayed three days a week. When not in Berners Street, FMB could be found in the countryside – Hampstead to be precise – where he had a home with his girlfriend, Emily Hill. She had modelled for him and they both feared scandal if seen together in town.

Madox Brown and Rossetti were not easy flatmates; Brown accused Rossetti of 'making the whole place miserable and filthy, [while] translating sonnets at breakfast'.

A few skips along from these Men Behaving Badly, we come to the double-fronted Berners Street home of the forger Henry Fauntleroy, who is surely the origin of the phrase 'Little Lord'. A banker by trade, he worked for a financial house that his father founded.

Henry became a partner and it was on his watch in 1824 that the bank ran out of cash. Fauntleroy was charged with forging signatures on trust funds and it was said he pilfereed £250,000, all spent on complete debauchery. Fauntleroy was sentenced to hang, despite the character witnesses of seventeen bankers and merchants. Later, rumours circulated he had escaped by inserting a small silver tube into his throat that stopped him being strangled and retired to live out his days in extreme comfort somewhere on the Continent.

We pause at the Sanderson Hotel a few more doors down to admire a place that took design seriously. In its courtyard are friezes by émigré Jupp Dernbach-Mayen, whose work we considered earlier. Jupp's mosaics are joined by stained glass windows by painter John Piper, whose soaring panel covers up the hotel's lift shaft.

NOBBLING NAGS

Now we move south, and cross Oxford Street into Wardour Street. Much has been said of how pleasant car-free roads were during lockdown, and as the city shakes awake, what can we learn? Let us consider how London was 100 years ago, before the domination of the petrol engine. There were at least 300,000 working horses, and with them came blacksmiths, vets and feed sellers, while the market gardeners had a ready supply of manure. So how about we bring back the horse?

This brings us to Wardour Street chemist Cecil Bishop, a horse lover who got tangled up with gambler Daniel Dawson.

Dawson met Bishop at his Soho apothecary, and spoke of a friend's ride who had been given a tonic that made the nag's feet swell. It meant a bailiff could not ride him away in lieu of unpaid debts – and the tincture soon wore off.

After making up a mixture, Dawson returned and said it had not been strong enough: instead the naive Bishop gave Dawson a phial of arsenic and suggested dashing it in the water trough of the horse he hoped to nobble. Having tested it on Lord Darlington's horse, Reuben, at the Brighton Races in 1808, he tried his luck at Newmarket – but was caught, following the death of six racers.

From Wardour Street, we cut west towards Piccadilly, to pause briefly outside the 300-year-old White's Club, St James's, which used to be the unofficial headquarters of the Tory Party, and was where Prince Charles held his stag do before marrying Diana Spencer in 1981.

It was on these steps that, thirty years before, some very ungentlemanly conduct took place. Labour legend Aneurin Bevan had been invited to dine by the Marshal of the Royal Air Force, Sir John Slessor. It was 1951, and they had worked together, successfully during the war in government, and got along very well.

Bevan had previously riled Tories in a speech, stating, 'no amount of cajolery … can eradicate from my heart a deep burning hatred for the Tory Party that inflicted those bitter experiences on me. So far as I am concerned they are lower than vermin.' *The Standard*'s Londoners' Diary editor Tudor Jenkins recalled, 'Few men [namely Bevan] were disliked so much at that time by the sons of the rich. The news of his visit quickly spread to neighbouring clubs.'

Mr John Fox-Strangways, supping champers at Brooks's directly opposite, decided to march over and land a haymaker on the politician. 'Bevan, Sir John told me, acted with great restraint,' recalled Jenkins.

Sir John was less easy-going. He laid a complaint against Fox-Strangways, who was also a member of White's. The club apologised and his assailant was forced to resign.

We shall now dash down St James's and across Pall Mall, in order to finish this walk by the river. Pall Mall's name comes from Italian: *palla a maglio*, which means 'ball to mallet'. Charles II was a fan of such a game (think croquet) and he had a Pall Mall Alley built, even redirecting traffic so the

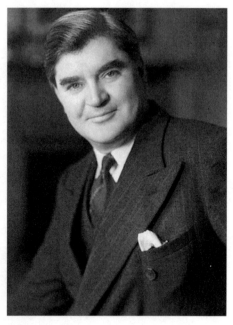

Bevan.

dust created would not interfere. Eventually, the avenue became known as a shady place to promenade – and 'mall' became a word used to describe a public space.

There is another Italian link to this fancy stretch: Pall Mall was home to Almack's, a club based at No. 50, and founded by a former gentleman's valet, William Almack. Opening its doors in 1764, it became the favoured watering hole of a group of dandy-ish, high-rolling fellows fascinated with all things Italian, earning them the nickname of 'Macaronis'. Later, the site would be home to the Marlborough Club, which had a strict membership policy: you had to be a personal friend of the Prince of Wales to grace its bars, restaurant and reading rooms.

St James's is home to a handful of gentleman's clubs whose walls have borne witness to conversations that have helped shape modern Britain. Let us consider that post-war crossroads, the 1956 Suez crisis.

Prime Minister Anthony Eden was dining at No. 10 when the news came that President Nasser was nationalising the canal. At the meal where this information reached the PM was Nuri El Said, who was the Regent of Iraq. El Said suggested the best move would be to flex the imperial muscle, a decision that not only saw Eden lose his premiership, but El Said lose his life.

The Athenaeum, Pall Mall.

The aftershocks of the Suez Crisis would lead to Iraq doing away with the Regency. El Said's end was extremely unpleasant. Tied to the bumper of his own luxury car by a gang in Baghdad, he was disembowelled, and then dragged slowly, still alive, through the streets by his enemies, who enjoyed taking the wheel of his car as they heard him screaming behind them.

Eden went, and was replaced by Harold Macmillan, a member of five different clubs in St James's. Macmillan would create his Cabinet from those he could share a cigar with at one of these establishments. The all-male group were not only all Etonians or Harrovians, bar two, but members of the same clubs Macmillan visited (his favourite was the Turf Club). The close-knit nature of governance then is illustrated by the following fact: after six months in power, Macmillan's government had eighty-five ministers – and of those, thirty-five were directly related to Macmillan by marriage, including seven members of his Cabinet.

LAUGHING ONE'S SELF TO DEATH

Just off Pall Mall, and where we briefly linger before heading across St James's Park, is Suffolk Street. It was here, in the 1840s, that the famous Garlands Hotel stood.

It was known for a classy reputation – a place that did not advertise its existence, but if you knew, you knew. Among those who certainly did know was Harriet Beecher Stowe, who wrote *Uncle Tom's Cabin* and the brilliantly titled *Dred: A Tale of the Great Dismal Swamp*. Others on the guest list at reception were DH Lawrence, James Whistler and Henry James.

One wonders if James and Anthony Trollope, who also was a regular, ever met at the Garland's bar, and if so, what the atmosphere may have been like between these two giants of Victorian literature. James had poured vitriol on Trollope's works, calling, for example, *The Belton Estate* novel in the series of Trollope's Barchester novels, 'a stupid book, without a single thought or idea in it ... a sort of mental pabulum'. He also questioned Trollope's habit of wandering off on a tangent, as was the vogue of great novelists of the time (think of the meandering passages in any Victor Hugo novel, and you see why it was a trend).

Trollope finished his earthly journey in the drawing room of Garlands. It is said he was laughing so much at his family giving readings of F Antsye's comic novel *Vice Versa*, that he had a fatal seizure. Perhaps James felt bad, because after Trollope was lying six feet under the earth at Kensal Rise Cemetery, he wrote, 'His [Trollope's] great, his inestimable merit was a complete appreciation of the usual. ... [H]e *felt* all daily and immediate things as well as saw them; felt them in a simple, direct, salubrious way, with their sadness, their gladness, their charm, their comicality, all their obvious and measurable meanings. ... Trollope will remain one of the most trustworthy, though not one of the most eloquent, of the writers who have helped the heart of man to know itself.'

Garlands no longer stands among us: it was destroyed by a Luftwaffe bomb in 1943.

THE FLYING SQUAD

After paying our respects to Trollope and heading across St James's Park, we come out opposite King Charles Street, home to George Gilbert Scott (the father of the Scott of red telephone box fame), who designed the Foreign Office's HQ, full of his crazy Victoriana. From here we catch a glimpse of Old Father Thames – and we will cast our minds back to the day a pig flew past this spot.

Telephone boxes.

Flying Pigs.

Lt Col. JTC Moore-Brabazon served in the Royal Flying Corps and then became a very right-wing MP whose Conservative tastes stretched to being the last member of the House to insist on wearing a top hat into the chamber. Before the First World War, he was mad about flying – and became the first in Britain to achieve a powered flight (a feat he pulled off on the Isle of Sheppey in 1909). In the same year, he won a prize of £1,000 for being the first Englishman to fly a mile.

While doing this act of derring-do, he steered his plane along the old river, dipping his wings in salute to the bankside crowds who had come along with the faint hope of watching this unpleasant man get wet. He took a pig along for publicity, strapping the unfortunate porker into a wicker basket tied on to a wing strut.

As we gaze out at the river and remember the time in 1909 a pig flew past this very spot, we shall use this vantage point to speak of the oldest continuous sporting event in the country, in which the Thames plays a crucial part. While the annual, brawny-shouldered, gin-and-it-soaked Oxford and Cambridge boat race enjoys both longevity and global fame, there's another that pre-dates it. It goes under the delightful name of the Doggett's Coat and Badge race.

Dogget's Race.

Thomas Doggett, an actor of Irish descent who was to become the manager of the Drury Lane theatre, established the contest in the 1710s. Taking place on 1 August each year, it required oarsmen to scull their way from London Bridge to Chelsea, with the winner receiving a new coat and a silver badge.

It is said Doggett wanted to say thank you to the Thames watermen after one rescued him from the waters when he'd taken a tumble into the waters while returning home late one night from the theatre. He even left money in his will to guarantee it continued after he had departed this mortal coil.

Sculling against an ebb tide must have been exhausting, and it is the Thames' tidal reach of 60 miles that helped power industries along its Westminster banks. We are by Millbank, whose name recalls the presence of watermills – the last of three was demolished in the early 1700s, around the time Doggett was watching his oarsman fly past.

One hundred years later, Millbank was the site of the largest prison in Britain. Built during the Napoleonic period and completed in 1821, it used a revolutionary design that housed prisoners in a circular building with a central point that could be used to observe them. Eventually demolished in 1890, it earned a reputation for harshness and a supposedly high level of security. It was, however, the scene of a daring escape by one Martin Sheen in 1864, as reported in the pages of *The Launceston Examiner*.

Above and below: Representations of Millbank Prison.

Right: Millbank Prison today.

Sheen, 28, described as 5ft tall with iron-grey hair and hazel eyes, a broken nose and broken right hand, labelled 'stout' by his gaolers, was a surgeon by trade. He lived in Wardour Street for many years until he fell foul of the law – and earned himself a ten-year stretch for forgery.

Following his conviction, he was first incarcerated at Pentonville, but following an escape attempt was transferred to the more secure Millbank. After serving eighteen months, he decided it really wasn't the life for him and was caught attempting more than a dozen flits.

Eventually, he cracked it: Sheen had managed to keep a knife about himself, despite regular searches, and used it to chisel away bricks in the corner of a cell on the top storey of the circular prison block. He made a hole large enough to squeeze through and then lowered himself down 88ft on a coconut fibre rope, made from matting stolen from the chapel. On one end was a hook fashioned out of a tin cup, and Sheen used it to circumnavigate a number of walls and roofs inside the prison. Eventually, he ended up in a garden after scaling a 20ft boundary wall, care of a weighted sandbag to hoik his rope over.

The Examiner said, 'For coolness of execution it has hardly been surpassed. Utmost vigilance is being paid to recapture the convict, but he is not known as a regular offender, of course the difficulty of recognition becomes increased ...'

Sheen was last seen scarpering westwards along the banks of the Thames, and we shall follow in his footsteps until we come to Tate Britain. Here, we shall remember the bitter winter of 1927. That year, London experienced a very white Christmas. It started on Christmas night and by Boxing Day had developed into a blizzard. More than six inches of snow fell across Westminster, and then came fierce gales that caused huge snow drifts. Roads, cars – all hidden beneath a huge white blanket.

But worse was to come.

On New Year's Eve there was a thaw, followed by rain storms of such severity they had not been seen for a generation. Furthermore, a North Sea gale whooshed up the Thames, giving it its highest tide in fifty years.

In January 1927 the Thames paid the art gallery a visit, swamping the building that housed sugar magnate Sir Henry's collection. A nightwatchman had to swim through submerged corridors to escape, and a set of Turner's drawings were ruined.

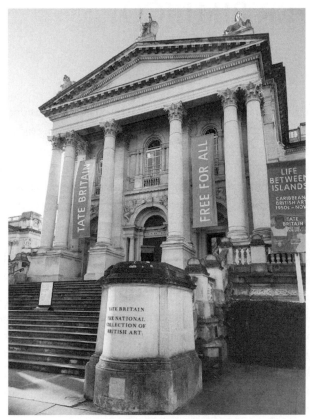

Left: The Tate.

Below: The
Tate floods.

IMPROPER PIMLICO

A nd it is now we find ourselves in Pimlico, and let us pause to consider this well-heeled neighbourhood's connection with the more rough, ready and achingly trendy Hoxton, out east.

Ben Pimlico was a publican in that eastern neck of the woods and became celebrated for a 'nut browne' ale he brewed. A boozer near what is now Victoria Station opened in the 1620s and decided the famous brewer's surname would make an excellent moniker. Whether Ben had any say in this matter has been lost in the mists of time.

And his surname, which would come to mean the entire area, is said to have derived from a tribe of Native Americans encountered by Sir Walter Raleigh in the 1580s. According to legend, an adventurer accompanying Sir Walt was given 'Pimlico' as a nickname, such was his interest in the women they encountered of this group, and he is said to have been the father of Ben.

We shall start our next raft of pavement-tramping historical gossip with a pint at the Morpeth Arms, in Millbank. The Morpeth, with nice views across the river despite Sir Terry Farrell's looming MI6 building reminding us all is never well, is named after the Victorian politico Lord Morpeth, who took the moniker from the Northumberland town he represented for a time in Parliament. An avid campaigner against all forms of religious discrimination, he championed the causes of Catholics and Jewish people.

Built in 1845 by a man called Paul Dangerfield, it had the custom of the wardens of the nearby prison in mind. A story the pub to this day likes to remind its visitors of speaks of another jail break from Millbank, but a less successful one than that which we previously mentioned.

Beneath the Morpeth are a series of cellars and tunnels. A convict, having worked once in the pub as a cellar man years before he was incarcerated, gazed across from his cage towards the backs of the pub he had known in happier times. He realised its proximity to the prison wall, and knew how its cellars and drains stretched out underneath the back yard. Our enterprising criminal realised he would not have to tunnel too far to reach a ready-made escape route. It is said his plan worked as far as getting into the cellars beneath the pub – but trying to find a further subterranean exit saw him get hopelessly lost. The story ends badly: he died, trapped in a small tunnel beneath the main bar. Having been likely to face a capital sentence for escaping, or being shipped to Australia, the poor man must have been desperate to get away. He was no doubt was torn between crying for help or trying to free himself, his liberty and life delicately balanced.

To please the tourists who have wandered along the Thames after looking at the Houses of Parliament and decided they fancy a bit of the old Ye Olde, the idea that the unfortunate (and unnamed) chap now haunts the pub has become one of those urban myths that is based on marketing rather than legend.

Pints sunk, ghost story shared, let us stroll along the Thames until we meet St George's Square. It is here we find

the statue of Corn Law campaigner William Huskisson, who is unfortunately also remembered as the man who was run over by Stephenson's *Rocket* in 1830 when the locomotive made its debut journey between Manchester and Liverpool.

The construction of the square, as with much of Pimlico's development, was slowed by the fact the land was marshy and often flooded – when housing was developed in the 1800s, spoil used from digging out St Katharine Dock was dumped there to provide a less soggy base to start from.

STEPTOE, STOKER AND SQUARES

As George III moved in to Buck House, the only building of any note around these parts was a Watney's Brewery. This slowly began to change when Thomas Cubitt – he of King's Cross Station fame – bought up leases from the Duke of Westminster and began creating squares and terraces that took their cue from Nash.

Cubitt was a clever chap. He set about building pubs before he started on the homes, to provide his building crews with sustenance. It meant that, in the 1830s, the area appeared as being one large site lined by various boozers sitting forlornly on street corners, while potential customers' homes had yet to be built.

Perhaps recognising this and being a bit of a Victorian prude, Cubitt's foreman, Thomas Cundy III, built St Gabriel's in Warwick Square and St Saviour's in St George's Square with the help of his father, Cundy the Second. He wanted to make his churches stand out from the impressive Cubitt terraces,

so decided to cast them in Kentish ragstone instead of the white stucco favoured by the well-heeled parishioner.

Now we head north: Pimlico's streets are packed with the great, the good and the not-so good at every turn. We could saunter for hours eying up the residences, but instead we'll rush past homes to the likes of Churchill, de Gaulle, Oswald Mosley before his arrest in 1940, Bram Stoker, Laurence Olivier and Kenyan freedom fighter and the country's first PM, Jomo Kenyatta, to reach Denbigh Street. Here we pay our respects to the actor Wilfred Brambell, or Albert Steptoe, as he surely is best remembered.

The Irish-born thespian moved to Pimlico after the war and remained in the neighbourhood until his death in 1985.

Sir William Cubitt.

Brambell became a bit of a go-to when casting directors needed an 'old' man along Steptoe lines – despite the fact he was in his 40s when the series debuted and was only thirteen years older than his co-star, Harry H Corbett.

Brambell's career as an actor included morale-boosting work in both wars. As a child, he entertained wounded troops returning from the trenches – and when the Second World War broke out, he joined the Entertainments National Services Association, taking his wry humour and delectable timing to bases throughout North Africa and Europe.

Our final destination today is Eccleston Square, where Douglas Douglas-Hamilton, Air Commodore, 14th Duke, Etonian and Oxford scholar, was born in 1903. Douglas-Hamilton had become a public figure of some renown for being part of the crew who flew an aeroplane over Mount Everest for the first time in 1933. In 1935, the duke ditched his title briefly and went to work in a coal mine his family owned to understand better the conditions of the people he employed. He even joined the NUM, under the name Mr Hamilton.

In 1936, he flew himself to the Berlin Olympics as an observer and was given a tour of Luftwaffe bases by a proud Hermann Göring. Rumour has it he was not a well-behaved guest – using the kudos of his title, he was given trusted backstage access and used the opportunity to indulge in espionage.

When Hitler's deputy, Rudolf Hess, crash-landed in Scotland in 1941, he demanded to meet with Douglas-Hamilton. The lord was sent to see Hess in hospital and at this point the Nazi henchman revealed his true identity. Douglas-Hamilton always denied having met Hess, and did not appreciate people believing it showed he had become chummy with the German air force command in the 1930s, due to both the RAF and the Luftwaffe having plenty of aristocrats in their officers' messes.

BUSINESSMEN'S BOTTOMS

From the flying daredevil Douglas Douglas-Hamilton's home we wriggle south until we meet Warwick Square, home to one of the most approachable architectural critics of the twentieth century, author and broadcaster Ian Nairn. In his 1966 publication, *Nairn's London*, he described his neighbourhood as 'the forgotten segment of Central London, Westminster-behind-the Abbey: the well-built, dull, regular streets of Pimlico, where after five years' residence you may still not be able to find your way home'.

Nairn was likened to William Cobbett and John Ruskin, the Victorians who saw the damage the industrial age wreaked on the countryside. He fumed about urban sprawl, coining the term 'Subtopia' as fields disappeared under speculative developments.

Nairn joined celebrated architecture guide Nikolaus Pevsner, helping with his books. Pevsner said Nairn was by far the better writer – but a bit too easy to voice his strong opinions, which did not suit the straitlaced approach of the Pevsner series. He described, for example, an elephant cast on the Albert Memorial as 'having a backside just like a businessman scrambling under a restaurant table for his cheque-book'. His light-hearted nature is illustrated by a TV series he made in 1972, *Nairn Across Britain*; a great beer drinker – he would die an alcoholic, aged 52 – he came across a railway signal box in Cumbria that he said would make a jolly home, suggesting the levers to change signals and tracks could be converted into handy beer pumps.

FLASH AND LOAN:
THE DOWNFALL OF A
PORNOGRAPHIC PROSE
PIONEER

From a writer of good houses to a writer of those of ill repute, we now switch eastwards to find our way to Petty France, on the fringes of Pimlico. So named because of the Huguenot refugees who gathered there in the seventeenth century after fleeing Catholic France due to their penchant for a bit of Calvinism on a Sunday, it was the London base of author John Cleland in the 1740s. Cleland is perhaps the most famous writer of titillating pornography in the English language. His novel, *Memoirs of a Woman of Pleasure: Fanny Hill*, published in 1748, was penned while he languished in a debtors' prison.

Cleland studied at Westminster School, travelled to Bombay as an employee of the East India Company, and while there got into a pickle after offering a haven to a female slave who was being mistreated by her owner. On his return to London, he became friends with author Thomas Cannon, and promptly borrowed £800 from him. It was this debt that saw Cleland sent down – and while incarcerated, he clearly had time to let his imagination do some wandering.

The result is considered by literary boffins to be the first pornographic prose novel written in English, and is known for its tremendous use of euphemisms. Cleland writes at great, great length of matters of the sensuous flesh, but does so without using any so-called 'dirty' words at all. He swerves biological terms for genitalia too, using such phrases as the 'nethermouth', 'wonderful machine', 'engine of love-assaults', 'stiff staring truncheon', 'sensitive plant' whose head is 'not unlike a common sheep's heart' – indeed. Such prose meant the autobiographical letters of Fanny, who we meet as a 15-year-old Liverpudlian orphan before being given a bedside seat to numerous exploits, was banned right up until the Lady Chatterley case in 1960. Cleland would be arrested for obscenity, the phrase 'stiff truncheon' appearing on his record as being the final straw for magistrates.

BARONET BUTT'S
HOUSE OF FARCE

A nd from here to another house of cheeky bawdiness: the marvellous
Victoria Palace Theatre, a few streets from Cleland's home.

A concert venue was first established on the site above a set of stables in
1832. It morphed into the Royal Standard Theatre, home to music halls, before
the current space was designed by Frank Matcham in 1911. Its design was
ground-breaking, with Matcham including a sliding roof on the auditorium

Victoria Palace Theatre.

that would be rolled back during intervals to allow fresh air in – and offer the audience a view of the night sky.

Impresario, horse racing dabbler, baronet and Tory MP Alfred Butt managed the programme: with its music hall past, it had a reputation for light-heartedness. Even when serious plays were produced, the audience would look for laughs. In 1934, the 83-year-old Rev. Walter Reynolds wrote *Young England*, a piece of stodgy patriotism of how the Boy Scout movement instilled moral values. It was universally panned, and to such a degree that it became a cult hit and saw 278 sold-out performances before transferring to other West End theatres. Lines such as a Scout mistress saying: 'I must go to attend to my girls' water' was roared out by a chorus of voices from the stalls, the owners of which having learned the awful script by heart.

Two years after this unintentional success, Butt, who represented Balham and Tooting from 1922, was accused of leaking details of the 1936 Budget and benefitting financially. He resigned and scurried off to Newmarket to look after his horses.

AROUND THE WORLD ...
BY HORSE-DRAWN TRAM

We commence by heading round the corner from the theatre and move onto Victoria Street, which is linked with another chap known for having an eye for a score.

The name Victoria describes an area that runs for about half a mile south of the high walls of Buckingham Palace, and the name for this 'hood dates from 1837, a year after Vic was handed the crown (at this point without the stolen Koh-i-Noor diamond from India).

It started with Victoria Square, built near the Royal Mews. Next came Victoria Street, and pretty soon after these royal-kow-towing trailblazer developments, the whole neighbourhood became synonymous with QV.

And while we gaze at Victoria Street, let's recall the appropriately named George Train. You may not realise it, but you have probably heard of Mr Train already. Jules Verne based his book *Around the World in 80 Days* on this chap.

An American adventurer, inventor, businessman, radical and crook, he ran sailing lines, helped organise the Union Pacific Railroad and brought trams to the UK, envisaging a horse-drawn public transport system across the city — and he proved its value by creating a tram line up Victoria Street and into town.

Born in Boston in 1829, he had been prepared for a life as a Methodist minister, growing up in an orthodox Christian family. But as a young man his calling was engineering and commerce. He came up with the idea for the tram line when a American émigré to England moaned about how hard it was to get around his adopted town of Birkenhead.

George Train.

It spurred Train into action. In 1860, he headed across the Atlantic and established horse tramways in London (and Birkenhead). It didn't always go smoothly: rails laid in Uxbridge weren't sunk into the thoroughfare, causing obstructions, and although popular with passengers, they were criticised for being impractical and he then faced the added expense of tracks sinking into the ground.

Back across the Pond, in 1864 and as the American Civil War raged, the Union Pacific Railroad was established with Train at its centre. Designed to take passengers from Missouri to the Pacific and seen by Abraham Lincoln as a way to unite states, Train had more base motives. He and fellow company directors put together a blag to turn a hefty profit.

They set up a separate firm as construction contractors to build the line – with a board that was exactly the same as UPR – and then awarded themselves the contract. They sent the US government a wildly overpriced bill and the scam was not discovered until 1872.

Train then got into radical politics, supporting a free Ireland and Republicans in Australia. He ran for US president as an independent in 1870 with a campaign that included a global tour, garnered plenty of press and inspired Verne's Phileas Fogg character.

A two-month stay in France saw him arrested for supporting the Paris Commune. He was saved by the novelist Alexandre Dumas, who got him out prison after an uncomfortable two weeks.

As with us all, his eccentricities became more pronounced as he got older. He held rallies (with the chutzpah to charge people to get in) and he'd make barnstorming speeches, calling on people to appoint him as Dictator of America. This was a golden era of lecture circuits, with the likes of Mark Twain and Charles Dickens speaking to thousands – and Train's firebrand skit was a jolly night out.

His energy eventually fizzled out and he fell into poverty. In his last days, Train could be found sitting in Madison Square Park, New York, giving dimes away from a sack beside him, and had a Golden Rule: only speak to children and animals.

SNAILS, HORSE BATHS AND QUEEN VIC

On that note, we turn tail and go inside Victoria Station, where once crawled animals when the Earth was a little younger in the grand scheme of eternal things. Six fossils of a snail-like creature called a nautiloid, estimated to be 50 million years old, were dug up when the navvies made the Victoria line. And even these slime-trailing slow coaches were babies in the grand scheme of things – they have been on planet Earth for about 500 million years and are still around today. Think of that next time you are stressing out about catching the train.

Before the station was built, the land was home to a tremendous white elephant. Irish Doctor Richard Barter built the Oriental Baths at 2 Victoria Street in 1862, believing his attraction would bring in punters hoping to wallow in health-giving waters. He gave his bathhouse a twist – you could bring your horse in and give it a soak, too.

Despite this unique offering, the baths did not prove to be popular, but the railways came to Dr Barter's rescue. Just three years after its completion, the building was bought by the Metropolitan Railway Company and they demolished it to make way for what is now Victoria Station.

For much of the twentieth century, Victoria Station was the gateway to Europe, considered in the same way the Eurostar is today. It was where a boat train called the Golden Arrow Express set off, whisking passengers to Dover and then to a ferry. It also means these platforms have seen a million tragedies played out, linked forever with the British soldiers and the First World War. It was where they set off alive, and where their bodies came back.

From 1936 Victoria became a staging point for left-wingers joining the fight in Spain against Franco's fascists. Volunteers had a fiver in their pocket and a ticket to catch the Arrow to Paris, where French comrades would then take them south … Special Branch lingered in cafes and pubs, trying to find a communist to follow.

Ernest Bevin summed up Victoria's reputation as a place that links London with the rest of the world when, as Foreign Secretary in 1951, he said, 'My policy is to be able to take a ticket at Victoria Station and go anywhere I damn well please.'

Let us follow Bevin's policy and shuffle down Underground for a few stops on the Victoria line, up to Oxford Circus to have a mooch round Marylebone. As we walk through the low-ceilinged hall at Victoria Tube Station, let us start by recalling an incident that took place in 2014.

Builders upgrading the place accidentally smashed a hole into the signalling room – and compounded their error in a cartoon-ish way by filling the place with quick-drying cement. It caused havoc with the trains and workers had to mix sugar into the gloop to slow its setting, then shovel it all out.

We've hopped on a near-empty Tube, and now, back above ground at Oxford Circus, we'll pop into Cavendish Square and hear how its development led to a change in the law regarding intellectual copyright.

Robert Dodsley started his working life as a footman. He became the author of a number of poems and plays and was championed by Alexander Pope, who lent him cash to set up a map-making firm. And there was money to be made in maps – although quite how original and well-researched each publisher's efforts were can be seen by a series of rival guides produced in the 1700s. Like Mr Dodsley's, they all showed a set of streets around Cavendish Square that had been included on one of his street plans in anticipation of building work. The economic meltdown that was the South Sea Bubble struck. They never were built. Map makers did not bother to survey the area for new editions and for years ghost streets confused the newcomer hoping to navigate this part of town armed with a street plan.

This copy-and-paste thievery was used by Hogarth in 1734 as an example of people stealing others' works, and led to an Act of Parliament establishing copyright at fourteen years. Those found breaking the new law would be fined 5s per imprint – a huge sum at the time.

Later that century, Princess Amelia, daughter of George III, lived in the square: her ailments included the painful skin disease known as St Anthony's Fire. Amelia, who would spend weeks in the sea at Weymouth to alleviate the complaint that manifested itself in giant, swollen red blotches across her body, fell in love with a Colonel Fitzroy. George III did not like the suitor and was having none of it – but the couple were inseparable. When she died, aged 27, she left her fortune to him.

Now to a Victorian convent on the northern side of the square that was smashed about in the Blitz. After the war, the nuns employed architect Louis Osman to rebuild it – and he in turn commissioned Jacob Epstein to create a piece of sculpture, Madonna and Child, to hang from its façade. The Mother Superior did not realise he was Jewish, and when she did she kicked up a fuss. Thankfully, in the face of stinging criticism, Epstein's work was reinstated and the piece is there today.

Jacob Epstein's 'Madonna and Child'.

FROM GREAT FILTH COMES GREAT BEAUTY

Moving westwards, let's stroll to Wigmore Street, home of Wigmore Hall. It is said to have some of the best acoustics for classical music in the world – which might not be surprising when toy consider that it was built as Bechstein Hall by the German piano firm, who had a shop next door.

They employed architect Thomas Collcutt (who also gave us the Savoy Hotel), but disaster struck in 1916 when the firm's assets were seized. The hall was then sold as 'an alien property'. It cost the Bechsteins £100,000 to put up, and fetched £56,000 in the fire sale.

From Wigmore Street, we'll pop down the thoroughly well-heeled Queen Anne Street. It was here that JMW Turner made his home in 1836 and it became known as Turner's Den, a filthy dwelling, stuffed full of paintings and the general flotsam and jetsam of his life.

One visitor recalled, 'The windows were never cleaned, and had in them breaches patched with paper; the door was black and blistered; the iron palisades were rusty for lack of paint. If a would-be visitor knocked or rang, it was long before the summons was replied to by a wizened, meagre old man, who would unfasten the chain sufficiently to see who knocked or rang, and the almost invariable answer was, "You can't come in."'

And Turner was just as unwelcoming to potential buyers of his works. He was also offered £100,000 to sell Queen Anne Street, with its rolls of musty paintings stashed in cupboards and propped up against easels and walls, a sale he refused by saying he'd been offered more. One wealthy collector managed to force his way past Turner's elderly servant, only to be met by the furious artist – who relented when the intruder pulled out £5,000 in cash.

And on the steps of the home of this cantankerous genius, let us for a moment close our eyes and let Turner's summer sunsets fill our minds.

JMW Turner.

SOUNDS OF THE SEAS

Nice, aren't they, those Turner scapes? Indeed. But now it is time to swagger round the corner into Chandos Street. It gets its name from the Duke of Chandos, a landowner and politician in the early 1700s. When he died, his son discovered his father's estate was in so much debt that he had no choice but to hold a demolition sale of their country pile, with literally everything available: walls, ceilings, as well as the family silver. It means that today some of Chandos's expensively good taste in art and architecture can still be found in other stately homes, even though his lavish yard no longer exists.

Right – back to the present day. Chandos Street gets a name check on page 417 of Zadie Smith's novel *White Teeth* – 'Let's get going,' he said, as a huge beer-pregnant Englishman, wet from the fountains, collided into him, out of this bloody madness. It's on Chandos Street', she writes. But because the characters are in Trafalgar Square, critics wonder if she might be referring to Chandos Place, which is further south.

While we are ruminating on this minor question, let us consider the story of Joseph Johnson, who lived in either Chandos Street or Place in the 1800s. Originally a merchant seaman, he was unable to return to the life of a sailor because of an injury, and not being liable to relief from any parish, Joseph took to making a living by singing songs of the sea with a small replica of HMS *Nelson* attached to his hat. 'He can, by a bow of thanks, or a supplicating inclination to a drawing room window, give the appearance of sea motion,' one witness described. Hats off to you, Joe.

GOING UP! FALLING DOWN!

And sitting a stone's throw east of old Joe's haunt is the magnificent Langham Hotel. (Blagged a free night, have we? Ed.)

Designed by John Giles (not the tough-tackling Leeds United midfielder but an architect who also designed hospitals and asylums), it was built in 1863. It cost a whopping £29 million in today's cash to complete. But what a magnificent sight it was! The Langham boasted London's first hydraulic lifts, 100 loos and thirty-six bathrooms … thirty-six?! Can you imagine?

During the Second World War, BBC staff would sleep there due to the ease of getting to Broadcasting House across the road. One such night, playwright and novelist JB Priestley had headed to get some kip after recording an episode of his morale-boosting series, *Postscripts*. He was woken by a producer, who asked if he'd mind standing in for someone on a World Service broadcast. Dutifully, Priestley got out of his pyjamas and went back to work.

Langham Hotel.

Left: Broadcasting House.

Below: JB Priestley.

Half an hour later, German bombers scattered their murderous payload over the city centre – and one scored a direct hit on the bedroom Priestley had been sleeping in, completely demolishing it.

The BBC itself tried to pull the Langham down in 1980 – Norman Foster had designed an office block in its place – but permission was denied. The old girl was sold on again as a 'do-er upper', this time to a hotel group, who splashed out £100 million on the job.

We shall now go to Great Portland Street for a pretend pint on the spot of the old Harp Tavern. It was here in the 1750s that the City of Lushington Club was formed – a drinking society that, it is said, gives us the word lush to describe someone who likes being in one's cups.

The City of Lushington was organised along the same lines as the City of London, a place not unknown for huge, boozy, indulgent meals. A lord mayor was elected, supported by four aldermen who looked after four wards named Juniper, Poverty, Lunacy and Suicide – a type of Hogarthian progress as the devil drink takes hold. It spawned a number of sayings: 'Voting for the aldermen' meant being blind drunk, while to be told 'Lushington was your master' would be a subtle way of saying calm it down there. In the marvellous *Green's Dictionary of Slang*, which traces 500 years of idioms and sayings and general language chit-chat, it says the word may have derived from the Bavarian '*Loschen*', meaning a strong beer.

Saying cheerio to the ghosts of the Lushington crew, we shall head a little south to the site of the former Middlesex Hospital in Mortimer Street. Only a chapel and a façade remain of a building that first opened its doors to the sick in 1755, replaced with a typical modern developer's flats and offices combo. Its medical school had the quaintly hilarious motto *Miseris Succurrere Disco*, which to the untrained Latin reader might translate as 'Misery is Aided by Disco', but is actually a highfalutin reference to something Virgil said about Queen Dido rescuing shipwrecked sailors.

The old entrance to this place of healing was graced by a set of murals called 'The Acts of Mercy' by the Edwardian painter Frederick Cayley Robinson (they are now along Euston Road at the Wellcome Trust). Cayley Robinson was a painter and decorator as well as an artist, perhaps making him an even dabber hand at getting paint on walls. It's hardly surprising – he lived for many years in Florence, so was steeped in Renaissance friezes. He got into set design, too, working at the Haymarket Theatre.

Having sat upon Turner's steps, let's depart for some more high culture.

JUST A BAD COLD

The Midd played an important role in trying to save Londoners during the 1918 flu pandemic: in one October weekend, sixty people collapsed in nearby streets and were rushed there by ambulance. The hospital's chief medical officer at the time was quoted as complaining that he was 'merely directing the traffic', sending victims to the emergency wards – intensive care units – or the mortuary. Writing BID – Brought In Dead – became a horribly routine entry in his notes.

How to tackle the flu became, as today, the stuff of claim and counter-claim. *The Times*, which said, 'the visits of the raiding Goths to London were but a summer shower compared with the deluge of germs we have just received', was not slow to offer possible remedies. Its health reporter suggested wearing 'a piece of cut gauze over the mouth and nose'. Such good advice was offset by his claim that smoking would see off the deadly virus. It proved a wildly popular piece of advice, as it prompted many shop floors to drop their no smoking rule. He added that drinking port and Burgundy offered relief and protection, too. One out of two isn't so bad.

The Middlesex Hospital.

RUNNERS, RIDERS
AND ROMEOS

From here, we pop along to Riding House Street, so named after the barracks of the Horse Grenadier Guards, who had stables there in the 1700s. The Grenadiers were a fierce bunch, chosen for their muscular frames – they had plenty of equipment to carry as they lobbed hand grenades from their charges.

Of the many titled officers, let us pause and remember James O'Hara, 2nd Baron Tyrawley. In April 1743, after a long and bloody career on the battlegrounds of the War of the Spanish Succession, O'Hara was made a colonel of the 2nd Troop. While stationed at Riding House Street, the married colonel had an affair with an actress called Mrs Bellamy. Their daughter, George Anne Bellamy (the birth certificate was meant to read Georgiana but the clerk messed it up) followed her mother on to the stage. She got her break when impresario Mr Rich of the Covent Garden Theatre heard her reciting passages from *Othello* to his daughters.

And Shakespeare would play a crucial role in catapulting her to fame.

In 1750 she won what became known as the Battle of the Romeos: during a twelve-day period both the Covent Garden and Drury Lane theatres put on competing productions of the Bard's tragic, Verona-based love story. Bellamy was cast opposite David Garrick, while Drury Lane boasted Spranger Barry and Susannah Cibber. Critics said the 19-year-old was 'young and beautiful, more physically appropriate for Juliet and more pleasing in the first half of the play'.

She had chutzpah, too: when overlooked for the role of Cordelia, she printed leaflets claiming the role had been stolen from her. She added that if the audience wanted her to perform, they should make their feelings clear when the curtain rose. Her hapless rival, Miss Wilford, had no choice but to exit stage left as the crowd bayed for Bellamy.

STAINED GLASS
AND CAPTAIN WEBB

Next, we head south to Wells Street, whose name derives from George Wells, a brick maker who owned fields in the neighbourhood. It boasts the The Champion pub, a Victorian boozer dating from 1860, and is Grade II-listed for its charming interior.

Its windows feature stained glass depicting heroes from the period – cricketer WG Grace, nurse Florence Nightingale, explorer David Livingstone and mountaineer Edward Whymper among others – but despite their look, they are recent additions. Commissioned by the Sam Smith brewery, they actually date from the 1990s and were created by artist Ann Sotheran.

Among those figures filling the boozer with coloured light is one Captain Matthew Webb: Webb became famous for diving overboard to rescue a seaman who had toppled into the Atlantic. Feted as a hero, he became the first man to swim the English Channel and is considered to have popularised swimming.

The Champion pub.

Sadly, his taste for derring-do and the publicity it garnered ended in unpleasant circumstances. He decided his next stunt would be to go over the Niagara Falls in a barrel. His body was never recovered.

Our final stop on this little turn is Adam and Eve Court, which runs parallel to Wells Street, and here we will recall the tale of master swordsman, pugilist and showman James Figg.

Born in 1695, Figg could today be considered as a mixed martial artist: he fought with sword, cudgel and his meaty fists. He became a heavyweight bare knuckle champion, and is considered one of the fathers of modern boxing. He was painted by his friend, Hogarth, and hung out with the Prince of Wales.

In Adam and Eve Court, he set up a fighting school and hosted displays of brutishness, including sword fights and cock fighting.

In 1725, Figg battered a challenger whose size and weight had made him the favourite – but who hadn't reckoned on Figg's skill and bravery. The crowd was not happy, and started to riot. Figg slipped away as the brawling mob got out of hand, and retired for a cup of cocoa at his lodgings opposite.

As the noise outside grew, he heard a furious knocking on his door. Assuming it was the mob coming to take revenge for his victory on the man they had backed, he leapt up, clutching his sword. Instead, it was his landlord, wearing his nightshirt, who politely suggested that in light of the evening's events Figg might like to find himself new place to stay.

He did – directly across the narrow Adam and Eve Court. He built a hall attached to his new home and used it as a school for swordsmen, proclaiming he was a 'Master of ye Noble Science of Defence'.

LIBERTY, MODERNITY, HABERDASHERY

And on that slash-and-thrust of a tale we leave Adam and Eve Court behind us and head south across Oxford Street, down through Ramillies Street (named after a battle in the Spanish War of Succession, since you ask) and come out in Great Marlborough Street, home to the world famous Liberty department store.

We'll pause to tip our face masks to the statue of Arthur Liberty, standing at the entrance of his emporium. The current shop dates from the period of Tudor revivalism in the 1920s. Builder Edwin Hall came up with a wheeze – he used recycled timbers from decommissioned Royal Navy ships.

HMS Impregnable, a Victorian battleship, was huge. But her design meant she was soon obsolete in the fast-moving switch from wind to steam. Instead, she became a training vessel, her 121-gun ports never carrying more than twelve at a time.

Liberty.

Liberty.

Marshall Street Baths.

Her ancient timbers, cut from 3,040 New Forest oaks, were sold off in 1921. They were joined at Liberty by those originally felled for HMS *Hindustan*, an eighty-gunner launched in the 1840s. From them, Edwin had all the ancient timber he needed for the grand haberdashers Arthur envisaged.

Next we take a walk along Fouberts Place – named after Henry Foubert who, not unlike James Figg ran a school to teach martial arts. His father, Solomon, had been a crack Parisian fencing trainer and Henry, on moving into England in 1679, set up an institute to teach the correct way to thrust and parry.

At the end of Fouberts Place we come to Marshall Street, home of the famous baths. The first incarnation was completed in 1850 before being revamped in 1931. The new baths boasted Sicilian marble – white, fossil-streaked rock, quarried for hundreds of years from around the capital, Palermo. The marble does not absorb humidity – making it perfect for keeping the Sicilians cool and resilient as cladding for pools.

Once the marble was laid, the Mayor of Westminster, Captain JFC Bennett, conducted the opening ceremony. A veteran of the First World War, he had served in the 2nd Battalion, Queen's Westminster Rifles – and his unit has helped shape the legend of the Christmas truces in the trenches.

With German troops within carol-singing distance, conversations struck up. One asked how Fulham was getting on in the FA Cup, saying he supported them as he once lived on the Fulham Road. The captain's comrades entertained their opposite numbers, reporting, 'We found old bicycles, top hats, straw hats, umbrellas. We dressed up and went over to the Germans. It seemed so comical to see fellows walking about in top hats and with umbrellas up. Some rode the bicycles backwards. We had some fine sport and made the Germans laugh.'

While the Marshall Street Baths are associated with good public health, right next door was once a dead-end yard whose name is self-explanatory: Pesthouse Close.

When the Great Plague swept through London in 1665, the owner of the land, William, 1st Baron of Craven, sat on the seventeenth-century version of the SAGE Committee. He constructed thirty-six homes 'for the Reception of poor and miserable Objects ... afflicted with a direful Pestilence'.

A plague pit was dug out back and its inhabitants have occasionally reappeared, dug up in recent years during building works.

FROM LEATHER
TO LENTILS

And so across to Lexington Street, and let us stop outside Mildred's veggie restaurant. Mildred's was a trailblazer, opening in 1988 when the veggie nosh option was basically lentil gruel.

Its owners, Diane and Jane, first hired a cafe that had really been a sex club. When they got the keys, they discovered to their mirth a fully padded S&M cell in the basement. The building was owned by porn barons, who would come in to collect rent in person 'with a glamorous blonde in a fur coat on their arm'. The landlords would slip wads of cash into the inside pockets of their cashmere coats before invariably asking for a bacon sandwich.

Further down Lexington Street, we pay respects to a victim of the Soho Strangler. This murderer committed heinous crimes in the mid-1930s and was never caught. The first death was that of French Fifi, a prostitute killed in Archer Street in November 1935. The second, Marie Cotton, lived in a Lexington Street flat and her body was discovered by her 15-year-old son, Remo. Suspicion fell on a neighbour who arranged male orgies at a place next door, and who had fallen out with Cotton over a mattress.

Then, three weeks later, a woman called Leah Hinds was killed in her Old Compton Street home. She was known as both Dutch Leah – a calling card for clients to make her sound exotic – and Stilts Leah, a more affectionate nickname used by friends on account of her penchant for extremely high heels.

The neighbour was no longer a person of interest. Officers later hoped to link the crimes with the wartime serial killer Gordon Cummins, known as the Blackout Ripper, but they failed to find enough evidence. The identity of the culprit remains a mystery.

Let's cheer ourselves up before we depart by heading to Brewer Street, which cuts across

Mildred's.

Lexington Street, and stop outside the O Bar. In the 1950s, the pub was called The Roundhouse and was home to musicians Bob Watson and Cyril Davies's skiffle venue. When Watson left to join the glamorously named Dickie Bishops and the Sidekicks, Davies turned the venue into the London Blues and Barrelhouse club.

Its first ever performance that featured an electric guitar took place in 1958, and was by a performer called Muddy Waters. Later, the singer Bob Davenport, whose delightful voice is much cherished, turned it into a successful folk venue.

We have now reached Soho on a zig-zag course set by Captain Random and face much historical treasure to pick through.

O Bar and Bob Davenport with Martin Carthy and Nigel Denver.

OCCUPE-TOI DE TES OIGNONS!

Let us go forth, steadily, from Brewer Street and swing into Ham Yard. Its name doesn't – surprisingly – come from a connection with pigs, but because of an inn situated there in the early eighteenth century called The Ham.

While there is no clear link to the butcher's trade, the yard does remind one of a story about a culinary master. French chef Alexis Soyer was a star in Victorian Britain – a foodie genius turned philanthropist. He came to London after a narrow escape from members of the anti-Royalist Trois Glorieuses during the Second French Revolution of 1830; he was a target as he cooked for the French prime minister Jules, Prince de Polignac. A group burst into his kitchens and shot dead two of his staff. He got the message and scarpered.

In England, he campaigned for the victims of the Irish famine, gave a contribution of a penny for every copy sold of his cook book, *Soyer's Charitable Cookery; or The Poor Man's Regenerator* (1847), improved the diets of Crimean War soldiers and invented the Soyer field stove, which the British Army used up until 1982.

In 1852, in Ham Yard, Soyer showed quite how big both his talent and his heart were: he set up a kitchen over Christmas and served 22,000 hungry people a free dinner. Nice work.

PAVING THE WAY
TO PARIS

Next up, Denman Street, home to the Piccadilly Theatre, whose owners boasted on opening in the 1920s that it was so big that if you laid all its bricks out end to end, they'd reach from London to Paris.

Its art deco interior has borne witness to a number of firsts: in 1934, it was taken on by Warner Bros, and the Al Jolson film *The Singing Fool* was screened. Never before had a UK cinema audience watched a talkie. They'd fitted a Vitaphone sound system, which worked by printing the soundtrack on vinyl and then attaching a record deck to the projector with pulleys.

Before the war the theatre became known for its cabaret shows but closed for the duration when hit by a Blitz bomb. Refurbished in the 1950s, by 1960 it hosted Les Ballet Africains, featuring the master drummer Professor Famoudou Konaté. Born in Upper Guinea, he was a child protégé and lead Djembe soloist for the company. Transferring from Broadway, it kickstarted the Piccadilly as the place to see the hot shows from New York. *A Street Car Named Desire* premiered there.

In 1983, Turin-born, world record-holding quick-change expert and magician Arturo Brachetti was booked in for a season with his new show, 'I'. It was meant to be another groundbreaker, with the stalls removed and a dinner and cabaret set up.

Brachetti learned magic from a 'Gospel Magician' monk called Silvio Mantelli and by the age of 15 had perfected a performance where he would change in the blink of an eye into a new costume. However, despite having the Almighty on side, Brachetti's big London break was a disaster. His show was riddled with technical issues. His tricks failed spectacularly, with audiences able to see exactly what should have happened and how. Dinner was served late, and mean journalists muttered mean things to readers and each other.

Brachetti wasn't defeated: he closed the curtains after a few performances and put it right. Renamed 'Y', his show won him awards.

Onwards: let's head to Air Street, featuring an odd corner plot, now redeveloped. There was a decades-long discussion through the 1800s about how best to bookend Nash's great Regent Street creation, and this quadrant was at the heart of it.

In 1840, after allegations of corruption in the Metropolitan Board of Works over this prized real estate set back improvements, 73-year-old retired architect Norman Shaw was appointed. In what is described as 'an astonishing burst of creative energy' by historian FHW Shepherd, 'he produced in a few months a design of heroic conception, as well as a number of schemes for the rearrangement of the Circus'.

It would, critics said, make Piccadilly Circus a wonder of the world by sorting out the mess of the roads round the centre and completing Nash's vision. But it was stymied by the stinginess of the Crown, who refused to chip in 'for the sake of either architectural effect or municipal improvement', which meant it was a non-starter. Shepherd described it as 'one of the greatest of all the many lost opportunities in the architectural history of London'.

And on that note, we'll stare dead-eyed at the advertising slogans blaring out across the circus, and paraphrase that quote from Evelyn Waugh: 'Piccadilly and its lights are very nice – if you can't read.'

We suspect Mr Shepherd and Mr Shaw would agree.

Piccadilly Circus lights.

THE UNGODLY BOREDOM
OF DON SEBASTIAN

G ood day! We parted company gazing up at the LED light pollution of the giant billboards in Piccadilly Circus, pondering on how advertising, that industry based on trickery and persuasion, had somehow managed to convince us that giant flashing product names should still be one of the 'sights' of London. Understandable, perhaps, for generations who remembered gaslit streets – but such a reason now doesn't hold quite the same heft as it did then.

We shall continue our scatty-footed trundle around our borough with a brief rest in the quiet sanctuary of the Our Lady of the Assumption and Saint Gregory Catholic Church in Warwick Street.

In the 500s, St Gregory was behind the earliest recorded attempt to bring Christianity from Rome to what were then these pagan shores, while, of course, the lady is Mary and refers to her heading upwards to meet St Peter at the end of her earthly life. The current church dates from 1789, although there was a smaller chapel on the land used by diplomats of the Portuguese court. One such chap was Don Sebastian Joseph de Carvalho, who would become a dictator back home. His character was such that he set a long series of tedious rules and regulations regarding the services held there. Yet it remained popular: Catholic churches were hardly thick on the ground from the Tudors onwards, but, due to the link with the Portuguese government, its congregation were allowed to quietly get on with it for many years.

The peace broke spectacularly during the Gordon Riots of 1780. A mob stormed the church and dragged whatever they could move into the street. They burnt the lot – although the Father just had time to save the altar plate before the doors caved in.

TEA, TOAST
AND TAGLIATELLE

Now for something mellower. Let's wander down Swallow Street, on the opposite side of Regent Street, and pause outside what once was the majestic Euro Snack Bar.

Established in 1920 and closed in 2004, surrounded by the backs of department stores, lap-dancing clubs and nondescript entrances to attic offices for businesses wanting a W1 postcode, it was a cherished secret. Shop workers, road diggers and women working in the strip clubs would sit in the original booths while browsing a menu that ranged from greasy spoon classics to Italian plates. One has not forgotten the salt and pepper shakers, the scratchy paper napkins and the identical receding hairlines of the men who worked the counter.

Suitably refreshed, let's sashay down Haymarket.

We'll start by remembering a tragedy that befell Sir William Wyndham's grand Haymarket home in March 1712. A fire ripped through the property, which he had only purchased a few months previously for £6,000.

Satirist and *Gulliver's Travels* author Jonathan Swift reported that two of Sir William's maids were caught upstairs by the flames – and leapt to their deaths. The servants' distressful endings were made worse by the fact they both landed on railings below the house, with one impaled by her head. It is interesting to note contemporary reports appeared to be more interested in the fact the maids were suspected of accidentally starting the fire, and that Sir William's poor wife lost £1,000 of clothing, rather than the distressing final moments of the domestics.

Let us leave this sad place and continue along the Haymarket. A little further down the road is the spot where in 1838 the Home Secretary, Lord John Russell, and friends exited a theatre on a cold night. A gang of urchins had created an icy slide for their amusement down the Haymarket slope, while waiting for the nobs inside the heated theatres to head home so they could cadge pennies. The unfortunate lord was knocked over by an excitable tobogganist.

Coincidentally (or maybe not), later that year, Section 54 of the Metropolitan Police Act – which has never been repealed – came into force. It decreed that one must not slide on ice 'in any street or thoroughfare, to the common danger of passengers'.

Portrait of Fyodor Dostoevsky by Vasily Perov.

Now we jump forward thirty years to join Fyodor Dostoevsky as he gazes with wonder at Haymarket's nightlife. 'Streets are lit by jets of gas, something completely unknown in our own country,' he wrote. 'At every step you come across magnificent public houses, all mirrors and gilt.'

The writer was bowled over by the crowds, and seems to have had beer-goggles on. 'You find beautiful women at the sight of whom you stop in amazement. There are no women in the world as beautiful as the English,' he adds.

'I went into a "casino". The music was blaring, people were dancing, a huge crowd was milling round. The place was magnificently decorated. But gloom never forsakes the English, even in the midst of gaiety. Even when they dance they look serious, if not sullen, making hardly any steps and only as if in execution of some duty ...'

A MARKET FOR MUSOS

Ah, but we did learn how to loosen up in the post-Victoria years, and to illustrate this let us now head to Archer Street, moments north of Haymarket. It was the go-to place for jobbing musicians for much of the twentieth century. Nestling in the middle of theatre and club land – the Apollo and the Lyric's stage doors open on to it – players hung out to pick up an evening's work. It acted as an outdoor social club, too.

During the Great Depression, it offered a support system for unemployed bands. International Brigadier George Green, who later died in the Spanish Civil War, wrote in the *Daily Worker*, 'Every day gather four or five hundred musicians ... anxious for tomorrow. This is not the Rhondda. Poverty does not show its access so openly. Sometimes a passer-by seeing a thronged pavement, will ask if this is a branch of the Stock Exchange. This is no Stock Exchange but a slave market, and here the slave who finds no master starves.'

The gatherings sometimes attracted the police and questions were asked in the House. One MP countered the chivvying of the downtrodden by the Old Bill, saying it was disgraceful that unemployed men looking for work should be asked to move on. 'Will the home secretary inquire why these men should be denied the right to assemble in a peaceful manner for desirable purposes?' they asked.

The end finally came for the Archer Street musicians in 1961 when, under pressure from businesses, they were banned, casting a London tradition into the past.

THE PREPOSTEROUS PARSON

We have previously paraphrased Evelyn Waugh, citing his dislike of the lights of Piccadilly, and there is another Waughian link to our next stop – Bourchier Street, a little Soho cut through linking Wardour Street with Dean Street.

It hasn't always had this moniker. In a pre-developed past it was called Milk Alley and Hedge Lane, and then for a time Little Dean Street. It was renamed once more, becoming Bourchier Street in 1937, in honour of the vicar of St Anne's, Soho, the Rev. Basil Bourchier.

Bourchier had preached in Hampstead Garden Suburb, a church the Waugh family worshipped at, and young Evelyn called him the 'preposterous Parson', amused as he was by Bourchier's extravagant approach to the Gospel.

Bourchier Street.

Bourchier moved to St Anne's and it was here his career took a turn for the worse. In 1933, he was removed from his post, in order to stop a scandal developing over rumours about his behaviour towards choirboys, which had become public knowledge. Whether this was true or not is lost in the mists of time. He was gay – and the unproven allegations about other behaviour may have been a homophobic attempt to smear his name.

He had a rectory in Soho Square, and his replacement, the Rev. Herbert Bamforth, moved in while Bourchier was away. Bamforth and his family explored the house, but his brother-in-law, a Mr Roe, recalled how when they reached the second floor, 'I immediately felt all about me the presence of evil so strong as to be almost tangible. I saw no ghost or anything that was strange in any way. There was no sound, no smell, sensation – none of the things which are the hallmark of a proper ghost story – only this fearful sense of evil.' The house had once been the lodgings of a mistress to the Prince Regent. She was murdered there and the crime, Roe believed, had left an 'evil stain'.

Bourchier died just three months after leaving Soho – and in his will he put aside £50 to pay for a doctor to check he was really dead before burial.

Leaving this sad tale behind us, we will head into St Anne's Court, another traffic-free cut through a little to the north.

The wealthy Victorian philanthropist Lachlan Mackintosh Rate built thirty lodgings to be let to artisans. He had plenty of cash and liked to sponsor craftsmen: he employed Utopian architect William Burges to build it – although it sadly no longer stands – and also got him to knock up a fancy pile in Dorking, Surrey, too.

Perhaps the echo of this continued into the twentieth century. The famous Trident Studios was at No. 17, where the Beatles recorded 'Hey Jude' and some of the *White Album*, and where its roster was essentially a *Who's Who* of 1960s and '70s music.

Another cool addition was the marvellously named sci-fi comic book shop, Dark they Were and Golden Eyed. Named after a Ray Bradbury story, the owner, Derek 'Bram' Stokes, had previously run a Gothic fanzine and started a mail order book company.

Bram brought to the UK hundreds of American titles never seen before and helped fire the genre's popularity that continues today. It became a cool counter-culture place to hang out. The shop also acted as an office for a time for the still-publishing *Fortean Times*, a terrific monthly read. *The Times* specialises in tales of extraordinary phenomena, and it meant the shop received its share of correspondence relating to odd events, making the arrival of the morning post always something for the staff and customers to enjoy.

The *Fortean Times* (FT) is inspired by the work of the author of *The Book of the Damned*, Charles Fort. He had an interest in weird news and weird happenings, his world made up of Yetis and Nessies, freak storms, giant sea monsters, spontaneous combustion, ghosts and the like. He liked to approach the topic with a healthy dose of scepticism, and this is something the magazine continues today. It asks its readers to 'enjoy adventure, curiosity, natural scepticism and have a good sense of humour', and it fills its pages each month with a range of thought-and-giggle-provoking yarns.

Today, St Anne's Court has a cool barbers' and a handy key-cutting and shoe repair-type ironmongers. Rumour has it that the actor who played Zammo in Grange Hill worked there.

BATTY LANGLEY AND OCCUPATIONS OF ILL REPUTE

O ne more stop: from St Anne's Court, we're exploring another little back lane known as Meard Street. It is here we find the grandly named Royalty Mansions. Now housing, it had humbler beginnings. Designed by architect Harold Woodington – who also happened to build the majestic Pavilion Cinema in Selsey on the south coast – it was originally designed for one-man tailor workshops supplying West End outlets with clothing and hotels with linen.

The mansions date from 1907, but the street has been there much longer and dates from the 1700s. Constructed by John Meard, who also contributed to housing in Great Marlborough Street and built (and possibly designed) the famous spire of St Anne's, Soho, which was hit by a German bomb during the Blitz.

Meard Street.

Despite his success and the longevity of the quality of his work, he comes over as a bit dodgy: he rose to be a Freeman of the City of London and a magistrate, but it was alleged that he used his position to avoid paying rates for himself and his tenants. He used a scam that saw him moving lodgers about his various properties so no rent records could be accessed. And this sleight of hand involved the wonderfully named Batty Langley.

Batty was a celebrated architectural writer and lived at No. 9 in the mid-1700s; he also had his brother Thomas, an engraver, working under his roof. But parish rates books from the period show that whenever anyone knocked to collect what was owed, they were told the occupants were 'out of town' or 'in ye country or gone away'.

Meard Street today has a hilarious sign on one of its poshly painted doors, saying, 'This is not a brothel. There are no prostitutes at this address.' The address was the home of the late artist, writer and dandy, Sebastian Horsley.

The next inhabitant of Batty's place was one Elizabeth Flint, who paid 5*s* a week for a furnished room, and was brutally described in the parish records as 'generally slut and drunkard; occasionally whore and thief', while in the 1960s it was home to the Golden Girl Club.

LEGS FOR THE LEGLESS

On this grubby note, we emerge in Dean Street and gaze thirstily at The Crown and Two Chairmen pub before continuing our virtual walk.

Dating from the 1730s – although the current building was put up in 1929 – it earned a reputation for the excellence of its drink. From 1895, German-born Theodore Hamberger ran the place and it became known for its European lagers, a change to the usual Kentish hoppy ales. Census records show that he passed the licence on to a compatriot called Charles Heinlee. He too had emigrated to London from Germany – and the death certificates of both men are registered in the same Hackney parish.

The Mittel Europe link didn't end there: The Two Chairmen was then run by Charles Schaufert, born in Frankfurt, who lived above the place with his wife Gertrude and children Beatrice, Louis and Harold.

When the First World War broke out, this popular West End boozer, which had been well cared for by three Anglo-German families, changed hands and transferred to a man with a more English-sounding surname. It suggests a sorry tale of how the war hit millions of people in millions of ways.

The Crown and Two Chairmen.

As we stand outside The Crown and Two Chairmen and consider the name's link to the craze for sedan chairs in the 1600s, let us also note the number of rickshaws in Soho today. The leopard-skin-seated, disco-light-flashing, mini-sound-system Euro-pop playing trikes gather around the area as they wait to take people for a (let's hope literal, rather than figurative) ride.

London's layers of historic development mean our streets are not laid out to make sharing space easy, and the rickshaws have attracted long-running complaints. Has it always been this way? Think of the Hackney coachmen, waiting for fares outside our Dean Street boozer. Notorious for bad language and diddling passengers, they worked their nags hard – the term hackneyed, to describe an expression that is worn or overused, comes from an allusion to a 'weak, tired horse'.

The drivers' approach was everyone for themselves: they'd fight with each other and, as Samuel Pepys noted, turned their powers of vituperation to 'affronting the gentry'. The 700 who worked during the reign of William and Mary paid £59 for a twenty-one-year permit, and then an annual tax of £4 – and, as it is today, when others started taking rides, they weren't happy about it.

The interlopers were the two men who sit on the pub's sign: chaps carrying another about in a sedan chair. First introduced in 1634 by Sir Saunders Duncombe, the name comes from the Latin *sedere* (to sit).

The sedan took off in the reign of Queen Anne, when passengers were attracted by the shilling-a-mile charge and the mobility in crowds. There were sedan chair ranks working day and night – although after midnight the fare doubled, and a boy would walk ahead waving a torch to light the way.

By 1711, 300 chairs were looking for fares and, like the Hackneys, they did not have a polished reputation. The pole-men, who grasped the ends of 12ft shanks, are described as being 'often drunk, often careless, and nearly always uncivil'.

Another complaint noted by Pepys was how Londoners did not like the idea of employing 'freeborn Englishmen as beasts of burden'. It meant the majority were Irish, about whom Soho citizens did not have the same qualms.

THE RADIO STAR

Now we turn into Bateman Street, and halfway down, find ourselves at the entrance of Bateman's Buildings. Home once to John Snow of cholera fame – he lived there as a student from 1836–38 – it was described in the late 1800s by the French writer and San Marino diplomat William Tufnell Le Queux in his novel *The Temptress*.

Le Queux was an early aeroplane buff who helped organise the first ever air meeting in the UK. He was also a radio fanatic, a pioneer of playing music over the airwaves and he ran a one-man broadcasting station at a time when radios had yet to be mass produced. He describes Bateman's Buildings as being a 'narrow and exceedingly uninviting passage between a marine-store dealers and the shop of a small vendor of vegetables and coals. Bateman's Buildings [is] lined by grimy, squalid-looking houses, forming the playground of a hundred or so spirited juveniles of the unwashed class.'

Let us scurry to the northern end, and here find a connection to one of Soho's most-celebrated residents, William Blake. A quick recap: the artist and writer's father was a haberdasher based in Broad Street. They had a house built on the plague pit we popped past in Pesthouse Yard (off Brewer Street) and in Blake's youth there were complaints of the smell of corpses that had been buried too near to the surface.

Peter Ackroyd writes of Blake going into the 'foul shambles of Carnaby Market', known for its female butchers. Ackroyd points out that one of the plates for Blake's *Jerusalem* depicts three women disembowelling some poor soul. He links Blake's imagery to the carcasses he saw being hewn in two by cleaver-wielding women.

At the top end of Bateman's Buildings, we spot the former studio of Josiah Wedgwood on the corner of Greek Street and Soho Square. It was here that Blake's friend and mentor John Flaxman worked. Flaxman's father was a Covent Garden plaster cast maker and Flaxman grew up in a shop full of figurines that children came to gawp at.

Flaxman and Blake got on – no mean feat, considering William's reputation for being difficult. Both were influenced by Gothic sensibility; they read the same novels, converting words into internal imagery and then sharing their visions through art.

Flaxman became one of the most influential English artists of his time; yet, as Ackroyd points out, while Flaxman is barely known today, Blake — anonymous while alive — rings out across the ages.

Left: The John Snow.

Right: William Blake by John Linnell.

SPAGHETTI. ART. SEX

From the corner of Soho Square, we shall head down Greek Street, once called 'the worst street in the West End' by a police inspector in 1906, who added it was where 'crowds of people gather nightly who are little else than a pest ... some of the vilest reptiles in London live there or frequent it'.

Perhaps that's behind a good deal of its charm. It's also the first street in the cabbies' mnemonic for Soho locations: they say, 'Good For Dodgy Women' to recall the order of Greek, Frith, Dean and Wardour streets.

Across Soho, Italian restaurants were known for occupying ground floors to serve food, while they ran brothels upstairs. The 1920s Greek Street and its surrounds had a sleazy current washing through it. The police were bent – Sergeant George Goddard ran a protection racket, and shook down the proprietors of every business they could put the squeeze on.

Goddard had tried to persuade the owner of Quo Vadis, Pepino Leoni, to use the upper rooms for the sex trade, an offer the restaurateur rather bravely declined to take up. Goddard would later be arrested, along with his friend and the notorious nightclub owner Kate Meyrick, of the 43 Club over in Gerrard Street.

Edward Carrick was an artist who liked the feel of Quo Vadis and believed it to be something like the Parisian restaurants where the Gertrude Steins, Ernest Hemingways and F Scott Fitzgeralds hung out. Eager to recreate such a Bohemian headquarters – and aware that forming a friendship with the generous-natured Leoni would no doubt help ease the rumbling tummy of the struggling artist – Carrick helped refurbish the place. Carrick used Quo Vadis for exhibitions, as had seen done in trendy Left Bank cafes in Paris. Carrick and artists who found favour with him or their spaghetti-boiling benefactor became known as the Grubb Group, and went on to stage exhibitions on the Quo Vadis walls right up until the outbreak of the Second World War, when their patron was interned as an enemy alien.

Now, to our left we note the House of St Barnabas. Today it is the base of a charity for the homeless and a private members' club, but it was a hostel after the Second World War. At one point it provided 800 beds for ex-servicewomen, and was financially supported by the actress Joyce Grenfell.

In early days, it was the headquarters of the Westminster Commission of Sewers. It was from a desk in this building that Sir Joseph Bazalgette began mapping out London's drain network, and it is said Dickens wrote *A Tale of Two Cities* there.

HOGS, OPIUM
AND MONKEY BUSINESS

After gazing at St Barnabas's beautiful terracotta exterior, we walk past the old Gay Hussar restaurant, established more than sixty years ago by Victor Sassie. As a teenager, he had worked in Budapest and decided to bring goulash to town.

But rather than being known for its excellence in Hungarian delights, the Hussar's fame was based on it being the meeting place of prominent left-wingers and where you could pick up a bit of gossip from the likes of MP Tom Driberg and the Welsh-born, London-based, Labour politician Illtyd Harrington. Intrigues bounced off the walls – and the venue's special place in the history of Britain's left is partly due to the disgraced MP Garry Allighan.

Allighan was elected as MP for Gravesend in 1945, and among his early contributions was a question asked to Air Minister John Strachey about what arrangements he was making to ensure airmen staying in private billets got a good Christmas dinner, as their 'landladies are not able to provide anything extra, while men attached to stations will be given a special menu'.

Such interventions were not the start of a long and illustrious political career. He was expelled from the House in 1947 for what he declared were 'divided loyalties' between his job as an MP and his previous work as a journalist. Allighan would slip political news he'd gleaned from attending behind-closed-doors sessions of the Parliamentary Labour Party to the *Evening Standard*. He would quote what had been said and by whom, and Labour MPs grew increasingly furious at the leaks.

Allighan would accidentally out himself by penning a story in *World Press News* that laid out how Fleet Street had MPs on the payrolls of newspapers. He added that 'some MPs knock 'em back at the bar and being less absorptive than reporters, become lubricated into loquacity'. The admission led Quintin Hogg MP – who later became Lord Hailsham – to ask the Committee of Privileges to look into it. Allighan was interviewed and MPs voted to expel the fellow.

He would move to South Africa, while the Parliamentary Labour Party found a more secure home at the Gay Hussar for intrigues to be mused upon.

The Gay Hussar.

Further down Greek Street we come across the house where Thomas de Quincey wrote *Confessions of an English Opium-Eater*. He had acquired a taste for the drug when he bought some from an Oxford Street chemist to alleviate toothache, and would slip into opium-induced dreams at No. 47. He squatted there, joined by the 10-year-old illegitimate daughter of a lawyer called Brown, who de Quincey knew through a money lender he frequented.

Portrait of
Sir Thomas
de Quincy.

As we stroll on, let us briefly imagine ourselves here on a day in 1950 – and gaze upon a young man accompanied by a monkey. The person in question is George Fage Senior, the well-known West End fruit and veg seller, and he has just bought the hairy chap from a sailor in a pub in Covent Garden.

He is walking the creature down Greek Street, showing it off as he makes his way to his home across the Euston Road. Named Sinbad, the monkey lived in the Fages' attic above their greengrocers shop at the bottom of Albany Street. Lulu, Fage's wife, hated the beast and he hated her. 'He had been taught some rude gestures by the old man … one of which could be politely called self-abuse,' his son, George Junior, recalls in his autobiography, *My Old Man was a Barrow Boy and Gran was a Piccadilly Flower Girl*. 'He always did this to Lulu, which made the Old Man roar with laughter,' he adds.

After a year, the creature had grown to an enormous size, so they gave him to London Zoo. 'Apparently he was so over sexed he killed two females in his efforts to mate,' says George.

The Fages were well known in Soho. George's gran Eliza sold flowers, and George Bernard Shaw bought bouquets from her. She is said to have been the inspiration for Eliza Doolittle in his play *Pygmalion*, later transformed into the musical *My Fair Lady*.

George Fage Senior was a trove of London songs. His son recalls the party pieces he would launch into, including the following ditty:

My sister sells kisses to sailors,
My mother makes gin in the bath,
The old man makes counterfeit tin-tin
That's how the money rolls in
My brother's a slum missionary,
He saves fallen women from sin,
He'll save you a blonde for a shilling,
That's how the money rolls in,
(Altogether for the chorus)
Rolls in, rolls in,
That's how the money rolls in.

GINGER, YOU'RE BARMY

Having enjoyed Greek Street and looked in on Dean Street, it would be churlish not to pause in Frith Street. It was at the top end of Frith Street, at the turn of the 1900s, that the tragic tale of Ethel Kibblewhite and the poet TE Hulme unfolded.

Kibblewhite's dad had a Queen Anne house on the corner of Frith Street and Soho Square, where he ran a stained glass window business. It must have been grand – it was previously the Venetian Embassy.

It became the unofficial home to the poet (and one of the fathers of modernism) in 1911. TE Hulme moved in and started a passionate affair with Kibblewhite. He hosted a salon in their sitting room, which was visited by the likes of Rupert Brooke and Jacob Epstein.

But Hulme was something of a womaniser, and while romancing the mistress of the house he shamelessly used it to meet friends, including the painter Kate Lechmere. They regarded themselves as a couple, although poor Kibblewhite did not know about her rival. Both love affairs came to tragic ends when Hulme was killed in action on the Western Front in 1917.

It was Hulme's interest in Lechmere that saw him get into a fight with the poet Wyndham Lewis. The pair quarrelled as Lewis also had the hots for the painter, who studied under Walter Sickert. Lewis declared he was off to kill his rival, an animosity no doubt further stirred by unfounded rumours that Hulme was trying to subvert Lewis's pet project, the Rebel Art Centre. The pair were in competition, both running salons where talkative, intellectual Edwardian types could vent.

Lewis set out to track down Hulme, with poor Kate following behind, begging him to calm down. He burst into Frith Street and grabbed Hulme by the throat – but it did not end well for Lewis. Hulme was stronger. He carried his assailant outside and hung him upside down by his trousers on a set of railings in Soho Square.

The Kibblewhite house illustrates nicely Frith Street's long-standing connection between arts and crafts and manufacturing. Places like Kibblewhite's father's stained glass studio thrived in the neighbourhood up to the twentieth century. In the 1850s the census shows a row of shopfronts boasting goldsmiths, jewellers and watchmakers. There are also metal workers' studios and engravers.

It was from one such business that poor John Green, aged 16, was caught pinching 15lb of lead from an artisan called Thomas Redaway. He got a seven-year stretch in Australia for his troubles.

It's well known that Mozart stayed in Frith Street when he was touring Europe as a child, and perhaps it was he who recommended the Austrian oboist Johann Fischer, who is in the rate books as having lived there a few years later. From his home in Frith Street, Fischer set out to introduce a new form of oboe into the UK – and Mozart composed *Twelve Variations in C on a Minuet of Johann Christian Fischer* in his honour.

Horns of a different type have echoed down Frith Street for decades, and while we're trying not to linger too long on the well-known landmarks as we saunter, it would be poor form to walk past Ronnie Scott's and not pick one of a million funny stories about the goings on.

Ronnie Scott and Pete King.

The carefully nurtured reputation of drummers being doolally comes to mind as we linger outside and recall the late Ginger Baker. He played at the club on numerous occasions from the 1960s onwards – and recalled how he and his band once disarmed a man brandishing a shotgun who'd come to make off with the weekend takings while the staff and audience scattered.

Another time, he was having a fag outside when a pickled and disgruntled punter went for one of the bouncers with a knife. Ginger waded in. 'I ran over to assist and Ronnie came running out to see what was going on – and accidentally hit me over the head. I said: "Oi, Ronnie, I'm on your side."'

Here's to Ronnie's, and may crazy drummers ring out at top volume over Frith Street again soon.

UPTOWN TOP RANKING

Let us complete the cabbies' Soho dictum ('Good For Dodgy Women' – aka Greek, Frith, Dean and Wardour) and head to the last name on that list.

Some background: the name Wardour comes from the Dorset–Wiltshire borders and is linked to a tooled-up baron who leapt upon our shores with William the Conqueror. The early Wardours set up shop on the fringes of the rolling hills of Cranbourne Chase, their name becoming synonymous with a district and a castle. They owned land in and around the town of Shaftesbury, where King Alfred had established an abbey in 888. Having put down roots and oppressed the peasants, the Wardour family headed to town and bought land in the 1700s.

The gorgeous town of Shaftesbury featured in the famous Hovis advert, with the boy on the bike, by Ridley Scott. This leads us to a little link between sliced bread and Wardour Street.

It would be churlish not to mention the film world when strolling along our chosen thoroughfare – it was the centre of the industry in the UK and still boasts film production offices. By 1926 there were no fewer than forty film companies based along its stretch. The Rank Organisation made its home there in the 1930s, and here is where bakers come in.

Founder J Arthur Rank was born into money. His father, Joseph, got into the business of milling flour in the late 1800s when he rented a windmill in Hull. He got the taste for it, and went round buying up as many mills as he could near ports and installed new electric processing systems. His wheeze was good: he soon established the biggest bread firm in the UK. Think a Victorian Greggs and you're close. As well as grinding and baking, he owned shops selling his produce in high streets.

As he became more successful, he began considering life's larger questions, and this led him to Methodism. He poured his wealth into promoting Christian values, and put his bread where his mouth was: he used profits for charitable purposes.

But more importantly for British film, he supported and inspired his son.

J Arthur had set up his own flour business but when it failed to reach the same heights as his father's he quit and went back to the family firm. During this time, in the early 1930s, he became involved with the Religious Film

Society, which showed movies with a Christian slant at Sunday schools and Methodist halls. The RFS opened his eyes to the world of film and the business opportunities it offered. He wanted in.

By the end of the Second World War, Rank owned more than 650 cinemas, five studios including Pinewood, and an acting school to nurture new talent. His business acumen saw him do something similar to his dad: while his father thought he should be selling the bread he baked, Arthur felt if he was producing films he should also own the screens they were shown on. He bought out the Odeon and Gaumont chains, giving his movies a huge platform.

It was the golden age of film and Arthur facilitated it, partly due to his belief that the people he employed were there for a reason. He left directors to get on with it. David Lean said of J Arthur's approach, 'We can make any subject we wish, with as much money as we think that subject should have spent on it. We can cast whichever actors we choose, and we have no interference with the way the film is made ... not one of us is bound by any form of contract. We are there because we want to be there.'

It was while the Rank Organisation was churning out the hits in the 1950s that a young man called Terry Nelhams came to the area looking for a break. He worked as a messenger boy for a Wardour Street firm called TV Adverts and while running about Soho he discovered the skiffle craze. Soon Tel had persuaded colleagues they should arm themselves with a washboard, a tea chest bass and an acoustic guitar. Called The Worried Men, they gigged in Soho coffee bars and clubs, until one day Terry was spotted by talent scout Jack Good. He took the lad on, with the condition he changed his name to something more pop – thus bequeathing the world the singer Adam Faith.

Another stand-out Wardour Street film company was Handmade Films. You would think a Beatle would be rolling in it, but George Harrison had to remortgage his house in 1978 to finance the Monty Python film *Life of Brian*. The firm would go on to produce *The Long Good Friday*, *Time Bandits* and *Withnail and I*, creating a slew of British classics and no doubt giving George a good return on his investment.

And finally, as we've name-checked Beatle George and Adam Faith, we should mention the Marquee Club, home to the British blues explosion and where Jimi Hendrix blew the audience's minds with his first UK show. Legend has it that he was already so well known for his fret-lickin' skills that 1,400 people queued up to get in without any promotion done. The queue included the Beatles, Eric Clapton, Jeff Beck and the Stones, all intrigued to see for themselves if this left-handed dude had really reinvented what you could do with a Fender Stratocaster played back to front (his father Al told Jimi that playing the guitar left-handed was the work of the Devil, which with hindsight, sounds possible).

The Marquee's stage played host to all the names – The Yardbirds, John Mayall, Led Zep, The Who, Jethro Tull … More recently, the address was home to Cuban bar Floridita, which as well as food and music had a cigar shop and cigar lounge. It happened to be the only venue in Soho where indoor smoking was allowed following the ban, something its many rock'n'roll ghosts surely appreciated.

TONG YAN KAI, THE CIVIL WAR AND THE WORLD OF KATE MEYRICK

We wandered along the length of Wardour Street, so now let us pause at the faux Chinese gates at the western end of Gerrard Street where it meets Wardour, and dive down a thoroughfare steeped in history. Now considered the centre of London's Chinatown, its Asian link is a recent invention.

Gerrard Street is called Tong Yan Kai by Chinese people, meaning literally Chinese Street. But Chinatown was originally in Limehouse – and only moved to the West End after the Second World War, when a handful of Chinese restaurants served food to Tommies who had developed a taste for the cuisine after returning from service in the Far East. A collapse in the Hong Kong rice industry then saw people migrate to London and set up homes and businesses in the Gerrard Street area.

Its name comes from Cavalier General Charles Gerard, who owned the land in the 1600s and used it to square bash troops. He fought at the battles of Naseby and Edgehill in the Civil War, and went on a murderous rampage through South Wales. He was finally beaten during the Siege of Oxford, and is believed to have gone into exile with Prince Rupert. From Holland, he plotted continuously to overthrow the Commonwealth, planned to poison Cromwell, and would eventually return to these shores with Charles II. He would then spend his days trying to take hold of lands and titles and being involved in various litigations – one libel case saw his sworn enemy, his cousin Alexander Fitton, imprisoned for twenty years for the cross words he had with the peer.

He did not enjoy much of a reputation: Pepys described him as a 'proud and violent man' who was a notorious 'cheat and rogue'. One of the scams he is accused of was not informing authorities of the deaths of troopers under his charge, so he could draw their wages. When this came to light, the man who accused him of the actions was fined £1,000 and stuck in the stocks. The petition his accuser presented to the House of Lords was ordered to be publicly burned by the common hangman. His troubles did not end there: he was then caught conspiring to murder the Duke of York, fleeing to the Continent once

Wardour Street.

more, before returning with William of Orange. He died, it is said, from a 'fit of vomiting'. An unpleasant end for an unpleasant man.

Perhaps the General set the tone. Deceitful deeds and wrongdoings have never been too far away from Gerrard Street.

No. 43 had been the home to the poet John Dryden in the 1650s. In the 1920s, it was the home to the notorious 43 Club, owned by society hostess and general wrong 'un Kate Meyrick. When Meyrick opened her establishment, it came to typify the outrageous behaviour of the well-heeled in the Roaring Twenties. Attracting gangsters and the nobility, she served five prison sentences for selling booze after hours and trying to bribe the Old Bill who frequented the place. In 1929 she did a fifteen-month stretch for passing brown envelopes to Inspector Knacker of the Yard, and it was the beginning of a sad end. She died in 1933 after contracting a nasty bout of the flu. Such was her mark on the area that on the day of her funeral, as her cortège toured the streets, every theatre in the West End dimmed their lights in her honour.

Later, another notorious club could be found on the stretch. Businessman Hew McGowan bought a bar in Gerrard Street in 1964 and opened the Hideaway. Brave (or perhaps foolhardy), he offered the Kray twins a 20 per cent stake, having heard they were keen to get a foothold in the West End. But then he got cold feet and told the twins the deal was off – an extremely unwise decision. They came round and told him they would now be taking a slice of his profits, regardless of whether they had invested or not, prompting McGowan to grass them up. The Krays were arrested and held in Brixton Prison while the trial came to court. It took three trials and significant nobbling of jurors before it came to a conclusion – which saw the pair acquitted. Once back on the streets, the brothers immediately bought the Hideaway, changed its name to El Morocco, and celebrated their freedom by throwing a massive party at the club.

Less frightening, but just as notorious, No. 39 was the original home of Ronnie Scott's jazz club. In 1959, he joined forces with Pete King and they took over what was a dingy basement used by cabbies and musicians to while away the slow hours. Scott borrowed £1,000 from his dad to get it up and running: when they first moved in, it had two billiard tables and served tea and sandwiches.

Scott and King built a small stage and managed to somehow get a baby grand piano down the front steps, with a lot of pushing, shoving, grunting and cursing. It soon gained a reputation – Harold Pinter, Peter O'Toole and Eric Hobsbawn were regulars. It was here that Scott found his natural talent as a jazz club host, wisecracking his way into history as he introduced bands. His self-deprecation saw him deliver one-liners such as: 'I love this club, it's just like home. Filthy and full of strangers.'

And while no one in the band can quite remember it to confirm it (those 1960s, eh), it is believed No. 39 was the site of the first ever rehearsal for four musicians, Jimmy Page, Robert Plant, John Bonham and John Paul Jones – who would, of course, form Led Zeppelin. The story goes that they played some spaced out rhythm and blues in the basement on 19 August 1968, and decided they might be on to something.

Chinatown.

THE UNFORTUNATE
FREDERICK THE DRUNK

After dilly-dallying down Gerrard Street, we shall head one block south and turn into Lisle Street, gazing thirstily at The Falcon pub on its corner. An ancient watering hole, it served customers long before its earliest recorded licensee, John Dent, registered his business there in 1839.

Lisle Street dates from 1682, when it was carved out from the garden of Leicester House. Its first inhabitants were builders, who established a co-operative featuring masons, carpenters, surveyors and plumbers.

Lisle Street.

Leicester House was on that northern side of what is now Leicester Square. It was built by Robert Sidney, the Earl of Leicester, in the 1630s, and contained a grand thirty rooms.

The Prince of Wales, who would later become George II, lived in Leicester House after a family row with his dad saw him booted out of St James's Palace. He would later be given the news at its garden gates that his father had died and he was now the monarch. His son, Frederick, also fell out with his dad. Fred was a wild drinker, slept with as many women as he could squeeze into the hours of the day, gambled when he was eating, drinking, having sex or sleeping it all off, and had a cruel streak highlighted by his love of dog and cock fighting, bear baiting and other general animal cruelty that did not require too much physical effort on his part.

Fred never made it to the throne, and died at Leicester House in 1751. His was an unfortunate death – he got hit in the neck by a ball while playing some form of proto-cricket with friends. The wound created an abscess in his throat, which duly burst and drowned him by filling his lungs with pus.

Later the house would be home to the 8,000-strong stuffed animal collection of Sir Ashton Lever (1729–88). Perhaps related to the fact Sir Ashton had a home full of dead creatures, he is also the father of the modern sport of archery.

DE PALEOTTI'S SWORD

Fred had seen Lisle Street rise in what had been Leicester House's gardens, and it was the scene of another 'noble' man's demise. In 1718, this yet-to-be-trendy backstreet was the scene of a series of events that would end in Italian nobleman the Marquis de Paleotti being convicted of murder.

Born in Bologna, he had been a soldier but after the Peace of Utrecht, ending the decades-long squabble known as the War of the Spanish Succession, de Paleotti quit the army and came to London to visit his sister. It was in the West End where his penchant for gambling and other vices took hold.

He racked up considerable debts, which the suffering sister paid off: when she had had enough, he was thrown into a debtors' prison. Seeing his plight, the kindly sibling anonymously bought his freedom, vowing it would be the last time. However, his stint on bread and water did not mend his ways, and he continued to spend money he didn't have on the French card game Faro, a precursor to poker.

One day in the spring of 1718, the marquis, checking his empty purse, told his servant to go forth and borrow some dough. His employee, who had been turned down by lenders across the West End on previous missions, declined the task – prompting the marquis to run the unfortunate man through with his sword, killing him instantly. The marquis was tried at the Old Bailey and sentenced to death.

During his defence, he showed an unenlightened attitude – claiming it was matter of deep disgrace that English law should hang a nobleman for exercising his right to do whatever he pleased to his servants.

He also told the court he believed it ridiculous that England's churches did not offer sanctuary to murderers on the run. Facing inevitable punishment, he then demanded he should not be hanged with other criminals, and instead should be strung up alone so his body would not be defiled by coming into contact with such riff-raff. His snobbish wish was granted.

On to happier times: in the early 1800s the street became home to a group of miniaturist painters, including friend to the stars Samuel John Stump. Miniatures had become quite the thing, led originally by amateurs: the self-taught brushwork of a footman called Gervase Spencer and apothecary Samuel Cotes were in demand.

Stump, from his base in Theatreland, took it one step further. He saw a market among the vanities of the stage set and did well producing likenesses of actors in character.

One hundred years later, Lisle Street's artistic bent continued when the Royal Society of Musicians moved in. Founded in 1738, it was backed by Handel. He handed over the gate money from his first ever performance of the *Messiah*, and bequeathed £1,000 to the society in his will.

Their Lisle Street home was designed by Thomas Hopper, whose work earned him a life subscription to the society. Hopper was a key figure in the English Gothic revival, and he designed magnificent castle-like piles for posh people who wanted to play at being medieval knights.

On to No. 5, once home to a series of MPs, including the nicely named Bulstrode Peachey Knight. He sat in the Commons between 1722 and 1736 and was hardly a Stakhanovite. Hansard records him voting just once during his spell.

It would become the address of monolinguist actor and theatre impresario Anthony le Texier: he moved to London from Paris after the Revolution and hosted dramas in his Lisle Street home, with him performing each part. His dashing looks and dress sense made him a hit, and in 1802 he cemented his trendy position by being backed by Lady Albinia Buckinghamshire, who paid for Francophile parties that featured reciting the works of Molière.

He had previously executed super-quick costume changes for his Parisian audience, but his English fans felt it was too 'pantominic', as one critic suggested, so instead he chose to simply switch voices as he read from his lectern.

SMALL IN STATURE BUT ALWAYS STANDING TALL

Now, let us recall the music hall star Little Tich, whose surname – shortened from Tichfield – gave us a word to describe someone short in his socks.

Little Tich.

Little T was 4ft 6in and renowned for his prowess as a dancer – his Big Boots routine and comic turns based on observations of working men thrilled Victorian and Edwardian audiences, and it earned him a residency in Paris. But disaster would strike: in 1927, while appearing at the Alhambra Theatre, Leicester Square, he got a blow to the head during one acrobatic routine. He felt giddy, and retired to The Falcon pub for a spirit-lifting restorative libation. Sadly, here he suffered a stroke from which he never fully recovered, dying a few months later aged just 60.

The stretch would later have another French connection when it became the UK base for France's trailblazing cinema firm, Pathé. Businessman Bernard Natan headed it up during the days Pathé newsreels were shown before features, but rapid expansion of the business followed by the Great Depression saw Pathé go bankrupt in 1935.

Natan was charged with fraud, accused of buying the company on the never-never and fleecing shareholders through a series of shell companies. A disgusting taste of anti-Semitism hung over his trial – he was also accused of changing his name to hide his Eastern European Jewish roots. Sent down in 1939, French collaborators handed him over to the Gestapo in 1942 and he was murdered at Auschwitz.

The 1935 Pathé fire sale saw the building bought by St John's Hospital for Diseases of the Skin, where surgeons held evening clinics so workers could come for advice without their bosses knowing – and therefore not be sacked for scratching at blemishes that might be the harbinger of a nasty disease.

WE NEVER CLOTHED

From where we left off in Lisle Street, let us pop into neighbouring Great Windmill Street. No surprise that this stretch cutting between Brewer Street and Shaftesbury Avenue derives its name from a windmill – it is marked on a map dated 1585 and was owned by a brewer called Thomas Wilson.

From this pastoral idyll we are going to plunge headfirst into a world of classic Soho cultural entertainment that, let's face it, is really what the street evokes.

Its long relationship with letting one's hair down in one way or another started back in 1744, when a gentleman called John Cartwright built a tennis court attached to a gaming house called Piccadilly Hall. By the 1820s, Cartwright's tennis court had become the site for theatre and circus performances – and would eventually morph into what is known today as the Windmill Theatre. A contemporary handbill offers an evening hosted by Christopher Lee Sugg, ventriloquist and conjurer. It also offered horsemanship, rope dancing and billiard tables – quite the night out. By 1832 it had become the Royal Albion, and circumvented the law by offering people a membership subscription for entry. It meant no tickets were sold on the door and it could avoid the whims of the licensing authorities' censors. Owner Thomas Cooke,

Great Windmill Street.

a circus impresario, fathered forty children while in residence – giving him plenty of free labour to shift scenery about.

One hundred years later it saw a brief attempt to become London's first art house cinema, advertising in 1931 that it 'will be run on a policy of revivals of films regarded as classics and will make an appeal to a specialised public'. It was not a great success, so owner Laura Henderson and her manager Vivian van Damm hit on the wheeze for a 'non-stop' variety show, featuring end-of-the-pier Vaudeville artistes who were facing harder times as the glitz of the movie industry took hold of the popular imagination, and young women in fetching outfits.

It was something of a last resort for Laura, who wanted to put on serious drama, but it would make the old playhouse famous.

'I started with an excellent play, Inquest,' she recalled. 'At least all the critics said it was excellent, but it failed to please, and I lost more than I care to confess. I thought if I lose all this over a good play, what am I going to lose over a bad?'

When films also flopped, they decided variety was the game, although Henderson recalled that its risqué slant was not what she expected. 'I was never allowed inside a theatre at all till I was married,' she said. 'Consequently I had no idea of what it was like. My husband took me as my first effort to a Gaiety Burlesque. I, like most girls of that period, had been taught to regard legs as something you might perhaps meet in your bath, but never elsewhere, and my horror at the legs – rows and rows of them – I shall never forget. It's true they were in tights, but they were undoubtedly legs. I had the shock of a lifetime, but was just bearing up when the principal came on with an enormous diamond star just in the middle of her thigh.

'This was more than I could bear, and I implored my husband to take me out, but he, being a wise man, said, "Don't be an idiot," and we remained.'

Uniquely, the Windmill Theatre stayed open during the Blitz, hence its motto – 'We Never Closed'. However, aware of the acres of flesh on show, some wags changed it to 'We Never Clothed'.

Opposite the Windmill is the stage door to the famous Lyric Theatre. But before the Lyric was built, it was home to a different type of theatre – it was the base for pioneering Scottish surgeon William Hunter from 1767. He built a house and surgery on the site, and would hold lectures, dissections, and general medical chit chat. While there is little remaining of Hunter's house The Lyric's fabric incorporates Hunter's operating and lecture hall in part of its stage.

At No. 41 we come across the site of Club 11 – so called because it was owned by a businessman Harry Morris and then ten bebop-playing jazz musicians. A drug raid saw officers find hashish and cocaine on customers and some broadsheet hand-wringing took place over the fact those arrested were young white men – undermining the racist idea that drug use was somehow something shady foreign types got up to.

Funnily enough, it was in a pub next door to Club 11 where GH MacDermott first sang GW Hunt's 'By Jingo', popular during the Russo-Turkish War of 1877 – and which has bequeathed us the word 'jingoism' to describe a narrow, nationalistic view.

Jack Solomons.

It wasn't always a case of hooray for Blighty in Great Windmill Street – the Red Lion opposite at No. 20 was a favoured boozer for Karl Marx. He regularly played chess there while enjoying inebriated bar stool preaching.

Finally, we'll pop past the former headquarters of Israel Jacob 'Jack' Solomons, one of the greatest boxing promoters ever to have stalked the streets. He came from a family of Petticoat Lane fish merchants and got into the fight game in the 1930s. From Great Windmill Street he set up twenty-six title fights, and brought Muhammad Ali to Britain twice (in which The Greatest beat Brian London and Henry Cooper).

His first big scorecard came in 1945 when he hired White Hart Lane and drew a capacity crowd. He had to pay a 48 per cent entertainment tax, but it put him in the business.

'I can never forget I was running around, attending to last-minute details and then a gateman wouldn't let me back inside for my own show. I told him I was Jack Solomons and that I was in a hurry. He replied: "And I'm Jack Solomons' grandmother, and I ain't in a hurry. Along with ye, mate, you don't get in here."'

Later he would put a photograph of himself chomping a cigar on the front cover of fight programmes. One cannot help but wonder if this might be why.

SHAKEN, NOT STIRRED,
AT SCOTTY'S

A nd so from Great Windmill Street to Coventry Street. It's the one with a yellow cards on the Monopoly board and its location on the board screams upwardly mobile but not quite there yet.

Dating from the 1680s, it was built for commerce and entertainment, a raison d'être that has defined it in one form or another for centuries. Its early life offered workshops and warehouses alongside booze, gambling and prostitution, and by the time the street had reached its 150th birthday its entrenched impolite behaviour was enough to set hands wringing at *The Times*.

On 24 March 1841 the editor criticised its 'infamous brothels', and called for police action. The Rozzers got on it, and so many women were nicked that a Westminster magistrate got fed up, stating, 'these women must be allowed to walk somewhere'.

According to reports, the area's prostitutes celebrated by going on a spree of ringing Soho doorbells in the middle of the night and swearing at the sleepy inhabitants who answered. *The Times* got wind of this and responded the following week: 'It is the duty of the police to see that [prostitutes] walk in such a manner so as not to annoy and insult peaceable persons and modest women, and that their "walking" does not extend to the knockers and bell-handles of the householders.'

The area's grubbiness brought down a rain of fire and brimstone in 1850 – a blaze tore through the tenements, factories, workshops and warehouses. Igniting in Mr Creese the Bootmaker's, it quickly destroyed a tailors', a stationer and a hosier. Burning for thirteen hours, other buildings that were homes to three other boot makers, a gunsmith, a poulterer and a carpet maker were destroyed.

From the ashes came many of the buildings we know today – heading up to and beyond six storeys, they were faced in a white granite or Portland stone cut in classical proportions. Until the façades were altered by garish marketing – the Rialto Cinema boasted the first ever neon-lit sign in the UK – they looked rather swish.

It was on the unfortunate fire-ravaged chicken seller's plot that Charles Hirsch, a bookseller, set up shop in the 1880s. He advertised his speciality as

French literature from his 'Librarie Parisienne' – but alongside the Gallic tomes were dirty mags, including a range of gay publications. A friend to Oscar Wilde, he alleged the poet and playwright was a good customer of his.

Now for a spot of sustenance and to where the famed Scott's seafood restaurant was located up to 1967. It started as an oyster warehouse, established in 1851 by fishmonger John Scott and now, based in Mayfair, is in the top five oldest remaining London eateries.

It enjoyed a celebrated clientele throughout its long tenure. It was here that James Bond creator Ian Fleming liked a dry Martini, shaken not stirred, and decided it should be 007's bevvy of choice. It is also mentioned in the movie *The Great Escape*: PoWs chat about how that's where they are making a beeline for once they've dug the bally tunnel.

Alongside Scott's growing reputation, the music halls and theatres gave way to night clubs and cinemas. The Roaring Twenties saw it shimmer – Fred Astaire, Charlie Chaplin, Rudolph Valentino, Noel Coward and the Prince of Wales were bar proppers along the stretch. It also attracted its fair share of oddness, illustrated by the following story.

It was with a sense of some understatement that a clerk described the events that left him 'feeling a bit dizzy' as he came round in a bed in Charing Cross Hospital one morning in 1922. He told doctors he was walking to his office job at 6 a.m. on 16 April in Coventry Street when a strange and semi-invisible shadow had leapt from the cover of a dark alley, made for his neck and sucked his blood till he fainted.

Doctors examined him and discovered he had been stabbed with what they described as a 'thin tube' – and suddenly London had a vampire story to feast on. Incredibly, the same day two other victims were admitted to the hospital, having been attacked in the same spot and in the same way.

Plod were at a loss, fuelling rumours that something was abroad. It was said that detectives secretly contacted a vampire slayer, who hunted down the monster, rammed the devil with a stake through the heart, and buried the body in hallowed ground in Highgate Cemetery. Whatever the truth, no one was ever charged.

Such gossip would have been exchanged across the rumbustious dance floor of Coventry Street's famous Cafe de Paris, opened by Martin Poulsen, a Danish-born waiter who had worked along the road at the Embassy Club. A friend of the Prince of Wales – His Maj would dine three times a week – Poulsen built a secret staircase leading from a balcony into nearby Rupert Street so such valued customers could come and go as they pleased without attracting attention when they were up to no good. It was also used to eject unruly guests who were lowering the tone.

Snake Hips Johnson.

Cafe de Paris.

Music was the thing, of course, and its reputation for world-class performers was helped by the excellence of a resident player during this time, the hefty, 24-stone American xylophonist Teddy Brown.

C de P also has tragedy ingrained: on 8 March 1941, a German bomb smashed into the building and killed at least thirty-four people. Among the dead was Poulsen, the beautifully talented Trinidadian saxophonist Baba Williams and band leader Snake Hips Johnson. The youngest daughter of former Prime Minister Stanley Baldwin was among the dozens who were seriously hurt. Waiters were seen washing the injured with champagne, as there was no running water to hand.

This awful tragedy was, of course, far from being a one-off. The West End had been absolutely pasted with high explosives from the spring of 1940 onwards, and council records show the extent of the damage.

Every raid, it was estimated, brought a minimum of seventy breaks in the water mains that needed fixing. This wasn't just an issue of getting water back into homes and businesses, but also providing firefighters with the tools to save the city. The fire brigade estimated they needed around 375 million gallons each day to battle the incendiaries raining down. The answer was to create a series of huge steel water troughs – across the West End and beyond, more than 1,400 were put in place. One was so large that after the war it became the swimming pool at the Oasis Baths, along New Oxford Street. London landmarks hit included the British Museum, which saw 250,000 books destroyed in the resulting blaze, and then there was the night-time raid that sent incendiaries through the roof of the Houses of Parliament. Three bombs had set off raging fires – but when firefighters appeared to tackle them, they could not find an unlocked door to get in.

Thankfully, an MP appeared from nowhere, brandishing a ceremonial axe. He hacked away at a side door, splintering its panels enough for the fire crew to break in and put the flames out. Such awful stories were frequent during the Blitz, and the Cafe de Paris did eventually shake the plaster dust from their hairdos and reopen.

Let's now pop into another basement music joint, The Flamingo. Found in the Mapleton Hotel, it was set up by pianist Jeffrey Kruger. His MO was a jazz club that did not revel in its seediness – somewhere one could feel respectable. It meant a strict tie-wearing rule, with Kruger stating, 'It is possible and preferable, I think, to be hip and keep a high social standard'.

It is also where Dame Babs Windsor got her first break: as an 18-year-old, Kruger employed her as a cabaret singer to replace his sister, who was unwell. She stood on hallowed ground – Billie Holiday had headed straight to the Flamingo after her 1954 performance at the Royal Albert Hall. She sang for lucky punters all night.

BOY, THE DEVIL POODLE

From Coventry Street southwards, along Rupert Street. It is named after Charles I's nephew, the seventeenth-century sword-wielder, Prince Rupert of the Rhine. He has rightly had a bad press over the centuries – he was an arrogant and angry fellow. His reputation was irreversibly damaged by the portrayal of his character in the *Ladybird Book of Oliver Cromwell*, who Rupert clashed with during the English Civil War. He was a child soldier, first taking up arms aged just 14, and would grow up to be a giant of a man for the period, standing at 6ft 4in in his socks.

He loved a dust-up and was known for being reckless – his cavalry charges during the Civil War steamed forward, hoping bravery married to luck would overcome tactics and discipline. He took this approach to the high seas too – charging boats under his command to rush forward into both English and Dutch fleets that heavily outnumbered his. It is not surprising, therefore, that he won no major battles in a long military career.

However, his reputation was such that the God-fearing Puritan ranks of the New Model Army believed Rupert was in league with the Devil, who manifested itself in his pet dog, a large white poodle called Boy. Cromwell's propaganda machine played on his supposed devilry. Boy went everywhere with Rupert, and was finally killed at the Battle of Marston Moor in 1642. Parliamentary soldiers were convinced of the mutt's dark powers, claiming the creature could sniff out hidden gold, catch bullets in his mouth, was impossible to kill, and had similar soothsaying abilities as Old Mother Shipton. Rupert also possessed a pet monkey, which drew similar superstitious ire from his opponents.

After the Civil War, Rupert fled abroad for a time but would eventually return – and it was in Restoration London that he would fall for the Soho-haunting actress Peg Hughes. They didn't marry, but had a daughter, the creepily named Ruperta. Being at Rupert's side was a lucrative position, and the prince funded his lover's taste for jewels, gambling and general hedonism.

It would be terribly poor form while in the neighbourhood not to stop off at the fantastic Blue Posts pub, run by sister-and-brother team Zoe and Layo Paskin, they of The End Club fame, who after building one of London's best clubs set up two incredible restaurants – The Barbary, in Covent Garden, and

Portrait of Prince Rupert by Gerrit van Honthorst.

The Palomar, which is in Rupert Street. If you are lucky enough to visit this Israeli fusion joint, check out the chef who plays his pots and pans with a wooden spoon as he serves up tasty morsels. The siblings saw the historic Blue Posts was up for grabs, right next door to Palomar, so they bought it.

There has been a pub on site since around 1739, and as was discussed previously in this column when we visited The Crown and Two Chairmen further north in Soho, The Blue Post's name is said to be linked with the sedan chair trade. A set of blue posts signalled a sedan chair 'taxi' rank, a place you could hitch a ride home.

The distinctive building, dating from the early Georgian period, has upper floors that are built out over an entrance into Rupert Court, an alley with a chequered history. As readers will know by now, your correspondent loves to duck into an alley, so let us pause our perambulations down Rupert Street and see what this court holds.

It is here the words of the poem 'London Lickpenny', written in the 1400s, spring to mind – namely, if you've got cash, London can be very judicious, and without it, you're stuck:

To London once my steps were bent
Where truth in no wise should be faint
To Westminster-ward I forthwith went
To a man of law to make complaint
I said: 'For Mary's love, that holy saint,
Pity the poor that would proceed.'
But for lack of money I could not speed.

For it was money and the law that kept a certain trade running in Rupert Court for many a year. While today thoroughly respectable, it was once known for its brothels and 'exotic' clubs – and many were said to have been run by the famous Messina brothers, the Maltese gang made up of five siblings who created a chain of brothels in London in the 1930s. They had been expelled from Egypt for running a similar racket in Alexandria, and set about making the Soho game their own.

When they arrived in England in the 1930s, they decided they needed to ditch their Maltese monikers and chose titles that today feel like the characters from an early edition of *Minder*. Brother Carmelo took on Charles Maitland, Eugenio became Edward Marshal, Alfredo lost the 'o' to be Alfred Martin, Salvatore swapped his charming Mediterranean tag for the more staid Arthur Evans, while Atillio did the same, christening himself Raymond Maynard. They bought property across the West End, including in Rupert Court, and after the war began trafficking women from Europe to work for them.

The police were at best not interested, and at worst complicit: they seem to have been persuaded to always be looking in the other direction as brown envelopes and services were offered. Things eventually got too hot for the boys in the 1950s, after a series of exposés by *The People* newspaper's crime reporter Duncan Webb, and they left the country before collars could be felt.

There were plenty of others waiting to step in – which leads us on to Bernie Silver. For a good twenty years, he was lead man in The Syndicate, a racket that ran Soho's strip clubs from the Messina days through to the 1970s. His stock included sleazy stage shows in Rupert Court, and he was to get a six-year stretch after it was found he rented out rooms above his clubs to women for immoral purposes, sent down for the crime of living off their earnings.

Briefly, let us stop on the corner of Rupert Court, where the steak house Garners once sat: a favourite diner of the Beatles, there is a famous pic taken on the Fab Four walking down the alley, about to tuck into. And Rupert Street was well documented in stills: these days were captured in a set of photographs by Wolfgang Suschitzky, best known as the director of photography on films such as *Get Carter, Entertaining Mr Sloane* and the Oscar-bagging *The Bespoke Overcoat*.

A photojournalist before he was a film man, he shot images across the West End, including Rupert Street in the 1970s and '80s. One such photo shows a bustling street market – and in the background, captured for posterity, is a shady-looking gent about to enter the Porno Cine Club.

Wolfgang Suschitzky.

THE WIDOW GOOLIGHTLEY, TURTLE SOUP AND SHERRY

Having meandered southwards, and out of Soho, we'll just follow our noses and have a wander about a set of backstreets between the Haymarket and Trafalgar Square – a stone's throw from the Soho beat, but a world away in look and feel.

Let's start in Oxendon Street. It appears on a map in 1585 as a patch called Scavengers Close. Already the streets and fields around had been bagsied by the great and good. This name suggests a scrap of a field with access for the lower classes to collect firewood and exercise livestock.

Henry VIII wanted it, and the Mercers Company laid legal claim to it, so he paid them off. At some point following, the delightfully named 'Widowe Goolightley' owned some kind of shack in one corner. By 1637, Mary Baker and her husband Henry Oxenden had a thirty-two-year lease and had a 'messuage [which was a dwelling house], cookhouse, tennis court and four acres'.

It became a bit of an attraction – a man called Simon Osbaldeston had been given a franchise to run a bowling green nearby. But after bringing in large crowds, his licence was changed to limit numbers. Instead, he opened another bowling green 'made to entertain gamesters and bowlers at an excessive rate'.

We have touched on this building in previous walks, referring to it as Piccadilly House. However, that is a moniker for map makers – if you were knocking about Oxendon Street in the 1600s, you'd have called it Shaver's Hall – because Osbaldeston was a gentleman barber to the Lord Chamberlain and would trim his beard regularly. Handy, as the Lord Chamberlain happened to be the person who granted licences for such places of jollity.

It also attracted crime: a Richard Woodgate was caught in 1780 with counterfeit coins after he enticed a woman called Mary Ann Smith to 'go with him' – and then ungentlemanly palmed her off with soft shillings. She didn't take kindly to it and, as his Old Bailey trial heard, she enlisted the help of a Bobby to tackle him.

Woodgate got eighteen months, which was an easier stretch than Mark Wood received for breaking into Captain William Hazard's home in 1783. He

Stone's Chop House, from *The History of Stones Chop House*, by Virginia Curle and William Feilding, 1985.

worked there as a servant, and one night decided to steal 39s worth of cloth. He was transported to Australia for seven years.

Shaver's Hall changed hands a couple of times and its bowling greens were eventually eyed up by town planners: Sir Christopher Wren recommended the area be developed, saying, 'by opening a new street from the Hay-markett into Leicester-fields' it would 'ease in some measure the great passage of The Strand, and will cure the noysomness'.

Sturdy houses and places to go – these streets saw action.

Thomas Hickford ran Hickford's Great Room between 1696 to 1730, which held boisterous auctions of all manner of house clearances, shipwrecks, bonds, animals, debts, and then in the evening became a dance-and-beer hall. Across the way was Stone's Chop House, a restaurant that opened in 1770 to serve meat to hungry upper-class types. They don't appear on rate books until 1778, suggesting, perhaps, they ran a cash-in-hand cafe, or Mr Stone took it over from someone else! No matter, it rapidly became an institution and remained so until it closed its doors in 1981.

Oh, the joys of the internet and a good key word to search! It appears that while Stone's is no longer slicing up slabs for hungry customers, there is a lively trade of items connected to it, including menus galore.

In 1972 you could get a fillet of smoked eel for 55p, stewed tripe and onions would set you back 80p, and if you had room, 35p buys you real turtle soup and sherry. They were famous for their pancakes, which had been served continuously since they opened. Here is the recipe, for four: 6 eggs, 6oz caster sugar, 2 tablespoons of double cream, 2 sliced cooking apples, 2oz raisins, 2oz of butter, half a teaspoon of cinnamon and a dash of rum. Yum.

Stone's was never known for being progressive, either in what it served – it was all solid traditional English fare that ignored whims from the Continent – nor with their attitude towards women. Females were only admitted in 1921, and even then were not allowed into a back dining room.

In the 1700s, when the chop houses were springing up across the capital, meat was the thing. Eating out was popular for both the cheap prices but also because with so many people living in lodging houses, there was a general lack of cooking facilities for the lower classes.

This was a domestic fact that lasted well in to the twentieth century. The writer CLR James, who moved to London from Trinidad in 1932 and settled in the West End while studying at the University of London, wrote columns he sent home to the *Port of Spain Gazette*, describing the émigré's life.

'The room itself is not so bad,' he wrote of his bedsit in a shared lodging. 'But whatever you do the loneliness of the room is dreadful. When you lock the door you are in a world of your own. You come in, you pass along the passage, you go up the staircase, you go into your room and there is an end of you. You see no one, you hear no one. You see nothing, all you hear is the cry of newsboys, or vehicles passing in the street. Who are living in the same house as you, you do not know. Your landlady brings your meals or sends them by maid into your room … it is when you appreciate what this means that you see why there is a cinema or theatre or a show of some kind every 50 yards in a London street. The million or two who have no homes in the strictest sense of the term want to get

CLR James.

out. They do not want to stay in those rooms, under any circumstances. To work all day and then come home to that would kill a normal person in five years. So he or she comes in and then, unless there is work to be done, goes off somewhere else, anywhere, out of the room …'

If the grubby student bedsits of the mid-twentieth century were bad, imagine what such dwellings for the working person were like decades before. No wonder Londoners lived their lives in public.

Taverns also served substantial meals alongside the chop houses. Slowly turning spits over open fires had large cuts hanging one above another – you can imagine the fats dripping from one slow-roasted carcass on to the next beneath. It would include the usual beef, mutton, veal, pork and lamb. The customer would take their knife and cut off what they wanted for their plate. The Chop House would supply accompaniments of salt, mustard, a bread roll and a jug of beer for the hungry Londoner to settle down and chew over.

For those who did have a working kitchen, such a meaty diet meant daily shopping trips to stock the kitchen. Hand bells would ring at dawn from the markets in the West End, to let the housewife – for it was the housewife, or servant in charge of a daily shop – that trading was ready to begin. Without any refrigeration, this daily trudge to the market was vital. There were no fixed prices and each person had to haggle with the trader.

Londoners' tables benefitted from the city's role as an international port and food from exotic parts was common. Beef was ever popular, but the average Londoner's table groaned under the weight of other meats, too: one such meal consisted of 'a leg of roast or boil'd mutton, dish'd up with same dainties, fowls, pigs, ox-tripes, and tongues, rabbits, pidgeons, all well moisten'd up with butter, without larding'. Another describes a first course consisting of 'a cows tongue, leg of mutton and colliflowers … a steak pye, a shoulder of mutton, a fire quarter of lamb and a dish of pease'.

Portrait of John Varley by John Linnell.

Now into Whitcomb Street. It is here that the Royal Watercolour Society is based. Its beginnings were somewhat turbulent for such a relaxing pastime. The Royal Academy was said to look down on watercolourists, so they split off in 1804. Two of the founding members were the Hackney-born brothers John and Cornelius Varley.

John, a painter and astrologer, was a friend of William Blake's. Cornelius was an inventor, which contributed to his style of painting. He was fascinated by optics and took the world's first telephoto image. He improved camera obscuras, worked on microscopes and manufactured his inventions to great acclaim.

Let's also mention his neighbour, Sir Henry Irving, who lived here between the 1860s and 1905. He was an actor and theatre manager, directing, building sets, casting and everything in between. He has become known for his classical Victorian style, and his memory is still connected to a certain manner of theatrecraft. His assent into the upper echelons of society was confirmed when Queen Victoria gave him a knighthood in 1895. Two years later, his great friend Bram Stoker wrote *Dracula* – and cited Sir Henry as the inspiration for the count.

Sir Henry Irving as Hamlet, from *The Idler* magazine, 1893.

Off we go again! Having traversed Whitcomb Street and its surrounding cut throughs around the back of Trafalgar Square, let us resume our constitutional in Orange Street.

An aside: when the name Orange Street comes up, your correspondent does not think of religious intrigue in the late 1600s, Protestant fears of a Catholic monarchy, nor sectarianism and pipe bands. No, instead, it conjures up imagery of red, green and gold record sleeves. Orange Street in Kingston, Jamaica, which takes its name from its London cousin, is the site of many a record shop and reggae studio. It became legendary in the development of the genre, with producers such as Prince Buster, Bunny Lee and Sir Coxsone Dodd based there.

But let our minds not wander. The West Central version is named after William of Orange, the Zeeland *Stadtholder* who became the king of these shores between 1689 and 1702. Let's also remember his wife, Mary, who was also his cousin. She died tragically early, aged just 32. Mary had proved to be a keen and effective ruler while King William was off fighting wars against his sworn enemy, Louis XIV of France.

We now walk past the Orange Street Congregational Church. It has a long history as a place of worship, and was the scene for the debut of a much-loved hymn, 'Rock of Ages'.

The story goes like this. The church had originally been built for Huguenot refugees in 1693. One minister, Jean Pierre Stehelin, could speak many languages – Hebrew, Greek, Latin, English, French, German, Italian, Danish, Dutch, Coptic, Armenian, Syriac, Arabic, Chaldean Gothic, Old Tudesco or Druid, Anglo-Saxon, Spanish, Portuguese and Welsh. Its learned reputation was underlined by the fact Sir Isaac Newton lived next door, and popped in to services.

The Wesleyan revival of the 1700s saw the Rev. Augustus Toplady take over. One day, while on a hike in the Mendips, Toplady was caught in a fierce storm at a place called Barrington Combe. It's a walk that leads you to the area's highest point, and is up the road from Cheddar Gorge. Its limestone geology is such that caves, clefts and hollows are common. Toplady sheltered, and as he crouched down, penned 'Rock of Ages'.

Now take a deep breath, because we're going up Charing Cross Road (CCR), a place so steeped in tales as to be worthy of a good deal of our attention. It's not that old – CCR is a Victorian invention to alleviate traffic issues caused by two narrow streets, with the boom of Charing Cross Station to the south making a fresh layout imperative.

But to carve this new highway would mean displacing 5,497 people living in slums – and all of them would have to be rehoused. Land on Newport Market was earmarked, described in 1880 by the *Evening Standard* in unglamorous terms: 'Gone are the glories of Newport Market; gone the glory of its Butchers-row. Fashion has this many a year forsaken its uninviting neighbourhood. Beau and buck know no more of its unsavoury haunts. Filth and squalor reign supreme in its courts and passages. Poverty and vice find within its dingy precincts congenial shelter. The old Market, indeed, exists; its walls are still standing. But how changed, how utterly changed, out of all form and semblance. Its shops and sheds are stables and slaughter-houses, its stalls and stands bricked over and built upon. Its very identity is lost; merged, so to speak, in that of Prince's Row, the narrow lane – foul among the foul – that surrounds and gives access to it.'

An argument kicked off when it became clear that Newport Market could only hold a fraction of the homes needed. The new road also swept away a huddle of ancient streets, as the *Illustrated London News* described: 'Steps have at length been taken for making a beginning of a long-needed public improvement, a new thoroughfare between Charing-cross and Oxford-street … In the course of another month a large portion of the following will have disappeared: Newport-court, Little Newport-street, Market-row, Market-street, Prince's-row, Lichfield-street, Hayes-court, and Grafton-street.'

The majority of the displaced families did not return, although some were housed in the newly built Sandringham Buildings by the Improved Industrial Dwellings Company. It was argued that creating more tenements would bring down the tone of the new thoroughfare, and the developers generally got their way. *Plus ça change.*

It was around these industrial buildings that a criminal fraternity evolved during the 1920s and they were well established and perfectly placed to exploit the opportunities arising from the outbreak of the Second World War. Some West End characters made fortunes out of rationing, and there were said to be various scams operated from back stairs offices and shop store rooms in Shaftesbury Avenue, West Street and Stacey Street, among others.

This included the sale of big bundles of coupons to small-scale crooks, who in turn might find themselves on the end of a swizz. It was not unknown for the bigger fish to sell the smaller fry envelopes supposedly packed with the sought-after coupons – only for the said small-timer to get to his hideout, open the envelop greedily and discover most of the so-called coupons were actually ripped up pages of *London Illustrated News* or the *Evening Chronicle*. Aware of their place in the criminal food chain, they would not return to complain, and instead passed the loss on downwards to anyone they deemed incapable of providing any form of comeback.

West End-based burglars made a packet from finding out where in the borough town halls the coupons were stored – and would brazenly take the whole lot to sell off for 6*d* a pop.

Opposite the old Newport Market you would find Hog Lane, offering an obvious link as to what trade went on there. It became an unlikely gathering point in the 1670s for a Greek community to form.

A resurgence of the Ottoman Empire in the 1607s saw Greek sailors in the London docks not keen to return to the Aegean, while other refugees from the Greek islands managed to find passage to London. In 1677, work began to build a Byzantine church for these new Orthodox Christians to use. Funds were short and the location was not near where the main body of Greek immigrants lived. It was eventually sold on: Huguenots moved in, it enjoyed a brief burst of Calvinism, and then the Church of England got the keys, before it was demolished in the early 1930s. Its hallowed land gave birth soon after to the St Martin's School of Art.

As Charing Cross Road bedded in, plans were laid to build the Royal English Opera House, now the Palace Theatre, in Cambridge Circus. It was the brainchild

Palace Theatre, Cambridge Circus.

of Richard D'Oyly Carte, the man who gave us Gilbert and Sullivan. Some thirteen years previously he commissioned the pair to write him a short comic opera. They proved their wordsmithery and musical know-how, and D'Oyly Carte was similarly adept at production, direction and theatre management.

They made their fortunes, and D'Oyly Carte bought the freehold of the land from London County Council for £32,000. His wife Helen laid the foundation stone in December 1888. He didn't muck about – his vision gave Londoners a 1,976-seat capacity venue with an orchestra pit for sixty-three musicians, although it was set at a wonky angle because the land was hemmed in by streets on either side.

It was forty-eight years later, and just across the way, that another impresario who was to bring much joy to London's theatregoers arrived in Shaftesbury. Hugh 'Binkie' Beaumont, born in Cardiff in 1908, became a colossus of Theatreland. He collaborated with Terence Rattigan, and worked with Cecil Beaton on set design. Beaton, the photographer, known today for his royal portraits, was a dab hand at creating make-believe backdrops. He won two Oscars for his set designs.

Binkie liked a musical. He brought Londoners lavish productions of *West Side Story*, *My Fair Lady* and *Oklahoma!* in the immediate post-war period, sharing theatrical sparkle with enthusiastic full houses. As well as such feel-good song and dance smilers, he brought *A Street Car Named Desire* by Tennessee Williams to the London stage in 1949, casting Vivien Leigh in the lead. He was criticised at the time by the Public Morality Council, who said it was shameful that 'servants and children are allowed to see it'. He could do serious, too, working with John Gielgud producing Shakespeare. Binkie strode through satisfied crowds leaving his theatre each night, a self-made bringer of joy to the many.

It later emerged that Binkie Beaumont was born Hughes Griffiths Morgan. He was the son of a Hampstead barrister, who went under the terrific title of

Morgan Morgan. When his parents divorced – he was but 2 years old – his mother married a Cardiff timber merchant. Binkie is said to have received his nickname as a child, which was South Wales slang that meant 'raggamuffin'. Poor Mrs Beaumont didn't seem to have much luck with the husbands, and Binkie's new stepdad passed away when he was still in short trousers.

But this cruel turn of fate was the start of a happier path.His mum took in a lodger, Major Harry Woodcock, who had been in the army's Entertainments Corps. He had become the general manager at the Cardiff playhouse – and it was through him that Binkie got his first job, aged 15, working in the box office.

Draw a line from Binkie's to D'Oly Cartes' and then northwards a couple of hundred yards and you have a random triangle within which has thrived decades of creativity. We shall explore St Martin's School of Art and the Astoria, and delve into what Charing Cross Road is famously associated with – the London book trade.

But before all that, here we are at No. 111, which was home in the mid-1500s to a popular wayfarers' hostelry called The Plough Inn. By the 1870s the pub had long gone, with just its derelict stableyard remaining. Champion pickle makers Crosse & Blackwell bought the site and used it for their expanding central London condiment empire.

C&B were a wildly successful catering story in the Victorian years and became synonymous with this patch. Edmund C and Thomas B had been apprentices at salted fish makers West & Wyatt, and bought the firm in 1830. By 1857, they were flogging 17,000 gallons of mushroom ketchup and shifting 120,000 tins of sardines annually from their West End base. By the time they took on No. 111, they had sauce mixologists beavering away in Soho Square, Sutton Place, George Yard, Denmark Street, Dean Street and Earl Street.

The firm, London's largest single employer in the 1850s, needed stabling for their horses, so at No. 111 they built a Romanesque multi-storey 'horse park'. The ground floor had space for eighteen vans and four nags, while ramps up to other floors provided more stables. Sadly, by the 1920s, the creators of many a vinegar-based meal-livener had sold up and the intriguing building was pulled down.

Along the road, the Astoria utilised the shell of a C&B jam jar warehouse for a cinema and dance hall. Now lost due to Crossrail work, let us remember the good times. It opened as a picture house in 1927 and was converted into a theatre by the 1970s. The 1980s saw it reborn as a gig venue that hosted all the names.

The Astoria played a key moment in London's acid house scene, too. In 1988 DJ Nicky Holloway put on a night called The Trip, and musicologists refer to it in hushed tones as a seminal happening in UK dance music history. The night would end with ravers piling out into the dawn to carry on dancing in the modernist fountains at the foot of Centrepoint, to the amusement of the Fuzz.

Now, on to books. The street has so many outlets worthy of mention, but let us not forget those now lost: Murder One, which specialised in crime and romance; the fabulously eclectic Quinto Books; art purveyor Zwemmer, and of course the famous 84 Charing Cross Road outlet Marks & Co., immortalised in the book based on the letters between Helene Hanff and Frank Doel. Where its bookshelves once stood is now a chain pub.

Still thriving is the biggie – Foyles, set up in 1903 by William F to sell surplus textbooks from a college course he had failed to complete. His daughter, Christina, inherited the firm and developed a reputation: an obituary called her rule 'paternalistic and autocratic', paying low wages while buttering up bright young employees by inviting them to happenings at the country abbey she called home.

Christina was behind the famous Foyles Literary Lunches. Hosted at the Dorchester, they were silver service stuff with amiable chat by a notable.

Christina hoped George Bernard Shaw would be her first guest but he turned her down, replying it was 'currently pointless to start anything new in England'. She would not be shaken off, and as the lunches picked up, she tried to entice him to chair an event in honour of HG Wells, who had also previously declined an invitation, stating: 'The letters I receive from my readers leave me no desire to meet them in the flesh.'

Shaw was equally caustic, he told Christina never to book two celebrities for one event. 'If you can get Shaw and Wells, get a lecture apiece out of them with a couple of tongue-tied nobodies thrown in as chairmen,' he said. 'What you propose is criminal extravagance to which I will not be a party.' He later wriggled out of another invitation after being sent a menu that was vegetarian, saying he couldn't bear the idea of hearing a room full of people eating celery.

From Foyles, we walk past the old St Martin's School of Art. How many tales of British popular imagination start with someone finding their voice here? We could revel in name dropping, from hosting the Sex Pistols' first gig to post-war lectures by tutors Eduardo Paolozzi of Tottenham Court Road mosaic fame and Anthony Caro. The likes of Katharine Hamnett, Frank Auerbach, Jeff Banks, Billy Childish, Antony Gormley, John Hurt and Carole Steyn all graduated from the CCR base, while Jarvis Cocker wrote the song 'Common People' after meeting a St Martin's student in its foyer ... But our interest is piqued by the following story.

Designer Gareth Pugh, who has dressed the likes of Lady Gaga, hosted a student fashion show at a strip club in Greek Street called Moonlighting.

A mosaic by Eduardo Paolozzi.

He was surprised to find a corridor backstage that led directly into the college's library. One hopes this is true.

Now we peer down the marvellous Cecil Court, a shaded cut-through off CCR that looks like a cliché of Old London and boasts a deep history. We could pause outside the tailor that supplied army uniforms to the poet Rupert Brooke, window shop at the smattering of antiquarian book and curio sellers, or dive into a bar frequented by Dylan Thomas (no surprise there) and Auberon Waugh ... But instead, let us go back to 1735, when Elizabeth Calloway ran a brandy shop here. She attracted rough custom and was not shy of a bit of criminality herself.

One fateful night she decided to over-insure her premises and burn the place down. Old Bailey transcripts reveal witnesses dived in to rescue barrels of brandy – all of which they found were empty – and noted the huge stash of kindling she had bought two weeks previously. Despite the evidence, she was found not guilty.

The Daily Journal reported that it took two hours for water to be sourced to douse the fire, which was long enough for the Prince of Wales to appear to see the incident. Tragically, the sole victim from this insurance job was the mother of William Hogarth, whose biographer Ronald Paulson described her death in the following way, 'she passed, of a Fright, occasion'd by the Fire. She was in perfect Health when the unhappy Accident broke out, and died before it was Extinguish'd.'

It was in these backstreets that our friendly Soho author Colin Wilson lingered while lacking a roof over his head. Here he went in search of the heavy-duty packaging that wrapped up the reams of high-quality tweed, twill, cotton and silk that the streets tailors used to make uniforms for the likes of Brooke. He recalled how with his friend, James, they would indulge in some dustbin raiding as the shops closed and the street lamps came on.

'We wandered up St Martins Lane and across Shaftesbury Avenue, into some narrow alley ways,' he would write. 'James led me into a dark cul-de-sac and struck a match. I was able to see several dustbins and heaps of brown paper.

'"Grab a few armfuls of brown paper. It's to make a pillow."'

'I did as I was told and we made our way back into the lamp light. Here James dumped his paper under a lamp, and folded it neatly into a small and compact bundle. I did the same. The paper had been loosely and carelessly folded; it was obviously used wrapping paper. James found two lengths of string and we bound our parcels tightly.

'"Now," James said, "to Waterloo."'

Brooke may have not liked being in uniform much after witnessing the slaughter of his generation in the trenches, and he equated the British love of dressing up with something rather rigid in his fellow countrymen's character.

Philosopher and historian RG Collingwood, whose work inspired many deep and wide-ranging thoughts among his readership in the interwar period, said dress was a form of language – and Brooke recognised that the tailor of Cecil Court spoke a fine form of the Shakespearean English in terms of clothing. 'When [dress] is rigidly uniform, the only emotions which it can express are emotions common to those who wear it,' he wrote. 'The habit of wearing it focuses the attention of the wearer on emotions of the kind, and at once generates and expresses a permanent "set" or habit of consciously feeling in the corresponding way.'

Brooke noticed that Americans 'walk better than we; more freely with a taking swing and almost with grace. How much of this is due to living in a democracy, and how much to wearing no braces, it is difficult to determine.'

Collingwood added that by wearing a uniform, you felt a sense of camaraderie with others donning the same togs as you – be it in the armed forces, at a black tie event, or the multiple street fashion cliques that drive the rag trade today. 'Dropping a uniform carries with it a curious breach in the emotional habit,' he observed. 'The consciousness of sharing uniform dress with a circle of others is thus a consciousness of emotional solidarity with them; and this, on its negative side, takes a form of emotional hostility towards persons outside the circle. To illustrate this from the history of parties and classes is superfluous.'

From admiring the decorum of Cecil Court, and its atmosphere of magnetic curiosity for the wanderer, we shall continue our story by heading a little southeast down Charing Cross Road, and past the Garrick Theatre.

We have discussed the building of the Royal English Opera House by Gilbert and Sullivan promoter Richard D'Oyly Carte, and the world of Binkie Beaumont. Now for the Garrick, which was another that owed its construction to the craze for these English librettos. This one was paid for by Gilbert, but the construction did not go smoothly.

Binkie Beaumont.

Rutland Barrington.

When builders dug down to lay the floor of the stalls, they discovered an underground river gushing beneath their feet.

One regular performer at the Garrick in its early days was Rutland Barrington, a baritone in G&S shows who played leading roles in *HMS Pinafore*, *The Pirates of Penzance* and *The Mikado*.

Barrington was a popular music hall comedian. He had the knack of twisting lyrics to reference something happening that day to the audience's amusement – and once recalled how, in 1908, he was due to do a gig during the FA Cup final.

'I determined to sing a verse giving the score at half-time,' he recalled. 'I had written an alternative two lines to suit whichever team had scored, but when the curtain rose for my turn, the news had not come. While I was singing the song I saw the stage manager in the wings waving a telegram. I got the envelope, opened it before the audience, and sang them the information that Aston Villa were a goal ahead. I do not think I have ever had a greater success with a verse.'

Now we leave Barrington's echoing voice in Charing Cross Road and scoot down William IV Street and to the junction of Agar Street.

Here we pause to gaze at Charing Cross Police Station, a cream, stuccoed piece of London classicism. Originally built as Charing Cross Hospital in 1831, its founding was the result of the good deeds of Dr Ben Golding. He had fifteen years earlier opened the doors to his home to treat the poor – and so great the need, work began on a purpose-built hospital. Designed by the revivalist Decimus Burton, it has a Grecian flavour with Corinthian pilasters and a portico at its entrance.

Burton's work was hit by an incendiary bomb during the Blitz, and the damage was captured by the artist RG Mathews. Mathews had been known for his celebrity portraits in the 1920s, painting Arnold Bennett and Joseph Conrad. When war broke out in 1939, he was commissioned by the War Artist's Advisory Committee to head into central London from his Hampstead home to survey and depict the scene. His work shows a huge crater that the hospital looks perilously close to toppling into.

The hospital closed for good in 1973 and in the 1990s, after a careful restoration project, the Old Bill took it on.

While we consider Charing Cross and artists, let's peer beneath our feet and mooch along the platforms of Charing Cross Underground. It is here you will find the woodcut prints by that very fine London artist and visual chronicler, David Gentleman.

Gentleman's illustrations have become synonymous with a visual style that captures the city. Known for his city-and-land-scapes, his designs for postage stamps, and much more besides, London Underground made the clever and far-sighted decision to ask him to help out at Charing Cross. The Underground bosses wanted to tidy things up with stations called

David Gentleman.

The Strand, Charing Cross, The Embankment and Trafalgar Square, and with a newly extended Jubilee line coming into the station, now was the chance.

Gentleman was commissioned to spruce up the Northern line platforms and hit on a wheeze to depict Londoners of 800 years ago as they made the Eleanor Cross, which gives the area its name. He began by carving out the images on wooden blocks in his Camden Town work room, and if you have the time to inspect the finished product closely, it's full of surprises. As well as peasants toiling away, Gentleman included our forefathers laughing, arguing, jostling, gossiping, alone, together, and everything else besides. The work still fascinates forty years later, while the original, ink-stained wooden carvings are stored on shelves on the stairs of Gentleman's Camden Town home.

Now we cross The Strand – don't get distracted – and explore Villiers Street, which takes us down towards the Thames. It is on this street that Benjamin Franklin lived during a sixteen-year spell in Blighty. Franklin, the Enlightenment politician and key mover in the American Revolution, was also known for inventing the lightning rod, designing spectacles and creating the fuel-efficient stove that took his name. He stayed at No. 36 and it was while at this address, in 1761, that Benji F created a 'glass armonica', an instrument inspired by watching musician Edmund Delaval play water-filled wine glasses. In later years he invented a stick with a grip on one end. Known as the Long Arm, he used it to hoik books down from high library shelves.

The Charing Cross printing blocks by David Gentleman.

Down the slope from Benjamin's old abode we find the site of a house belonging to Samuel Pepys. Handily close to the Thames and Whitehall for his naval work, it was later demolished to be replaced by the Salt Office, the government body charged with collecting tax on the seasoning. Its proximity to the river also meant Villiers Street boasted warehouses, although when the Embankment was built, it found itself too far from the quay.

Instead, the old Salt Tax HQ became a boarding house and its reputation sank. In 1923, landlord Alfred Frederick 'Fred-Fred' Joyce was found guilty of using it as a brothel.

Deep below this building you may hear the gentle pop of a cork being pulled from a bottle. It's home to the famous Gordon's Wine Bar, that den of good grape, tucked into the cellars of buildings that once stood above. Established by Angus Gordon, the bar dates from 1890 and has been allowed to mellow like a fine vintage.

In 1972 wine buff Luis Gordon bought the business from the Gordon family – they were unrelated, but in a nice dash of fortune shared the same surname – and the place continued much as before. It is said that after closing for six months for what regulars were told would be a revamp, the decades' old cobwebs that haunted every nook were left in situ.

Gordon's Wine Bar

From Gordon's, we just have time to stick our heads down the tunnels underneath Charing Cross Station, and pause outside Heaven nightclub. It earnt a brilliant reputation for its gay nights, but also acid house raves, Land of Oz and Rage, which have gone down in the sub-culture's folklore.

And it was also here that New Age hippie met acid house in the early 1990s, with the result being an event called Megatripolis. Its organisers sought to create a rebellious, left-field festival vibe in a West End club, and there was a fair dollop of rather silly, spaced-out philosophy shared across the dance floor. The Megatripolis team invited speakers such as the LSD-infused beat poet Allen Ginsberg, professional dope smoker Howard Marks and American spiritual guru Baba Ram Dass to spout stuff at pie-eyed trance heads.

And on that hedonistic and slightly confused note, we shall briefly linger here a while longer to talk ice cream. The London–Italian food link goes back centuries – for example, the famous White's Club, established in 1693, was a chocolate-eating venue by Francesco Bianco, who changed his name to Francis White. In 1757, Dominico Negri had set up Gunters, an ice cream and sorbet outlet, in Berkeley Square where waiters would bring sweet, cold refreshments out to your carriage.

Almost a century later, Carlo Gatti arrived from northern Italy and began plying his trade on West End streets, wheeling a barrow selling coffee and waffles. He recruited others from the Alpine province he came from and created a string of stalls and cafes.

His business took off – he soon had 1,000 operators – and in the 1850s got into importing ice cream. He sold it from Gatti's Under the Arches, and was so successful that when he died in 1878 he was a millionaire.

His work paved the way for other Italian ice cream sellers to make their mark: a once-common sight on our streets, the song 'The Hokey Cokey' comes from their cry '*ecco un poco*', meaning 'here is a little bit' – which they would say as they gave dabs of their wares to children to tempt them to buy a portion.

Now to Northumberland Avenue, found on land once owned by Thomas Walker, a grocer who ran an inn called The Christopher around the 1500s. The 10th Earl of Northumberland, Algernon Percy, gives the street his name: he married its owner, Lady Elizabeth, in the mid-1600s.

Percy was the offspring of the Earl of Northumberland who was implicated in the Gunpowder Plot against James I – his dad had been caught up on the fringes of the planned terror attack. He was fined £30,000 and held in prison at His Majesty's Pleasure. While not directly involved, he was considered a courtly representative of English Catholicism, and had met James before he moved from

Scotland to London to sound out if there was much chance of a more tolerant society. Despite James's apparent openness to the idea, he soon backtracked once he'd got the crown on his head – and Northumberland, as a well-known Catholic, copped it when the plot was uncovered. However, while the key surviving conspirators suffered such deprivations as having 'their privys cut off and burnt in front of them, to illustrate how they would never beget heirs', before being hanged, drawn and quartered, Northumberland was treated lightly. Banged up in lavish surroundings until 1621 – his prison quarters included a private cook, study, library, great chamber, two dining rooms and a 'withdrawing' room – he was finally released from his gilded cage to retire to his magnificent home at Petworth, West Sussex.

Later, violent politics would again come to the street his son built: the Wilkes Riots of 1768, caused by popular radical journalist and politician John Wilkes's expulsion from his Commons seat, saw a mob try to burn down the earl's home. The quick-thinking of Hugh Percy, the then 1st Duke of Northumberland, saved the building. He opened up the nearby Ship ale house and proclaimed a free bar, softening the rioters' fury.

The Avenue has historically been linked to hotels, although more recently government buildings. We'll stop by what was the Hotel Metropole, dating from 1885. Edward VII was a regular and it enjoyed a well-heeled clientele. It hosted lavish dinners for both the Aero Club and the Alpine Club – two societies whose members were au fait with derring-do.

The Aero Club was established in 1901, indirectly due to a mechanical fault in a Renault 4.5 car. Vera Hedges Butler had promised her dad, Frank, a spin with their friend Charles Rolls, of Rolls-Royce fame, in her vehicle. But the engine blew up before they got started.

Her dad, one of the first car owners in the UK after importing a Benz in 1897, was disgruntled – but Vera saved the day. She proposed, instead, they go on a balloon trip, and such was their delight, while in the air, they proposed over a glass of champagne to establish the Aero Club, similar to the Automobile Club they had already set up.

The Alpine Club had similar tastes for adventure. Founded in 1857, it made its base at the Met. Irish naturalist and politician John Ball was its first president. He made detailed guides to Alpine climbs and was known for his enjoyable writing style.

A Cambridge graduate who was denied a degree because he was a Catholic, Ball travelled the world to study natural history and botany. The Alpine Club did not just hold jolly, port-fuelled sessions at the Met to discuss climbs they'd done and planned to do. The members put their minds to creating a new, ultralight rope. The result was a creation made of Manila hemp, treated so it would not rot, with a red thread of yarn running through it. To join, you had to be proposed and seconded, and fulfil the vague rule that you had completed 'a reasonable number of respectable peaks'.

And the hotel's links to dangerous pursuits continued in the Second World War: Room 424 was made the headquarters of MI9 – the military intelligence unit set up to help Allied PoWs. It was here that Lieutenant Airey Neave appeared for work not long after escaping from the dreaded Castle Colditz in 1941.

He had crept out of a hole made under a stage in the camp's theatre, which led into a German guard room. Here, he donned a uniform and boldly marched out the front gate. He got to Switzerland four days later, and then worked for MI9, dedicating his time to helping other PoWs escape.

From the corner of Northumberland Avenue, we cast our gaze at a modernish building overlooking Trafalgar Square. Called the Grand Buildings, it is on the site of what was the Grand Hotel, which met a dusty fate with a wrecking ball in the late 1980s. The owners of the site, Land Securities, then began a huge rebuild (it was their scaffolding and building materials that were used as weapons during the poll tax riots of 1990).

But from such inauspicious beginnings came something of great beauty – an intricately carved doorway by the renowned sculptor Barry Baldwin. Grand Buildings features twenty-seven images: called The Endangered Species, the 20ft-high piece has a host of animals gazing out towards Trafalgar Square – and among them are a gaggle of Homo sapiens.

Barry Baldwin's gargoyles.

Barry, who is not only a master craftsman and a stunning artist, has a wicked sense of humour, too – he has included other visages, and they are based on the architects and builders who worked on the project, as well as an ex-girlfriend of his. His humour is such that many are pulling expressions that could be described as Goon-like, which leads us nicely to the other end of Northumberland Avenue and the famous Playhouse Theatre.

Built by impresario, actor and theatre manager Sefton Parry in 1882, part of the playhouse was squashed beneath Charing Cross Station when it collapsed in 1902. Parry was a globetrotter – in his early years he had enjoyed a stint in New York, working at the famous Barnum's Museum, a mixture of a circus and zoo. He is said to have witnessed the famous fire that burnt Barnum's to the ground in 1865 – a blaze called the most devastating ever seen in the city, when the museum's animals jumped from upper windows to escape, only to be shot by police officers as they landed. Two beluga whales boiled to death in their tank, while a fireman used an axe to kill a tiger that had broken loose, before rushing back into the inferno to rescue a woman who weighed 400lb, carrying her out on his back.

Such escapades must have influenced this showman. He knew what the public wanted and Parry was a success wherever he went. Later, the theatre he built gave a stage debut to Alec Guinness, was used to record *The Goon Show* and featured a number of performances by the Beatles.

Now we shall take a little detour and meander down Great Scotland Yard, linked forever with being home to plod. It seems to have acquired its name because it was a base for visiting nobles from up north when they had business to attend to in the great metropolis, although records also show land here was owned by a Mr Scott, so perhaps its moniker comes from the fact it was Scott's Land.

When Robert Peel established the Met in 1829, its HQ was in Whitehall Place – but a back entrance, also used by the government cab licensing authority, was in GSY and it soon became the way in if you were visiting the forces of law and order.

In 1884, the Irish Republican Brotherhood planted a bomb here that severely damaged its façade – and blew a whopping great hole in the nearby Rising Sun pub. The publican, rather than bemoan his bad luck and loss of trade, instead dusted down the bar and reopened immediately – charging customers a penny to come in and survey the dramatic damage the Fenian group had caused. They also laid one at the foot of Nelson's Column, which failed to detonate – and it was this campaign of terror that led to the formation of the Special Branch.

This leads us nicely on to Savoy Place, behind Victoria Embankment Gardens. It is here you will find Savoy Hill House.

Completed in 1880 by the Savoy Building Company, it boasted a Turkish bath house in the basement. It was used by the BBC as a studio in the 1920s, and more recently as a base for the Institution of Electrical Engineers (IEE), formerly the Society of Telegraph Engineers, now part of the Institution of Engineering and Technology.

In 1876, the Royal Institution commissioned sculptor John Henry Foley to create a marble of electrical pioneer Michael Faraday for their headquarters, then in Albemarle Street. Foley was an esteemed Irish artist, whose other works included the statue of Prince Albert for the Albert Memorial (which, as you will know, is surrounded by elephants that from behind were described by architect-critic Ian Nairn as looking like a drunk businessman scrambling beneath a restaurant table for his chequebook).

Foley's Faraday was copied in bronze to now stand guard outside the IEE in Savoy Place, and this leads us nicely back to Irish Republicanism, as Foley had dotted the Emerald Isle with commissioned works that would not, over time, prove popular. One such piece was that of Ullik Canning de Burgh, or Lord Dunkellin, a British politician who Foley created a statue of to sit in Eyre Square, Galway. After Irish independence in 1922, many of Foley's works, depicting Anglo-Irish lords and landowners, attracted the ire of Irish freedom fighters.

Members of Galway's Town Tenants' League marched to the city hall and dissolved the council after failing to persuade them to deal with grossly unfair rents. Called the Galway Soviet, they knocked the head off Foley's statue of Lord Dunkellin and then dragged the piece to the banks of the River Corrib, where they shoved the effigy beneath the fast-flowing waters.

The land the bronze Faraday gazes over has its own rebellious past, as uncovered by archaeologists: traces of tiling used for a floor of a great palace dating from 1246 were found in 2014. They came from a grand house built by Peter, the Count of Savoy, which was further extended by his descendants.

Like the sculpture of Lord Dunkellin, it attracted the ire of those with a rebellious streak: the palace was badly damaged during the Peasants' Revolt of 1381. Later, in the seventeenth century, the area had fallen into disrepute, a haunt of criminals that were so notorious that cockneys called all wrong 'uns 'Savoyards' in honour of this Thames-side spot.

Savoy Place, overlooking Victoria Embankment Gardens, was not only as the haunt of the Savoyards, but also another bunch of troublemakers who hung around the area. They were called the Mohocks, and these were rich tearaways, not those unfortunates forced into criminality because of their financial circumstances.

The Mohocks scared the life out of Londoners in the 1710s: a street gang, they specialised in wandering about The Strand and environs, stabbing and slashing random passers-by. Lady Strafford said at the time, 'Here is nothing talked about but men that goes in partys about the street and cuts people with swords or knives, and they call themselves by some hard name that I can neither speak or spell ...'

Her account reveals that one day they set upon a Mr Davenant, but the plucky victim turned the tables on his attackers, overpowering a couple and getting them nicked. Unfortunately, they managed to bribe their way out of custody the same night, and were back in the streets, claiming, according to Lady Strafford, to have found Mr Davenant and in revenge had cut off all his hair with their swords.

'They are said to be young gentleman,' she added, 'and they never take any money from any they assault.'

Mr Davenant's experience was confirmed by Jonathan Swift. 'Young Davenant was telling us at court how he was set upon by the Mohocks,' wrote the satirist. 'It is not safe to be in the streets at night because of them. The Bishop of Salisbury's son is said to be of the gang. I came home early to avoid the Mohocks.'

After these grim memories of unwanted set-tos, let's stop for a restorative cuppa, and hear about the family who did much to promote our national brew.

The Twinings family hailed from Gloucestershire, and had earned their living as weavers: but a recession in 1684 decimated the trade, so the family upped sticks and headed to London. Thomas Twining could read the tea leaves and saw that he needed a new living – and in 1706 he bought Tom's Coffee House, found just off The Strand.

Twinings Tea.

He sold coffee, rum, brandy and arrak, the clear spirit that turned milky white when water is added – but what made the family name was his decision to trade in a new-fangled tipple called tea. They soon became the go-to establishment for all things tea-related: the family sold something called Gunpowder Green, due to the fact Thomas rolled the green tea leaves into tight balls that looked like lead shot. It wasn't cheap, selling at what today would be £720 per pound.

His son, Daniel, exported tea to America, and so played an unexpected role later in the Revolution as his company's products were dumped in Boston Harbour. By 1717, the Twining family were so successful they'd bought up more properties along and behind The Strand. Grandson Richard would become the head of the London Tea Dealers' Association and it was his political influence in the drawing rooms of Georgian London that persuaded William Pitt the Younger that the best way to counter a burgeoning trade in tea smuggling was to cut duty on their product.

And it was Richard who, in 1787, built a fancy doorway to their Strand headquarters, featuring a golden lion, two Chinese figures and their name in a new typeface. They still use this logo, which is said to be the oldest in continuous use in the world.

STANLEY'S STAMPS

Suitably refreshed, let us take in another old-time firm whose life and times is intertwined with The Strand. Our story starts down in Plymouth, Devon, where in 1840 pharmacist William Gibbons lived above a shop and became father to a new arrival called Stanley.

When Stan had reached his early teens, the pastime of stamp collecting was in its infancy and he was an early enthusiast. Joining his father in the chemist trade, Stanley was given a small table in the shop where he could start selling stamps, his dad recognising a profit could be turned from this new-fangled craze.

Stanley's little sideline was successful enough for it to expand and eventually was more profitable than the chemist it was based in. One day, two sailors entered with a kitbag stuffed with stamps from South Africa, which they had won in a raffle when on shore leave in Cape Town. They were happy to accept £5 for the lot – a deal that reaped Stanley a profit of over £3,500.

By 1874, Stanley's stamps were flying off the shelves and he set up an office in London, working as a mail order business. In 1891, the famous stamp emporium took on a headquarters at No. 435, The Strand, and has remained on the stretch ever since.

Now we move back down into Victoria Embankment Gardens, having walked past Charing Cross and a space once known as the Adelphi Arches, after a block built by the celebrated Robert Adam that once stood there. The old Adelphi buildings were demolished in 1936 – a sad end to something that today would no doubt be celebrated as a serious piece of London heritage.

Adam, whose facades would set a trend for the Regency period, created a bold, bold plan, to say the least. Backed financially by his brothers, he decided he wanted to build a row of grand terraced homes overlooking the river. Below the

Stanley Gibbons.

residences would be wharves and warehouses, while behind would be well-built but smaller dwellings, no doubt to house the people who would make sure these large swanky des reses were suitably well staffed and kept spick and span.

But the plans did not go well. From the off, Adam got into a squabble with the City of London over the ownership of part of the Thames riverbank. After carving out various tunnels and cellars, in 1772, engineers discovered they were 2ft lower than they should be. The cellars had been designed with a deal to lease them to the government to store gunpowder, but no contract was signed and the Ordnance Office backed out. Eventually, Adam and his brothers had to get Parliamentary permission to sell off the project via a lottery, saving themselves from bankruptcy but badly damaging their reputations by doing so.

While the project attracted ridicule rather than rakes at first, it would eventually become the address for Thomas Hardy, George Bernard Shaw and John Galsworthy.

And it is by the former Adelphi site we pause and bow our heads in respect. It was here, in 1875, that the body of a young woman was found. No one came forward to claim her. No identity was ever discovered. Poor Jenny, as she was named, was a prostitute and drug addict, and was found to have been strangled. Police searched for the perpetrator, but no one was ever caught. It has been said that poor Jenny's spirit can still be sensed on a patch that became known as Jenny's Hole, on the north-western corner of the gardens.

And it was from about where Jenny's Hole stands that journalist Michael MacDonagh witnessed the shooting down of a Zeppelin on 1 October 1916, which he described as 'probably the most appalling spectacle associated with the war which London is likely to provide'. He watched as the hydrogen-filled balloon erupted into an inferno above Blackfriars Bridge. 'I saw high in the sky a concentrated blaze of searchlights, and in its centre a ruddy glow which spread rapidly into the outline of a blazing airship,' he noted.

The Zeppelin, Number L31, would eventually crash land 13 miles away in Potters Bar.

There are other reminders of the Great War in this little park – including a striking memorial to the Imperial Camel Corps, a unit formed in 1916 to take Tommies across the desert of North Africa. Made up of veterans from the disaster at Gallipoli, its number included Major Cecil Brown – who also happened to be a sculptor on Civvie Street. The designer of numerous medals, he joined a cavalry unit as he liked sculpting horses and wanted to work with them to improve his understanding of their physiology. It is his piece that graces a plinth of Portland stone, marking the contribution his unit made in battles across Egypt, Sinai and Palestine. It includes 346 names of those who lost their lives while serving their country from the back of a camel.

And just across a patch of lawn we can find Scotland's poet, Robert Burns, perched on a tree stump with the air of a man about to create his next verse. This piece was made by John Steell, a Scottish artist: erected in 1884, Steell had practised the poet's likeness. He'd already produced versions of Rabbie for parks in New York, Dundee and New Zealand, and after his Embankment piece he created a bust of the poet for Westminster Abbey.

Robert Burns.

While we are enjoying all this free public art, we shall pop along to a memorial for Henry Fawcett, by the artist Mary Grant. Economist and political thinker, Fawcett had suffered a devastating injury aged 25, when a loaded gun blew up in his face and blinded him.

It was while he was recovering that he fell in love with the trailblazing doctor Elizabeth Garrett, but she turned down his advances to concentrate on medicine. Henry persuaded her sister Millicent, of suffragist fame, to tie the knot instead.

Fawcett was at the famous Oxford Union debate of 1860 over Darwin's controversial book, *On the Origin of Species*. He was asked whether the bishop, Samuel Wilberforce, there to argue the case against evolution, had bothered reading Darwin's tome. He replied, 'I would swear he has never read a word of it', unaware that the bishop was standing right next to him. Wilberforce was ready to scold his critic – but on noting it was Fawcett, and that Fawcett was blind and so had not realised Wilberforce had heard every word, the churchman held his tongue. We are still none the wiser whether the bishop ever did wade through Darwin's world-changing work.

IT WAS A DARK
AND STORMY NIGHT

Ah, the fresh winds blowing up the Thames! What a way to clear a morning head. We have discussed how this area around The Strand and the Thames had been the haunt of male gangs in the Georgian period. Called the Savoyards and the Mohocks, these cut-throat scallywags were either stealing whatever they could lay their hands on (the Savoyards) or randomly assaulting passers-by (the Mohocks).

Now we hammer a final nail in the coffin of this environ's reputation with a tale of a later period to illustrate that things did not improve rapidly, this time from the pen of author, politician and diplomat Edward Bulwer Lytton.

A supporter of Jeremy Bentham's philosophies, he was elected to Parliament in 1831 and became Secretary of State for the Colonies. His written works are not so well known today, but many of his phrases are: he coined such terms as 'the great unwashed' and 'the pen is mightier than the sword', and he started a novel with the evergreen line, 'It was a dark and stormy night ...'

He also persuaded Charles Dickens to change the ending of *Great Expectations* – he read a draft and was furiously disappointed that Pip and Estella did not get together, so told his friend he must rewrite the last chapter.

Prime Minister Benjamin Disraeli said of Bulwer Lytton that 'he never wrote an invitation to dinner without an eye to posterity', and in his book, *Pelham or Adventures of a Gentleman*, Bulwer Lytton describes an incident that took place in Victoria Embankment Gardens, an area many used for cheap encounters, after one such feast. The meal, with six mates, was 'at once incredibly bad, and ridiculously extravagant – turtle without fat, venison without flavour, champagne with the taste of a gooseberry, and hoc with the properties of a pomegranate'; they drank 'with the suicidal determination of Romans' and they strolled to Charing Cross to see what mischief they could get up to.

'We had just passed the Colonnade, we were accosted by a bevy of buxom Cyprians, as merry and drunk as ourselves,' he writes. They engaged in 'amicable and intellectual conversation' until his friend, Dartmore, realised his pocket watch was missing – 'a bouncing lass, whose hands were as ready as her charms, had quietly helped herself to a watch which Stanton wore …'

Stanton's accusations were met with a barrage of gutter language. 'The b– counter-skipper never had any watch,' the retort from the accused came. 'He only filched a two-penny-half-penny gilt chain out of his master, Levi, the pawnbrokers' window, and stuck it in his eel-skin to make a show; ye did, ye pitiful, lanky-chopped son of a dog-fish, ye did …'

A scuffle ensued, with the chums eventually turning on their heels for the safety of a late-night tavern in Covent Garden. 'As when an ant hill is invaded, from every quarter and crevice of the mound arise and pour out an angry host, of whose previous existence the unwary assailant had not dreamt, so from every lane, and alley, and street and crossing, came fast and far the champions of the night,' wrote the shaken novelist.

Let us clear our minds of such grotty behaviour, turn southwards, and gaze at Hungerford Bridge. The one we are looking at now dates from 1864 – it replaced the original by the Victorian genius Isambard Kingdom Brunel, which was built in 1843.

Brunel posted two brick piers in the fast-flowing currents and then hung four sections on chains between them. Once completed, it cost half a penny to cross. However, his work did not last long – when Charing Cross Station was planned, Parliament granted permission for a railway bridge. But the design did not go to waste. It was sold – minus the brick piers, of course – for £5,000 and reused over the Avon Gorge in Clifton, Bristol.

The name Hungerford comes from a well-connected family who owned the land since the 1300s. Walter, the Baron Hungerford, was the Speaker of the House of Commons under Henry V, although his grandson was to fall out of favour with Henry VIII, having his head removed from his neck after being accused of the not inconsiderable crime of treason.

Later, members of the family opened a market here in the 1700s. It included a large number of fish stalls, which they hoped would take on Billingsgate due to it being that much closer to the West End.

Sir Christopher Wren bought a part of the site and built a covered market area, hoping to rival Covent Garden's piazza.

In the late 1800s, after Charing Cross Station was completed, it became synonymous with the concept of being in the centre of London – distances from the city were measured with the entrance to the station as the starting point. And the station's growth caused all sorts of problems in the surrounding streets.

You may recall that Charing Cross Road was built, alongside Northumberland Avenue and Shaftesbury Avenue, as crucial congestion-busting projects during the 1870s and '80s.

There was an unforeseen side effect of the train boom at Charing Cross, which included the opening of a cut-and-cover Tube tunnel linked to the District line from 1870. Its success inadvertently gave its rival, the horse-drawn omnibus, a helping hand.

The new roads made it quicker for the cumbersome bus to make headway. Added to this, the floor fell out of the maize market during the 1880s and '90s, partly due to trains making it cheaper to transport the grain to London, pushing the cost of a sack of grain to record lows. As this was a major outgoing for any omnibus firm, the cheapness of horse fuel meant they could peg ticket prices way below that of the Tube. It ensured it was accessible to even the lowest paid.   Perhaps this is why we talk of 'the man on the Clapham omnibus', instead of 'the man on the District line from Charing Cross'.

An aside: the earliest citation of this phrase to describe a Londoner of average means, wants and opinions was made in the *Journal of the Society of Arts* in 1857. 'So thoroughly has the tedious traffic of the streets become ground into the true Londoner's nature, that ... your dog-collared occupant of the knife-board of a Clapham omnibus will stick on London Bridge for half-an-hour with scarcely a murmur,' it said.

Let's march on Parliament Square while we have the omnibus swing voter on our minds.

BRIAN HAW AND THE
HUMAN CANNONBALL

Let us breeze past the statues of the famous – Gandhi, Mandela, Fawcett, Churchill, Peel, Lincoln, Palmerston, Smuts and Lloyd George – who gaze in judgement at the Houses of Parliament and pause at the place where a peace campaigner joined these exulted ranks.

The late Brian Haw set up a tent on the Square in June 2001, and would spend the next ten years at his post, protesting about British forces fighting in the Middle East. From a Christian background, his father was a British soldier who liberated the Nazi death camp at Bergen-Belsen.

Haw spent time in Northern Ireland during the Troubles, and visited Cambodia to see first-hand the brutality of the Khmer Rouge's genocide. Police and politicians were desperate to get rid of him – even making it a law

Brian Haw.

The Royal Aquarium.

that no protest could take place within half a mile of Parliament without the say-so of the Old Bill. Various attempts to have him removed failed, although the Met sent seventy-eight police officers, costing the tax payer £27,000, to take away his placards.

He missed just one night at his post following an arrest – and he returned refreshed the following day. So, button-covered hats off to Brian, who died of lung cancer in 2011. He didn't manage to clock up as many days as Concepción Picciotto, an anti-nuclear campaigner who spent thirty-five years outside the White House, but death does tend to get in the way of the most carefully laid plans.

From here, let us move north to Tothill Street, and pause at the site of the long-gone Royal Aquarium. With nothing on the yet-to-be-invented telly, the Victorians were adept at creating distractions – and the Royal Aquarium set out to do just that, with mixed results.

Its reputation was such that it became the butt of music hall jokes – celebrated entertainer Arthur Roberts poked fun at the fact that the aquarium had become a cruising ground for upper-class men with a taste for working women, penning the following ditty:

I strolled one day to Westminster,
The Royal Aquarium to see;
But I had to stand a bottle
just to lubricate the throttle
Of a lady who was forty-three.

Roberts' ascent into the limelight started when he was spotted busking at Covent Garden (the fantasy of many an aspiring Marcel Marceau) by an impresario, who gave him £1 a week to perform in Great Yarmouth. As well as nationwide success, in 1907 he led other end-of-the-pier types in what became known as the Music Hall War. He protested against their precarious living and founded the Variety Artists Federation.

The aquarium he joked about was opened in 1876, backed by department store founder William Whiteley. He believed it could rival Crystal Palace, offering a range of attractions in order to part the wide-eyed visitor with tuppences. Inside, you would find palm trees, fountains and sculptures in a central hall, with smaller side rooms for food, drink and games. There was an art gallery, ice rink, theatre and thirteen huge tanks filled with the wonders of the sea. However, a design flaw in a water-refreshing system – which had been built in the foundations, making repairs tough – meant they were often empty, leading to much ribbing from the likes of Arthur.

Its reputation as a place where the amorous and skint could make a deal reached the front pages due to the case of serial killer Thomas Cream. One day, he met aquarium employee Emily Turner, and told her he was Major Hamilton, well-spoken and of private means – no doubt a nice catch. They dined at Gattos in The Strand and enjoyed a show at the Alhambra Theatre. As a parting gift, he gave her a box of cough medicine.

Poor Turner's suspicions that her major might not be all he said he was emerged after she felt ill having sucked his lozenges. Worried she had been poisoned, the box reached the desk of the Yard's Inspector Jarvis. He ascertained she had been on a date with the notorious killer.

Cream's murderous spree stretched from Canada to the USA and then to Britain. He set up a doctor's practice in shady neighbourhoods and then murdered prostitutes who came to him for abortions.

Using Turner's description, Jarvis caught his man. As he approached the hangman's noose, Cream told an expectant crowd he was Jack the Ripper – an unlikely claim, as it appears he was in prison in Illinois at the time of those crimes.

While we look at where the aquarium once stood, it would be remiss not to speak of the wonderful Zazel, the human cannonball. Born Rossa Richter in 1863, she gave the first demonstration of this escapade at the age of 14 at the aquarium, accompanied by an orchestra. An acrobat and tightrope walker, she travelled the world performing her death-defying stunts. Truly an all-rounder, when not risking her life for others' enjoyment, she composed and sang operas.

Now, another short stroll to St James's Park, to look at the fabulous Duck House. We have spoken about the pelicans donated by the Russian Ambassador to Charles II previously, and while they were strictly for viewing, these birds were not so fortunate.

Charles ordered a series of small canals to be built for wildfowl to swim along, making them easy targets for the royal table. The canals created a small island, and Charles invented the post of Governor of Duck Island for his friend, Seigneur de Saint-Evremond.

Later, John Burgess Watson, an architect with a taste for English rural whimsies, was appointed to build a cottage there, and he included a club house for members of the recently formed Ornithological Society of London. It stands today, nestling among the reeds, and is surely one of the most liveable follies in London.

The ducks that swim around it unmolested now can consider themselves lucky – their ancestors were destined to be a king's feast, but before then, the birds were threatened by an even stickier end. When James I laid out the park, the king thought it a good idea to place two crocodiles he had been gifted in the lake. Understandably, the wildfowl were none too impressed.

From Bird Island, St James's Park, we shall head south towards the Thames. Our route leads us down Orchard Street, so named because it was once home to the apple trees for monks living at Westminster Abbey.

This thoroughfare was home to the eccentric author Thomas Amory in the 1700s, a renowned polymath whose works covered a range of natural sciences. It was from his home in Orchard Street that he penned *The Memoirs of John Buncie*, in 1766. It told the story of the title character, who was married seven times. Each wife described encompassed Buncie's idealised vision of the traits a woman should have.

It seems he never had much luck meeting someone who covered all bases – he lived the life of a recluse, only heading out of his house after dark. It did him no harm: he lived to 97 – a very good innings for the time.

And now on to Victoria Tower Gardens, where we shall consider a decades-old mystery. As we wander through the little park nestling west of the Houses of Parliament, we shall pause by the Buxton Memorial, and consider the fate of eight British leaders who decorated its plinth.

This striking piece of Victoriana dates from 1856 and celebrates the MPs who fought to have slavery abolished. It was paid for by Charles Buxton MP, the son of Thomas Buxton, who, along with the likes of William Wilberforce, Thomas Babington, Henry Brougham and Stephen Lushington, was a key campaigner to outlaw slavery.

The Buxton Memorial.

Costing £1,200 to build, the design included eight figures who had ruled Britain – starting with the Briton Caractacus, followed by Constantine the Roman, it also found room for the Dane Canute and Saxon King Alfred until it reached the age of Victoria.

Originally in Parliament Square, in 1949, after a tweaking of the road layout, the statue was put into storage. And while in the care of the London County Council, tucked away in a shed somewhere, the fountain caught the eye of unscrupulous persons unknown. Four of the figures were stolen, never to be retrieved.

And that was not the end of the memorial's woes. It reappeared in the gardens in 1967 – and after just four years enjoying its new, Thames-side view, the remaining four figures were filched. Eventually all eight were replaced by fibreglass looky-likeys, but the mystery of what happened to the originals remains.

If only, some might say, it was this easy to dispose of those making decisions on our behalf today.

EXOTIC FRUITS
AND BABY DRAGONS

Now we head west and gaze at the elegant span of Lambeth Bridge. Londoners have been heading north to south and south to north at this spot for centuries. It was built at the site of an ancient ford and is said to be the site of an important Roman crossing.

It became known as the Horse Ferry in the medieval period, when a shallow-bottomed boat was stationed there to link the archbishops at Lambeth Palace and the Palace of Westminster. The first bridge was built in 1860, but did not last – the steep approaches were too tricky for horses, and the five suspended sections soon rusted, making it necessary to replace the span in 1932.

What remains of the original bridge are the striking obelisks at each end, which are topped with what at first glance looks like pairs of that odd Victorian architectural obsession, the pineapple.

Ah, the pineapple – a symbol of great wealth and status after Columbus brought the fruit back form the new world. Their high price in Georgian and Victorian times was such that to have a pineapple was the height of sophistication – or extravagance, depending if you were sitting or serving at a dinner table. And pineapples are everywhere in London architecture, so it stands to reason that the obelisks at Lambeth Bridge should include such finials – especially as, legend has it, they were included as a tribute to the great horticulturist John Tradescant the Younger. Chief gardener to Charles I and celebrated botanist, he grew the first pineapple in England and introduced such beauties as the magnolia and cypress pine to Britain.

His family's estate stretched through Lambeth up to Westminster, where the bridge is found, and as well as collecting plants, he and his father, John the Elder, were avid collectors of curios. The items hoarded by the Tradescants – which they named rather grandly the Museum Tradescantiarium – ranged from Native American artefacts and ancient manuscripts, to coins and taxidermy of weird-looking creatures they'd shot on their travels. It was claimed they also owned a piece of wood from the cross Christ was crucified on, a mermaid's hand and a baby dragon.

The collection caused grief for the family after John the Younger's death.

He had struck a deal with Elias Ashmole, the man who would establish the Ashmolean Museum at Oxford, to take his collection once he had passed.

However, it appears John got cold feet and his wife Hester tried to undo the deal. Meanwhile, Ashmole was not so easy to put off. He moved in next door to the Tradescant house and cut a hole in an adjoining wall, which he used to remove choice items against Hester's will. He countered accusations of sneaky behaviour by besmirching her reputation and asserting that her compost heap was so large that thieves had used it to scale his garden wall to steal his hens and roosters.

Things did not end pleasantly for poor Hester. She was found dead, in mysterious circumstances, face down in a pond in her back garden. With her out of the way, Ashmole took the collection.

Meanwhile – back to the pineapples. On closer inspection, the idea that the obelisks were topped with John the Younger's fruit quickly crumbles. Instead, the finials are pine cones: considered ancient symbols of good luck. Civil engineer Peter Barlow decided he would like four of them welcoming travellers on to his bridge.

RIGHT HOOKES

'Lying in bed,' wrote the writer-philosopher GK Chesterton, 'would be an altogether perfect and supreme experience if only one had a coloured pencil long enough to draw on the ceiling'. As we do not yet possess such a wondrous thing, let us shake a leg and turn heel up Horseferry Road and chuck a right into Dean Bradley Street to gaze at the Robert Hooke Science Centre, which is part of Westminster School.

As we are celebrating our city, it would be bad form not to consider the man the centre is named after. Hooke – – sometimes referred to as London's Leonardo – was one of those fascinating polymaths, a jack of all trades and master of them, too. Astronomer, scientist, mathematician and architect, his work changed the face of the metropolis.

After the Great Fire, he was appointed the Surveyor to the City of London, teaming up with Sir Christopher Wren. Hooke's role in landmarks including St Paul's and the Royal Observatory is often overlooked – Wren has stuck in the public mind – but his fingerprints linger over so much. He worked on The Monument, which was built not just to mark the start of the fire, but, typically Hookeian, as a place to mount a telescope.He included a basement laboratory, too.

It was Hooke who suggested giving London a grid-type pattern with glorious avenues and squares, but saw his dream scuppered by property owners who wanted to keep their land and perhaps steal a few yards from neighbours in the chaos. Hooke had the unenviable job of acting as a mediator in disputes – new streets ate into people's yards, while adjoining walls were a source of bitter arguments. He earned a reputation not only as a first-class scientist but a wonderfully calm and balanced settler of disagreements. He also cared deeply for the plight of those fire-forced refugees squatting in Lincoln's Inn Fields and Covent Garden, insisting authorities cracked on at superfast speed with rebuilding.

Sadly, it appears there are no contemporary images of the great man to be found, and this leads us on to a little mystery. He was a founding member of the Royal Society, so it is unthinkable that no portrait was created. We know artist Mary Beale painted an image she called 'Portrait of a Mathematician' – and it matches the descriptions of Hooke.

Hooke had fallen out with Sir Isaac Newton, as professional rivalry got in the way. They argued over the properties of light (as you do). Beale's portrait included a model of the Solar System, which is said to have incensed Newton, who felt Hooke was somehow claiming ownership of astronomical research (he wasn't). When Newton was appointed head of the society, and was overseeing a move from its headquarters, the painting was simply left behind.

The Beale work reappeared in the 1960s and was sold – rather hilariously, as a picture of Sir Isaac. It then reared its head at Sotheby's in 2006. A deep-pocketed private collector won the bidding war and it is again hidden from public view. The mystery of whether this is indeed a painting of Hooke, remains.

Now let's meander past the old Horseferry Road Magistrates' Court, an imposing 1960s building that to your correspondent's eyes represents everything horrible about cheap modernism: it wasn't even functional, with a reputation for its mechanics breaking down. Beaks hardly raised a brow if they heard a suspect was late because they were stuck in a lift.

It was the scene of the case of Lord Justice Richards, who was accused of flashing on a commuter train. He was acquitted, after showing the court a pair of Calvin Kleins to illustrate the unreliability of witnesses. This was, he said, his preferred style of underwear, and not the kegs described by the accuser.

Nearby, we can see the former headquarters of the Gas Light and Coke Company, which first illuminated London streets in the 1800s. They built an HQ on the site of a market garden owned by a chap called Bower. On Christmas Day 1814, they turned on the taps from Horseferry Road and Westminster was lit up, marking a key moment on the path to modernity.

REGENCY SPLENDOUR

All this jibber-jabber is making your correspondent peckish – so let us rest our wearies at the famous Regency Cafe, in Regency Street.

This celebrated diner was opened in 1946 by Antonio Perotti and Gino Schiavetta, Italian émigrés who had worked in numerous cafes and restaurants before banding together. The family link remains: Marco Schiavetta, Gino's son, and Antonio's daughter Claudia, are now at the tea urn.

The Regency serves the grandest and best-value breakfasts in town. It is famous for its homemade steak pie, which has fuelled generations of diners, and its interior – the original art deco tiles survive. It means it is regularly used for film and photography shoots. As well as lovely tea and a cracking atmosphere, it has another enjoyable selling point: the many, many pictures of Tottenham Hotspur players that grace the walls.

The Regency Cafe.

Lutyens.

Gino and Antonio were committed fans, and that has been inherited by the current owners. Tottenham's Anglo-Italian star of the double-winning period, Tony Marchi, would bring such team mates as Jimmy Greaves and Danny Blanchflower in for a stamina-building plate of chops. For those of us (your correspondent included) of the Spurs sect, we sit on hallowed chairs.

Suitably full of both fry-up and a feast of mid-twentieth-century interior design, we turn around the corner into Page Street and ponder how the tastes and fads in architecture trundle in a circular fashion. It is in Page Street we first glimpse a striking block designed by Sir Edwin Lutyens. Built in the 1930s, Lutyens' traditional Arts and Crafts vernacular was, by then, out of fashion. Thankfully not before the Duke of Westminster employed Lutyens to build new homes for workers in Page, Vincent and Regency streets.

Lutyens used a clever trick with red bricks and white render, creating a vertical chess board. That was his secret, recalled architecture critic, Nikolaus Pevsner. He called Lutyens 'without doubt the greatest folly builder in England' and added, 'the British have a fascination for the folly like no other country'. He went on to say that the Brits need not be ashamed of that fascination, as 'to appreciate a folly a degree of detachment is needed, which is only accessible to old and humane civilisations'.

These delightful flats by this delightful architect were sold by the Duke of Westminster on a 999-year lease for a shilling to Westminster Council in 1935 – and it would lead them to a role in the 'homes for votes' scandals that hit the council under Dame Shirley Porter. They were at the centre of an unlikely court case in 1990, prompted by Westminster's intention of selling Lutyens' 532 flats to private owners. The current duke argued that his gran and grandad had handed the council a 999-year lease on the agreement that they would be let at low rents to the 'working classes'.

The council claimed such a definition did not exist anymore and considered, on the sly, that this was an opportunity to get rid of a swathe of Labour-voting tenants and replace them with wealthier private residents. The courts went with the duke.

STAND AND DELIVER

Leaving Lutyens, the duke and Shirley P behind, we now walk down Marsham Street, once home to Jonathan Snow, a businessman in the 1770s. He has left us descriptions of the fields stretching west, slowly being nibbled away by grand homes and peasants' hovels.

Snow was heading home from south London to Marsham Street late on 19 October 1774, accompanied in his coach by a vicar and two others, when they became embroiled in a high-speed chase and gunfight with a pair of highwaymen. Snow told the Old Bailey during the trial of two men called Tomlin and Knight, 'We had heard of a robbery that night in Gunnersbury Lane and having arms we determined not to be robbed'.

As they crossed the Thames, they noticed 'a couple o' fellows' and decided they looked like they were up to no good: a correct assumption. Snow said, 'They tried to force the coach to stop, while the passengers implored the driver to whip the horses up to speed.'

Pistol shots were exchanged while a hand-to-hand battle on the move unfolded. Despite the evidence, the jury voted to acquit.

Meanwhile, Snow's neighbour, William Gardner, also attracted the law's attention. He was identified by publican Thomas Ellis as having visited his hostelry in Kennington and, after drinking more than his fill, he stumbled out into the dark night.

As Ellis went to clear up, he noticed six green-handled knives and forks were missing. Suspecting his customer was up to mischief, he took a constable to Gardner's Marsham Street home. Lo and behold, there on a shelf was the missing cutlery. Gardner told the court he had been 'very much in liquor', and had found the knives in his pocket a day after getting home from an almighty bender.

He accepted responsibility, but claimed he had absolutely no recollection of where he'd been or what had done, a defence that the Old Bailey was not overly moved by. He got a seven-year stretch in Australia.

From the shady past of Marsham Street, we head over to St John's Smith Square to gaze at the lovely church – now a concert hall – at its centre. Its noteworthy towers, in each corner, are rumoured to have been placed there to please Queen Anne.

St John's Smith Square Church.

Poor Anne. She was said to have loved a drink and had a bit of a temper on her. No wonder: she had eighteen failed pregnancies and suffered from gout and rheumatism.

During her reign, the '50 Churches' project to bring more places of worship into London got under way, and builder Thomas Archer came to Queen Anne with designs and a request to get started. Anne, in her cups, took unkindly to the poor Archer, and was unimpressed by the stunning Baroque details. Exasperated, Archer politely asked her what she wanted the church to look like. She responded by kicking over a foot stool, and when it landed with its legs in the air, she replied, 'I want it to look like that.'

If you look at St John's today, you will see why Anne is said to have unduly influenced this church's look.

From Anne's edifice to a piece of architecture that did not fare so well, around the corner in Marsham Street, home to the Home Office. The current building dates from 2005 and was designed by post-modernist architect Sir Terry Farrell. It provides an interesting example of the changing whims of architectural tastes. The blocks Sir Terry's designs replaced were three towers by Eric Bedford, chief architect to the government for public buildings, in the 1960s.

They in turn had replaced defunct gas holders, which had been decommissioned in the 1940s and converted into huge bomb shelters. They were designed to withstand a direct hit by a 500lb bomb and beneath the gas holders were war rooms for critical civil service staff – beginning Whitehall's long association with Marsham Street.

The gas cylinders were owned by Westminster Gas Light and Coke Company, who, as mentioned, illuminated the streets. While here, let us pause for a moment and remember the people who worked for the firm during the Second World War.

The thousands of merchant seamen who gave their lives during the six-year conflict contained a good many from the WGLCC: they brought in vital fuel for the war industry, and lost many in doing so. Of the long list of ships sunk, let us pay respects to the crew of SS *Gasfire*, a 2,972-ton collier that was launched in 1936.

In October 1940, a German E-boat torpedoed the boat off Great Yarmouth. The ship managed to struggle home, but she lost eleven of her crew. She was repaired, and went off to do her duty again. But she had no more luck – on 21 June 1941 she struck a mine off Southwold, Suffolk, and went down with those on board.

The gas holders came down by the end of the 1940s, and by 1960 work on the three ugly sisters began. It didn't take long for them to be seen as examples of excessive British Brutalism, and they were criticised for creating a nasty backdrop for Westminster Cathedral.

It was not always so: Bedford's work was feted when they first opened (it took ten years from the first spade in the ground to civil servants swishing in to the marble-clad entrance). The three towers, linked by corridors three storeys up, boasted express lifts and escalators, and stunning views from the thirteen floors. But its interior as well as its exterior quickly became unloved, with successive politicians complaining that it was a depressing place to run the Home Office from. This prompted their demolition.

Sir Terry's designs are made up of three buildings and named after Elizabeth Fry, Mary Seacole and Robert Peel, figures chosen for their influence on Home Office policy. Like their predecessors, they too were feted when they opened, partly for the fact they were no higher than the buildings around them, and also simply because they were not Marsham Towers. Yet, as we have seen with even Sir Terry's designs, which can be found across central London at places such as Charing Cross and the MI6 building on the southern banks of the Thames, architectural criticism often grows as time whittles away the sheen of the new and trendy.

How long until a generation arrives that decides such works are no longer fit for purpose?

LOYAL CITIZENS, USEFUL WORKERS, SOLID CHRISTIANS

Now we amble north a little and come to the Grey Coats Hospital, at the top end of Horseferry Road. Its founding was an inadvertent product of the Great Fire of London. After the disaster had left so many homeless, there was an exodus towards the old medieval areas of Westminster. People were pushed west, and among those desperate, homeless Londoners a fair few turned to crime to meet their daily needs. The fact that criminals could seek sanctuary in Westminster Abbey is also said to have been a draw for those who had committed capital offences – and this was in an age when a long list of petty misdemeanours could see you swing.

And how to deal with this influx of new parishioners' offspring kept Church authorities busy. The answer was found in 1698, when eight kind-hearted members of St Margaret's Church each put 65p in a pot to found Grey Coats. The aim was to help build 'loyal citizens, useful workers and solid Christians'.

A disused workhouse in Tothill Fields was bought and converted. Children were taken in to learn their lessons, given in an austere regime to build up their constitutions. Queen Anne gave the place her blessing, and her royal arms still stand above the front door, next to casts of children decked out in the original Grey Coats uniform.

The benefits of the school may be numerous, but not all those enrolled felt so. In 1801, the pupils had had enough of their bossy tutors and went on a rebellion that saw them occupy the building. The school had to call out the militia to break the siege.

Grey Coats.

Peering in to the Grey Coats courtyard, it's rather fun to imagine the pupils throwing their quills and ink from windows at their oppressors.

In nearby Caxton Street, you could once find the Blue Coats school, set up by the Church of England congregation of 'ye Parish of St. Margaret Westr', as the school's history reveals, around the turn of the eighteenth century. An annual stipend was paid to fund it, with the aim of countering free schools being set up by Roman Catholics. The Blue Coat founders agreed their school would be run 'at their own annuall expense, wherein fifty poor boys of the said Parish, whose Parents were not able to be at the charge of their teaching, were and still are carefully taught to read, write, cast accounts, and also catechised and instructed in the Principles of our most Holy Religion, and put out when fit to trades whereby they might act honest livelihoods in the World'.

Hearty stuff. Now, there is a whiff of mystery over who actually designed the school. It was said to be in Wren's style, and was completed a year before the final stone of the lantern at St Paul's was laid. Historians wonder if Wren, perhaps, could also have designed this enchanting building. There is no record of who did – but whether he drew it with his hand or not, it's influenced by Wren. There is something uniquely English about this Corinthian column'd place, and it's vibe of old, steadfast and enduring London made it the subject of a watercolour that can now be found in the Victoria and Albert Museum.

During the Second World War, the Committee for the Employment of Artists in Wartime funded artists including John Piper, Sir William Russell Flint and Rowland Hilder, to capture scenes that were quintessentially British. Stuff to rally the spirits, to stoke the home fires. Polite market towns and neat village greens, the solid square tower of a Norman church or the spire of something a little more recent. Duck ponds and rivers, mountains and moors, and then industry and city life. All were captured in a project known as 'Recording the changing face of Britain' and managed by the National Gallery.

Its director, Sir Kenneth Clark, decided in September 1939 he wanted to record an England yet to be soiled by the grime of war. He knew the landscape would change, be it through bombs, invasion or the defence of the realm. Added to this, the likes of JB Priestley and HV Morton had already chronicled an England undergoing rapid change, driven by the car, with new roads stretching out and falling destructively across hills and valleys, ignoring the ancient routes that had been there before. He wanted those with an eye for such things to get out there and capture it – and saw the benefits of such work to the war effort.

It was a very productive scheme. Sir Kenneth saw over 1,500 works pass completed across his desk. He had employed ninety-seven leading artists, and thousands saw the works at shows at the National Gallery – it ran three times due to its size and popularity, before embarking on a nationwide tour. In 1949, the V&A were given the collection and loaned out the pictures to town halls. In 1990, they recalled the lot and it now resides as one complete collection.

Among these bucolic scenes to remind the nation what they were fighting for is a beautiful watercolour of Blue Coats. It creates a more peaceful image of the school than was always the case.

ELBOW GREASE

We will be discussing the marvellous chronicler of London, Henry Mayhew, in greater detail shortly. In his study *London Labour and the London Poor*, he came across two brothers who had been 'Grecians' at the Blue Coat School. It was aimed that the Grecians – as the old boys were known – would find some decent employment after finishing their studies, with one lucky student being sent annually to Cambridge to further their education, and another pupil making the journey to Oxford, although only once every three years to the Dreaming Spires.

These brothers had not gone down the path leading to a life of gentlemanly occupations and leisure. Instead, they walked the streets working as 'Grease-removing Composition Sellers', a trade that consisted of selling their home-made, patent, cloth-cleaning mixtures, by street hawking them to scruffy-clothed shoppers.

In those days, silk and woollen clothing was more expensive, but more durable. Their upkeep was seen to be a key skill in any housewife's armoury. This entailed finding grease-removers, who would gather crowds around them while they demonstrated on the tatty coat of an apprentice sidekick how their mixture would rub away the most stubborn of stains, like the Victorian version of the Daz washing powder man.

If their patter was strong, they could work a good profit. The substance used to scrub away those oily accidents was made up of clay, 'beaten up and worked with two colours, red lead and stone blue'. This mixture could be dried and placed on silks for five minutes before being vigorously brushed away, leaving nothing but the pristine colours beneath, or it could be spread on woollen clothing with cold water and then rubbed off, again removing any careless spills.

The Blue Coats grease removers, Mayhew felt, had a strong sales pitch, and enjoyed sidelines selling household cleaning products they could pick up as they went about their business. This included 'plate balls', a ball made up of whitening, a farthing's worth of red lead and an ounce of quicksilver.

'No tarnish can stand against my plate balls,' the brothers declared. 'If, in this respectable company, there should chance to be any lady or gentleman that has no plate, then let him make an old brass candlestick shine like gold, or his tin candlestick, extinguisher and all, shine like silver. You have only to rub it on what has to be restored … four a penny!'

INTERPRETING THE BIBLE
AND THE DISCOVERY
OF THE PROLETARIAT

Now we wiggle north-east until we reach Ambrosden Avenue, home to the magnificent Westminster Cathedral. Built on what was once a marsh called Bulinga Fen, it had been drained by a group of Benedictine monks. The land, known as Tothill Fields, has been used for bull-baiting, housed a maze during Elizabethan times and then became the site of a prison.

The Middlesex House of Correction opened in 1834, and was home to convicts whose crime did not warrant transportation. It was the subject of study by our social scientist and journalist friend Henry Mayhew, and his famous tome *London Labour and the London Poor*.

Westminster Cathedral.

He did not hold back with stark criticism, so it is interesting to note he described the prison as progressive: not a hard thing to be when you consider the diabolical conditions of Victorian lock-ups. While the wardens banned inmates from speaking to each other, and used the punishment of reduced rations to make it stick, Mayhew noted that convicts had only been whipped twice in five years.

The regime saw a gun fired at 6.25 a.m. to get everyone up and at 'em – and then the day was spent hard at work. A hive of industry, inmates made caulker materials for the hulls of boats fuelled by meals a day of gruel, bread and water, although twice a week meals included potatoes with tinned mutton or beef and a vegetable soup thickened with marrowfat and flavoured with ox head.

Mayhew described how the youngest convict was aged 5, banged up for stealing 5s 9d from a shop, while most were teenagers. The majority were pickpockets, but lesser offences also warranted sentences, such as the game your correspondent called Knock Down Ginger as a child, namely ringing a doorbell and running away. Perhaps the most bizarre crime he came across was that of two boys, 10 and 11, who were serving time 'for spinning a top'. One can only imagine where this heinous piece of antisocial behaviour was committed to earn time inside.

Before we continue with the physical geography of this patch, it's worth spending a moment in the company of Mayhew. His reportage of street traders, published in 1851, are an extraordinary 'account of the lives, miseries, joys and chequered activities of the London Street Sellers' as one preface to a modern edition trumpets.

We could fill many a paragraph trawling through his conversations with our London forebears, but instead of talking about his subjects, let's spend a moment thinking about Mayhew himself. His landscape is 'a vast underworld living by its muscles, its wits or its misfortunes', writes Stanley Rubinstein in an appreciation of Mayhew, penned exactly 100 years after his tome came out.

'With a skill amounting to genius he has drawn from his subjects their own story and recorded it in their own words, and he convinces us that he has recorded it truthfully, and that on the whole they spoke the truth. Even their fictions are truth of another kind: he was tolerantly aware of a disposition in the Irish to romance. Here we cannot help believing it is the authentic voice of the men and women, the boys and girls, who made the living in the streets 100 years ago.'

Mayhew's work had a three-pronged approach. He was a social investigator, concerned with poverty and then crime: he believed if the truth about the lives of so many were made public, something would be done to improve their loot. He wrote, 'It is but right that the truthfulness of the poor be generally should be known …'

It took him ten years to complete his studies, which were published in 1862. Mayhew's range of achievements are many, and are not only about his skill as a chronicler of London. The son of a London solicitor and one of seven brothers, he ran away to sea from Westminster School, where he had been bullied. He returned to join the family trade, as it were, but the study of law bored him and he decided the world of literature was more to his taste.

Mayhew, it is said, had little sense of business or managing his personal finances. Coming over as something of an empathetic dreamer with a drive to seek ways to build a better world, and coupled to his drive to embark on big, seemingly low-paying projects, he found it hard to reap a regular income.

Before settling on recording the voices of those he shared London with, he turned his house upside down after deciding to embark on a series of chemical experiments as he tried to make and market a dye that he believed was the hue of the ancient Tyrian purple. After the publication of his tome, he fell into a law suit against a printer – a case that cost him money he could ill afford.

His work was pilfered by others with little acknowledgement and certainly no financial recompense. His travails were undertaken with him solely supporting himself and living a very hand-to-mouth existence while doing so. There was no profit motive at the centre of his earnest investigations, which have left us such a vivid picture of a London swallowed up by the passing of time.

Mayhew left other legacies. He was a co-founder of *Punch* magazine, which, on his death in 1887, printed the following lines:

The record of the age's course will tell
Of him whose name a double honour bore
Comrade of Punch, and champion of the poor.

Now, back to the prison Mayhew visited. This seemingly progressive place – in the awful landscape of Victorian prisons – closed in the 1880s, and the land was bought by the diocese. Cardinal Manning could see the prison from the bottom of his garden and believed it would be an excellent spot for a new church, as well as vastly improving his view.

The land was bought in 1884, and architect John Bentley started work on a Byzantine-style building that would, on its completion, boast 126 different types of marble hewn from quarries in twenty-four countries across five continents. Some parts were recycled pieces from ancient Greek and Roman buildings.

Alas, Bentley would not see the interior of the cathedral finished before his death in 1902, and his passing left something of a mystery. The scheme called for a range of mosaics and reliefs – but Bentley had kept the ideas mainly in his mind's eye. It meant the job of decorating continued well into the twentieth century, and includes the first professional commission of the sculptor Eric Gill.

Gill, aged 31, was asked in 1913 to produce a series of fourteen reliefs for the Stations of the Cross. Gill was unknown and saw the job as a way to promote his work, so he put in a low bid of £765 for the lot. Slowly but surely, he created the panels and put them in situ – but not to the type of response his works receive today. Various critics – including the cathedral's own architect – called Gill's work 'neither suitable for the peculiar light of the Cathedral nor the Catholic public', 'cold as the mind that produced them' and 'hideous, primitive and pagan'.

Gill ploughed on with his design, and said he believed the bouquets outweighed the brickbats, 'especially when you take into account the infernal business of taking all the panels down again'.

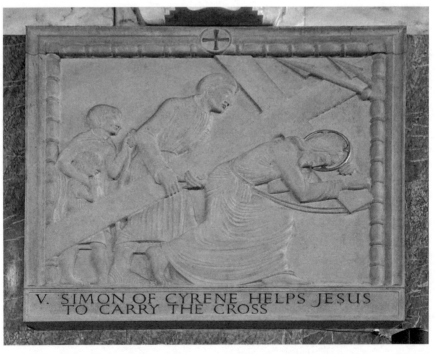

Westminster Cathedral.

A *TITANIC* FEAST

Now we leave the quiet serenity of this house of God and head north into Belgravia, halting our progress in Belgrave Square. This glorious late-Georgian masterpiece, consisting of four cream terraces, has history seeping out from beneath every front door. Today, it is home to numerous embassies and consulates, and let us pause for a moment outside No. 24, now home to the Embassy of Spain.

It was here that Lord Pirrie, chairman of shipbuilders Harland and Wolff, resided. In July 1907, he hosted a small dinner party to which J Bruce Ismay, managing director of the White Star Line, was invited. Lord Pirrie and Ismay were locked in conversation about how Ismay's rivals, Cunard, had just launched the world's two biggest ships, *Mauretania* and *Lusitania*. As the wine flowed, the pair drew up the designs for three ships to outdo Cunard – and from this idea came the ill-fated RMS *Titanic*.

Now we'll pop a little further along the square to No. 45, home in the Victorian period to the marvellous racehorse owner, Caroline Agnes née Horsley-Beresford. Using the pseudonym Mr Manton, as ladies weren't meant to own stables of racers, she was both feared and admired for her eccentricity. Her friends were jockeys and her rough manners shocked the society circles she was rich enough to move in. She was described as being a 'very grand dame to the tips of her fingers, her appearance and her dress are extraordinary. She is accustomed to call a spade a spade, to swear and curse like a trooper. Her fat and red face and dyed blonde hair are familiar figures on every racecourse, where she is known by her racing name of Mr Manton.'

She earned notoriety at a young age, when, at Royal Ascot, she was part of a gang who hissed at Queen Victoria. It concerned the monarch's treatment of Lady Flora Hastings, a lady-in-waiting the queen believed had been impregnated by a Tory MP. Poor Lady Flora was taken for a medical examination under Her Majesty's orders, as she had a swollen tummy. The doctors found she was still a virgin – and the swelling was due to a liver tumour, from which she soon died.

Horsley-Beresford's home is now used by the government of Malaysia, and can be seen in the 1954 Gregory Peck film, *The Million Pound Note*, in which the actor watches the paper fortune flutter away on a stiff breeze from the doorstep.

GREEK KINGS
AND DEAD HOUSEKEEPERS

From swish old Belgrave Square, let us take a sideways glance at Belgravia before tramping north to Park Lane.

Just around the corner from the square you will find Lower Belgrave Street. Pause outside No. 46, the former home of Lord Lucan and the scene of the death of his nanny, Sandra Rivett, who the peer was suspected of murdering. This case, which still intrigues due to the fact no one has ever proved what happened to Lucan after he fled the scene, has been well covered. Instead, we shall walk to Chester Square to recall a similarly horrible incident that is not so well known.

In 1946, the exiled King of Greece, George II, decided to make his home at No. 45. His housekeeper, Elizabeth McLindon, moved in to get things shipshape for his arrival. But when the king turned up, there was no sign of Elizabeth, and many of the rooms were locked.

The police arrived and found her body. They discovered a note from an Arthur Boyce, asking Elizabeth why she had not been in touch – and so they sought him out.

Boyce claimed they were engaged, but detectives discovered he was a bigamist and conman. They also heard from an army friend of Boyce's, who said his service revolver had gone missing – and he suspected Boyce had taken it. Suffice to say, the gunshot that killed Elizabeth came from this weapon.

It came out that Elizabeth had found a wedding invitation with Boyce named as the groom and another woman as the bride. She confronted him – and he killed her. Boyce claimed Greek Republicans had attacked Elizabeth after coming to the house to look for the king. The jury thought otherwise, and the Chester Gardens killer was sent to the gallows.

Let us move on to brighter topics, and head north to Park Lane.

Its current layout was created by pinching 20 acres of Hyde Park in the early 1960s to build a racetrack of a dual carriageway. If we look carefully we will see, at No. 90, a blue plaque marking the residence of Moses Montefiore. This fascinating character rose from being the grandson of a poor, Italian-Jewish immigrant to the highest echelons of society. Elected the Sheriff for the City of London, he became a respected philanthropist and fought for civil rights.

Montefiore got into banking but was swindled out of £30,000 in his early 20s and had to start afresh. The scamster, Elkin Daniels, used a wheeze involving raising multiple loans on the strength of one cheque. The burden of making good these promises fell on Montefiore's shoulders, while Daniels hot-footed it to the Isle of Man.

Fortunately, Daniels was arrested and brought back to face trial. His capture, however, caused consternation on the island: there was a Manx law that made such deportations illegal. Snatched at night and dragged to a waiting boat, Daniels's fate gave the heebie-jeebies to many, wanted for crimes on the mainland.

This early setback did not faze Montefiore, and he built a fortune, he then put to good use. He became a key social reformer – Charles Dickens noted his work in his diaries – and campaigned to abolish slavery. He organised loans to pay off sugar cane producers – a vile thought, but at the time a vital piece of realpolitik needed to get the 1833 Slavery Abolition Act passed.

Accounts portray a humble man with a laugh in his heart, illustrated by the following story. Montefiore sat at a posh dinner next to a lord of the realm, who casually said he had recently returned from Japan, where they 'have neither pigs nor Jews'. Moses replied, 'In that case, you and I should go there, so they have a sample of each.'

Moses Montefiore's blue plaque.

THE HUNGER MARCHERS

From this nineteenth-century Park Lane philanthropist's abode we peer across the way to Hyde Park, the green space that has become, for Londoners, a huge open-air political talking shop.

When Wall Street crashed, the economic chill was quickly felt in London. By 1930, 250,000 men were on the dole in the capital. In 1931, hunger marchers led by the National Unemployed Workers Movement came from the north-west, a 2,000-strong contingent who were followed five years later by the famous Jarrow Crusade.

The Met were on standby. The NUWM's links with the Communist Party meant the police smelt trouble, and they were keen show they would be obliged to crack heads if the feeling took them.

There had already been clashes en route, and tensions raised by scaremongering in the right-wing press that suggested the marchers were possibly armed with cudgels, certainly armed with anger, and needed putting firmly back in their proper, servile places. The famous communist Wal Hannington could see what was coming, and he put the word out to Londoners also feeling the pinch.

Wal's call to arms saw 100,000 gather in Hyde Park on 27 October to welcome the marchers and ensure there was safety in numbers. The police did not get the message. Around 2,600 officers, many part-time bobbies made up of sorely inexperienced specials and the occasional thug in uniform looking for a leftie to vent his anger on, arrived and promptly began a running battle with anyone in their way.

Tensions remained high: Hannington spoke at a rally in Trafalgar Square later that week and once more police raised batons against those attending. The fighting stretched over a huge expanse of Westminster. Battles raged in Whitehall, Westminster Bridge and along the Embankment, west along The Strand, north to Charing Cross Road and east into Piccadilly.

Onwards then, from those fighting for equality to those who represent inequality in the Londoner's mind's eye. We head now into Mayfair, where we shall consider a particular facet of this neighbourhood.

Mayfair is tucked in (as if by a butler) between Park Lane, Oxford Street, Regent Street and Piccadilly. Home to the seriously wealthy, it has around

350 residences and nine out of ten employ full-time servants. Behind these stone façades, iron railings and original shutters, there are more people in domestic service today than in the Georgian period.

Our entry point is by the Dorchester Hotel, which leads to Hill Street. Recent research shows that households here have a minimum of four staff working full-time. Larger spreads – the £50 million mansions – enjoy a complement of nanny, butler, driver, gardener, maids, bodyguard, personal trainer and the glue to hold it together, the housekeeper.

At the eastern end of Hill Street, we come to Berkeley Square, a plane-tree'd space whose nightingale Dame Vera Lynn sang about. Today it's home to offices, supercar showrooms and the 250-year-old private members' club, The Lansdowne.

Jeeves, who for Wooster performed single-handedly all the jobs mentioned earlier while simultaneously getting his boss out of scrapes, was stationed with Bertie in Berkeley Mansions, Berkeley Square. The address is, however, a figment of PG Wodehouse's ticklish imagination.

Jeeves's imaginary stomping ground has not always been the sole preserve of the wealthy. At the turn of the nineteenth century, just 20 per cent of its 1,500 homes were owned by rich folk. Today the figure is nearer 90 per cent.

The Code of the Woosters.

TWEET TWEET, BRUM BRUM

Ah, Berkeley Square, where the possibility of hearing a nightingale sing is today drowned out by the revving of a supercar's engine. We shall recommence our wanderings from the steps of No. 44, a grand eighteenth-century mansion that is home to the Clermont Club, a thoroughly respectable place of which to be a member. But if we peer past the top-hat sporting, livery-strutting doorman and in thorough the impressively panelled front door, we are looking at the scene of some rather unsavoury practices in times past.

In the 1950s, this address was home to an underground card club, run by the eccentric John Aspinall. Remember, at this time you were forbidden to lay a bet anywhere but at a racecourse – so Aspinall found a steady stream of Mayfair-dwelling clientele who wanted to settle down with a good vintage, a gaggle of like-minded peers and fritter some paper away. Its membership roll was impressive – as well as lords, it was of the haunt of James Bond creator Ian Fleming and the billionaire businessman turned single-issue politician James Goldsmith.

But hidden behind Aspinall's charm and grace, something dodgy was afoot. His card players were unaware that Aspinall was working with the notorious gangster Billy Hill – and had hit on a wheeze, imported from Marseilles crooks, to fleece those at the tables.

The con worked like this: a deck of cards was run thorough a handheld mangle, which made miniscule alterations in the bend of each card. Resealed in cellophane, the doctored packs would then be dealt out to an unsuspecting guest, while a plant would come in, read the cards and win big.

The figures Hill and Aspinall took at 44 Berkeley Square were impressive: on their opening night, they scammed £14,000 – around £300,000 today. Their biggest score came in 1958, when they took more than £300,000 from the unfortunate Lord Derby, worth £7 million now. Aspinall spent his money wisely, using large sums to finance a growing collection of elephants, gorillas and rhinos.

LAUGHS AND THE ENLIGHTENMENT

Now we move north-west a few streets to Upper Grosvenor Street and it is here we will discuss the ongoing attraction of Sir Humphry Davy.

Ah, Davy! A poet scientist, a polymath who straddled the Georgian and Victorian periods and whose talents helped revolutionise London and the world. He lived at this address for forty years, and it was from here he gadded about town, enjoying a vigorous intellectual life coupled with plenty of partying.

The son of a Cornish woodcarver, not only did he push, push and push again against the limits of scientific knowledge, he did so with pizazz. At the Royal Institution, he used theatrics to bring alive a topic on the chemistry of manure, and made crop yields, tanning and dying sexy themes for discussion. Fiddling about in his laboratory could produce unexpected results: in 1799, he took a deep gulp of nitrous oxide, giggled a lot and decided to call it laughing gas. He recommended it to doctors as a handy anaesthetic – a suggestion they painfully ignored for some time.

His lectures drew huge audiences at the Institution's Piccadilly base, and he used them to highlight links between art and science, stating, 'The perception of truth is almost as simple as feeling the perception of beauty; and the genius of Newton, of Shakespeare, of Michelangelo and of Handel are not very remote in character from each other. Imagination, as well as reason, is necessary to perfection in the philosophical mind. A rapidity of combination, a power of perceiving analogies and of comparing them by facts is the creative source of discovery. Discrimination and delicacy of sensation, so important in physical research, are other words for taste; and the love of the magnificent, the sublime, and the beautiful …' Samuel Taylor Coleridge was so impressed by this eloquent scientist he told friends he went to hear Davy lecture to 'renew my stock of metaphors'.

Davy's impact lives on – and a mark of his reputation during his own time is that he was immortalised in music hall song. Charles Rice, 23, was an attendant at the British Museum during the day, and a pub and inn crooner at night. In 1837, he kept a diary, noting how he kept an eye on the Elgin Marbles between nine and five, before knocking off to swan about West End boozers at night. One of his more popular songs recalled Davy's place in the collected memory of Londoners a decade after he had died.

'What are mortals made of?,' sang Rice ...

By analyzation, I've tried all the nation;
defined each gradation, and proved every station;
with Sir Humphry's best, best chemical test;
And I've found out what mortals are made of!

THE NOBLE ART
AND NOBLE ARTISTS

Now, before we scoot northwards, we find ourselves by Park Lane, and it is here where we can consider the story of Gregson the Pugilist.

Lord Elgin, who had pinched the Marbles that our bar stool lyricist Rice gazed upon while dreaming up his ditties, had a house in Park Lane. It was here the priceless Greek antiquities, hacked from the walls of the Athenian Temple, lay while Elgin tried to chisel £76,000 in cash out of Prime Minister Spencer Perceval's government. Elgin would finally be successful in 1816, but only after accepting around half that fee for his stolen goods.

Gregson had a sideline away from the ring. He would pose for groups of gentlemen artists who wished to sketch his magnificent form. Contemporaries described him as being 'six feet two inches and all admired the beauty of his proportions', and he had plenty of takers. The sketchers, members of the Royal Academy, asked Gregson to take up a variety of classical Greek poses – the discus bloke, the muscle-flexing Apollo, the chap clasping a shield and javelin …

The life drawing session was a success, and it led to Gregson being invited to Lord Elgin's Park Lane garden, where he was asked to repeat the whole process in the nud and in front of the Marbles so flesh could be compared to stone. Such was the triumph of this second outing, the academicians repeated it a fortnight later – but this time invited four more boxers along to sketch before enjoying bouts between the models.

BEER, BLOOMERS, BALLOONISTS

And on that heady mix of physical prowess and sculptural beauty, we peer across into Hyde Park and imagine being on this spot exactly 170 years ago.

We would be gazing upon the Crystal Palace, the work of gardener-turned-architect Joseph Paxton, whose other claim to fame is that he cultivated the Cavendish banana, the most widely eaten type of the yellow, boomerang-shaped fruit sold today.

Work on the palace, which held The Great Exhibition, started in September 1850. It was a large job, and done in record time. Steam pulleys raised thousands of girders to hold the 900,000 panes of glass, and thousands of workers busied themselves creating the spectacle.

A steel engraving of the Crystal Palace, artist unknown, courtesy of the Wellcome Collection.

But as it ever was, is and always shall be, there were some teething issues. The palace leaked in rain storms, and thousands of sparrows took up residence. The birds could only be removed by poisoning them, an act that was met with disgust from the wider public.

Prince Albert, a prime exhibition advocate, came to visit as the building neared completion. A bell was rung as the prince approached, and 2,000 workmen downed tools. *The Times* reported that 'it was a remarkable spectacle to see so large a body of people approaching in so many different ways, some slipping down columns, others skipping along joists, and balancing themselves dextrously along girders'.

The reporter noted how the workmen hushed as the royal carriage approached – but before the Prince Consort drew up, a brewery waggon pulled by dray horses entered the site, with 250 gallons of beer. The workers realised it was a little thank you for them, and when the prince's carriage followed, he was treated to a particularly enthusiastic reception.

As well as those who had come to look at the global wonders held within, the palace attracted cranks, causes and chaos. A gang of 'Bloomers' invaded in September to lead a demonstration against the restrictive dress women were expected to wear. The Bloomers, named after feminist Amelia Bloomer, advocated wearing baggy trousers in a Turkish fashion, and the billowing cotton leg-coverings became a symbol for the fight for equal rights. Sadly, the Bloomers' attempts to rally support were met with hoots of derision.

Then there is the story of balloonists, the Grahams. A balloon was tethered by Batty's Hippodrome, at the northern end of the park. As Mr and Mrs Graham fired up the heater and lost ballast, the balloon snagged a post and a hole was torn. Still, the balloon went upwards in a jagged fashion, swaying as it rose and fell – and then made a beeline for the upper panes of the Great Exhibition. With metal anchors trailing, disaster was in store. As thousands gathered to watch, the Grahams chucked sandbags overboard – some crashing through the glass roofs – and the basket thumped its way through a length of flagpoles, causing further chaos. Thankfully they gained height, scraping the top of the palace as they did so, and were blown eastwards.

The Grahams's journey continued along Piccadilly, where they took down chimneys and gables, before coming to a precarious rest on a roof. The balloonists, thankfully, managed to scramble out to safety.

GETTING A HIDING
IN THE PARK

Hyde Park, of course, has always been a place for the discontented to rally, the beginning or end of many a protest and, of course, home to Speakers' Corner, the ultimate stage for many a Bar Stool Preacher, Free Thinking Philosopher or Alley Cat Rabble Rouser.

In that dark decade of the 1930s, Hyde Park's place in Londoners' collective psyche as a meeting point was cemented. Its open fields became a natural gathering spot for the advocates of the competing political philosophies of the period to meet in person. It offered the slim chance of changing the opinion of someone with diametrically opposing views, and if that wasn't possible, perhaps administering a bloody nose to make them think twice about spouting off in public again.

Later, at a National Unemployed Workers Movement demonstration, the fascist thug William Joyce – who became known as Lord Haw Haw for this wartime broadcasts from Berlin – took to a soapbox stage by the banks of the Serpentine and launched into his ugly shtick. In the crowd was a young Jewish woman named Esther Cohen, and after hearing Joyce spout forth his anti-Semitic nonsense, she decided she would like to shut him up.

The woman, who was quite the beauty, sweet-talked her way down to the front, and then past the thugs providing security back stage. Before Joyce's black-shirted henchmen could react, Esther strode up to Joyce and without pause delivered a swinging right hook to the bridge of his nose. As blood and gristle burst forth, and a commotion kicked off, Esther fled through the park, where she ran into friends and neighbours who had heard Joyce was around these parts and were coming down with a crew to see them off. Esther's antics spread like wildfire, and she was carried aloft on shoulders, surrounded by burly communists, past the fast-disbanding fascist rally in celebration.

We now leave the park and stop in Connaught Place. If you look at older buildings here, you will notice spacious first-floor balconies. A nice touch, one may think, offering a south-westerly aspect that captures the afternoon sun. Sadly, these balconies have a less innocent history. They were installed to allow clear views of the gallows at Tyburn, across the way.

The place has enjoyed its share of notables who have made it their home. Randolph Churchill, Winnie's father, who held numerous positions as a Tory MP, lived here. While Winston is known to have spent time covering the Boer War as a reporter, it is to Randolph's sister, Lady Sarah Wilson – who used Connaught Place as an occasional London base – that we turn now.

Lady Sarah followed her army officer husband to Mafeking, and was promptly caught in the siege by Boer troops. *Daily Mail* owner Alfred Harmsworth had seen his correspondent arrested by Boer soldiers as he had tried to sneak out to file a story. Harmsworth recruited Lady Sarah to send despatches, and her reports covered everything from the deprivations of life under siege to the spirit-raising Sunday afternoon bicycle races.

A little further along, we stop to consider another Connaught Place resident with connections to the African continent. It was here the fabulous Lady Idina Sackville lived, before heading to Kenya in the 1920s and becoming a key member of the so-called Happy Valley set – a group of colonists who formed a racy, debauched social whirl whose key aim was the pursuit of partying.

Idina became the byword for society shakers during the flapper period: she married five times. She went to Kenya with her husband, Lord Kilmarnock, in 1924 – and divorced in 1929 after she discovered he had been fiddling the family books as he fell into big, big, gambling debts.

Lady Idina's free-thinking approach to sex, drugs and jazz filled the newspapers, and her impact seeped into literature, too. James Fox's bestseller, the 1982 murder mystery *White Mischief*, is based on adventures in the Happy Valley set. Nancy Mitford was inspired to include a character called 'The Bolter', based on Lady Sarah, in three of her novels, and Evelyn Waugh's *Vile Bodies* was also influenced by what she got up to, and with whom.

EAT MY FEET

Let us pick up from our last stop, Connaught Place, and walk north into Connaught Square. It was here that the celebrated nineteenth-century ballerina Marie Taglioni lived between 1875 and 1876. She performed what was known as 'Romantic' ballet, and in her later years taught ballroom dancing to children and must-know steps to society ladies.

Taglioni is considered to be the first ballerina ever to dance fully 'en pointe' – a product of a tough training regime imposed by her father, the choreographer Filippo Taglioni.

Filippo sounds like a tiresome task master: his daughter had a slight stoop, so he made her work out rigorously, watching her hold every position while he counted to 100 during two-hour sessions in the morning and afternoon.

The esteem she was held in was such that after her last performance in Russia, her worn-out shoes were sold for 200 roubles, stewed in a thick creamy sauce and ceremonially eaten by a group of dedicated dance fans.

After the Second World War, this piece of Tyburnia – the gallows were where No. 49 now stands – lay half empty. Connaught Square's potential was noted by the property developing aristocrat Lady Colwyn, wife of Lord Colwyn, a notorious playboy who was court-martialled for 'acts of gross indecency' with youthful Italian men while serving in the Mediterranean.

Now, Lady Colwyn had become friendly with a builder by the name of Charlie Taylor, a Paddington wide boy with a range of interests, many of them on the wrong side of the law. He and his friends had numerous scams on the go during the 1930s, '40s and '50s. One such trick during the Second World War saw Charlie dress up in a suit, tie and bowler hat, and head into a furniture shop on the Harrow Road. He knew the shop was known for selling black market furniture – so he pretended to be a civil servant with a forged search warrant. When he came across the surplus household goods tucked away in a basement, he allowed himself to be bribed to keep quiet.

He also played the system, winning contracts to deal with bomb sites: he'd make up non-existent workers and claim wages from the government for them. It was one of many earners.

Having befriended Lady Colwyn – to the extent that he was having an affair with her behind the lord's back – Charlie won a contract to kit out the grand houses in Connaught Square. He'd agreed to supply fixtures and fittings, and made a hefty mark-up using reclaimed pieces from London's bomb sites. They included a job lot of boilers from West End hotels, which further bumped up the Paddington wide boy's cut.

Across the road from Connaught Square, we now peer down Portsea Place. Behind the door of No. 16 was the home of Olive Schreiner, feminist and vigorous anti-war campaigner during the Victorian period and into the Edwardian era. South African-born Olive was a political trailblazer, fighting for equality between the sexes and battling racism. As well as her numerous books, Olive's letters reside in archives at Edinburgh and Leeds universities.

The range is enormous, from personal correspondence between herself and doctor and social reformer Havelock Ellis, with whom she had a thirty-five-year love affair, to a letter penned to the *Evening Standard* in 1887, describing how late one night she was harassed by a policeman on her doorstep, 'He turned round shortly, and said, "What's going on here, what are you up to here?; I won't have this; what are you doing here?"' – and he threatened to haul her off to the nick if she didn't slip him a few bob.

'Someone who was expecting me opened the door and he slunk down the steps with the look of unsatisfied greed,' she noted. 'There are in London some hundred thousand women who are unable to defend themselves against the hands of the police.'

From Portsea Place, we cross the Edgware Road and head to Bryanston Square. It should be noted that many of the streets around this patch have Dorset place names – a legacy of land owner Henry Portman, who built the area and was born in that gentle county.

In 1936, it was where Wallis Simpson resided as she waited for Edward to hand back the bling to the Beefeaters, and during the Second World War these Georgian blocks were home to the US Army. The garden, whose railings had been removed as war-effort scrap metal, was used as a car park for the officers' Jeeps. The square today boasts a set of benches installed in 1954, and they are seats with a story: each is made from timbers gleaned from HMS *Iron Duke*, the flagship of the Royal Navy under Admiral Lord Jellicoe.

Jellicoe's career of campaigns included the Anglo-Egypt War and the Boxer Rebellion, before commanding the British fleet at the Battle of Jutland in the First World War. He was criticised for being too cautious – the British outnumbered their opponents, but did not destroy the German Navy.

Questions were asked whether the advantage should not have been pressed to win a victory akin to Trafalgar, although, as First Lord of the Admiralty Winston Churchill pointed out, if Jellicoe had misjudged it and the battle had been lost, so would the war.

It appears the famous battleship was recycled into numerous other objects: when the *Iron Duke* was scrapped in 1946, teak planks from on board found second lives as carved bookends – popular mementos no doubt for those who served on her. You can still buy them at antique auctions in the Home Counties for about £100 a pop.

WHEREFORE ART THOU?

Now we head one block east to Montagu Square. This address has been home to some marvellous types, including novelist Anthony Trollope, Ted Hughes and Ringo Starr, who bought No. 13. Jimi Hendrix moved in after the drummer, and at the start of their relationship John Lennon and Yoko Ono used it as a clandestine base.

A less well-remembered but equally fascinating resident was stinking rich amateur actor Robert 'Romeo' Coates, who lived at No. 28. Coates won fame for enjoying great confidence in his thespian abilities – so much so that he proclaimed himself as the best actor in Britain.

He loved playing Romeo, but his unique talents meant he struggled to pass auditions. No matter. Instead he poured a fortune into producing plays with himself cast in the lead role.

He sounds an unmitigated hoot – he would continuously forget his lines, filling scenes with made-up dialogue instead. He loved dramatic deaths, and would repeat such moments three times in one performance. His reputation meant he sold out theatres – audiences wanted to see if he was as bad as was claimed.

Robert Coates dreaming of his turn as Romeo by The Caricaturist General, 1812, The Wellcome Collection.

Coates believed he could improve Shakespeare: in one performance, he used a crowbar to pry open Capulet's tomb and changed the ending. One poor lead playing opposite him was so embarrassed she had to be carried off, while *The Times* reported theatregoers at a performance in Richmond needed medical treatment after laughing too much. It didn't help that he insisted on designing eccentric costumes, appearing in diamond-studded pantaloons that once split open to reveal more than you'd like to see on stage. Many believed Coates could not be so blind to his own failings, and was parodying the serious world of Georgian Shakespeare productions.

The theatre was, in a way, the death of him: he was a victim of a hit-and-run accident as he left the Theatre Royal, Drury Lane, and he died soon after, aged 76, at his Montagu Place home. A life lived well, bringing much joy to others.

A BRIEF VISIT TO
THE PICTURES

We leave Montagu Square to make our first port of call on nearby Edgware Road. We could spend a lifetime wandering along this street full of stories. Yet we won't dilly-dally on the way, as Marie Lloyd once sang at the long-lost Turnhams Music Hall, found further up the stretch. Instead, we pause briefly outside Nos 51 to 53.

Look carefully – you can still see telltale signs of the Gala Royal Cinema, an art deco offering from the late 1930s. By the 1960s it was known for its art house and European films, but dwindling audiences meant its programmers spent the 1970s screening increasingly dubious risqué flicks and its projector stopped whirring in 1979.

Its demise is a well-told tale along the Edgware Road, which once boasted five purpose-built cinemas. The street's reputation was such that, while we now associate Leicester Square as the epicentre of cinematic traditions, for Edwardians, Edgware Road was the place to go.

It all started with Montagu Pyke – a man whose notoriety deserves recalling (and whose name today blesses a pub in Charing Cross Road). Known as the 'Cinema King', Pyke cashed in on the craze for moving pictures and fleeced a lot of people in doing so. Along from where the Gala Royal would later be, he opened the Recreations Theatre in 1909. After a spell of people watching in the neighbourhood, he decided a cinema was worth a punt.

Later, he would describe the attraction of this new entertainment: 'It is appealing not only to men and women of every class, but to men, women and children of all ages. The Picture Theatre, if it has done nothing else, has brought delight to the minds and souls of thousands upon thousands of mites in this great Metropolis, some of whom look upon it as the one oasis in the desert of their dull and sordid lives.'

Pyke, whose previous jobs included commercial traveller, gold miner and unsuccessful stock market dabbler, had a talent for enticing investors. His cinemas soon dotted the capital. Unfortunately, he also had a penchant for dodgy book-keeping. In 1912, his business was exposed as a pyramid scheme – he used fresh investment to pay dividends and award himself a £10,000-a-year salary.

From here, we duck back into Marylebone and dawdle outside the glorious Seymour Street Baths and Laundry. Built in 1935 by St Marylebone Council, it boasted a roof copied from a seminal piece of 1920s Bauhaus-style design – an aircraft hangar with stunning, futuristic concrete arches at Orly, France.

Perhaps more useful for the working people who populated the area and lacked such amenities at home, architect Kenneth Cross included a state-of-the-art laundry and bathhouse. There were fifty slipper baths, twenty-five washing troughs, eight washing machines, fifty drying horses, mangles, ironing tables and even electric irons.

Now we head north, to Homer Row. It was here in 1916 that TS Eliot settled at Crawford Mansions, soon after completing his (first) landmark statement in modernist poetry – the publication of *The Love Song of J Alfred Prufock*. In poor J Alfred, Eliot created a tragic example of manhood, suffering from physical and intellectual apathy, struck by the emptiness of life and haunted by unfulfilled sexual desires.

ONE SOLUTION: REVOLUTION!

From Eliot's retreat we take in Cato Street, famous for the conspiracy named after this nondescript terrace. In 1820, Prime Minster Lord Liverpool had come to personify Establishment brutality – the Peterloo Massacre of 1819 meant revolution was in the air.

From Cato Street, radical Arthur Thistlewood hatched a plan to assassinate Liverpool and his Cabinet, hoping to replace the government with a 'Committee of Public Safety'. Thistlewood, a former farmer and soldier, had been radicalised travelling through France and the USA. He became a marked man on his return for his involvement in the Society of Spencean Philanthropists, named after radical thinker Thomas Spence.

Thistlewood was on the authorities' radar, having been charged with treason for attending a rally at Spa Fields, Islington, in 1816. Protesters at the meeting had planned to storm the Tower of London and the Bank of England.

He tried to flee to America but was arrested as he boarded a boat on the Thames. However, his trial collapsed as the prosecution relied on the testimony of a government spy with a criminal record, which did not impress the jury.

Thistlewood, with a bit of government-baiting cheek, then wrote to the Home Secretary, Lord Sidmouth, asking for £180, the price of three tickets to America, to be refunded. When Sidmouth failed to respond, Thistlewood challenged him to a duel – and earned a year inside for breaching the peace.

It did not reform him, and he became a key figure in the Cato Street Conspiracy. It transpired that those involved had been persuaded to act by George Edwards, apparently a fellow revolutionary with a firebrand tongue.

But Edwards was a police agent and the Bow Street Runners stormed their Cato Street base. Thistlewood escaped – after running an officer through with a sword – but was soon caught. He was hanged a month later at Newgate Prison.

There is another link to the Cato Street gang nearby – Castlereagh Street, named after Lord Castlereagh, who served in Liverpool's government. Deeply unpopular, Percy Shelley namechecked him in *The Mask of Anarchy*, his poetical response to the Peterloo Massacre.

Castlereagh never got to see Shelley's combustible take down. The poem wasn't published until 1832, ten years after Castlereagh had taken his own life after his enjoyment of same-sex carnal encounters were discovered. Shelley's poem had been spiked by *The Examiner* magazine, with the editor claiming the public would not be 'sufficiently discerning to do justice to the sincerity and kind-heartedness of the spirit that walked in this flaming robe of verse'.

STEAM PLAYER

From Castlereagh Street, Marylebone, we point our visages to the western sun and cross Edgware Road. As we do so, let us briefly cast our minds back to a spring day in 1829, and strain our ears to hear a puff-puff-puffing above the neighing of horses and the clatter of carriages. It was in this year that Edgware Road became a test track for a remarkable inventor, Dr Goldsworthy Gurney.

Gurney, who as well as being a mechanic earned a living as a surgeon from his Soho base, was fascinated by the idea of building a steam-powered carriage. Gurney had experimented with burning hydrogen and oxygen together – and by the late 1820s had decided the future lay in a personal, self-propelled form of transport.

He built himself a steam carriage in his garage in Albany Street, and set off up Edgware Road with the aim of reaching Bath (he made it). Travelling at a stately 10 miles per hour, he chugged past our present stop with a trailer attached to his contraption, which bore four passengers and extra coke to help keep the steam up.

Gurney would later give evidence to aParliamentary Select Committee in 1831, praising the virtues of his invention. But he faced a strong lobby from those in the horse and cart industry – the select committee was formed under pressure to consider how much of a nuisance this new-fangled idea would be, how they might affect the roads and what tolls should be levied if they were given permission to continue.

Gurney argued four wheels caused less damage than four hooves, and claimed that running the invention cost less than keeping a 'coach and four'. Oh, innocent days!

Now we dip into the area known as Tyburnia, further west of Edgware Road, and admire the architecture of Norfolk Crescent, and Oxford and Cambridge Squares. The area is named after the lost river that flows from the heights of Hampstead out west and snakes through the patch until meandering through royal parks and on to the Thames. These squares were laid out for the Church of England by Samuel Pepys Cockerell – the great-great-nephew of the diarist.

Cockerell had an eye for the fancy: his most-celebrated creation is Sezincote House, built for his brother out in Gloucestershire. It is festooned with Oriental imagery – inspiring John Nash, who built the Prince Regent his Brighton Pavilion.

Cockerell – who laid out much of Bayswater and then drew up a masterplan for the Tyburnia area for the Bishop of London – did not live long enough to see it completed. Instead, from 1827, surveyor George Gutch took over the scheme, and would remain district surveyor for the area for the next fifty years.

Much of the neighbourhood was laid out in a simplified grid system, except for one north-to-south stretch of streets. And the reason these the streets seem to have incongruous wiggles built into their route? Because they follow the now subterranean path of the old River Tyburn.

These glorious examples of late Georgian and early Victorian squares attracted a fair number of the well-heeled. Caricaturist and author George du Maurier lived at No. 17 Oxford Square in the late 1800s: du Maurier was known for his biting cartoons in the periodical *Punch*, and for penning the Gothic novel *Trilby*, which featured the character Svengali. Not only was he the grandad of the more famous writer Daphne, five of his grandsons are said to have been the inspirations for JM Barrie's *Peter Pan*. Du Maurier's neighbours included Queen Victoria's diplomat to both the Russian and Ottoman empires, Lord Currie.

Currie lived at Oxford Square with his wife, Mary Lamb, who wrote scandalous doggerel-like poetry under the pen name Violet Fane. The pair married in their 50s and had no children, meaning Lord Currie's title – he was made Baron Currie of Crawley for his services to the Empire – was never passed on.

And while many of the streets were sought after, attracting gentry, parts of Tyburnia soon slipped into acute poverty. Old Bailey court reports reveal some of the larger homes became known for prostitution from the 1830s, made worse when Paddington Station opened in 1854.

CANAL PURSUITS

The Grand Union Canal also made its presence felt. When Paddington Basin, a few streets north of the squares, opened in 1801, associated industries and warehouses soon sprang up. Contemporary reports describe hundreds of carts lining up each day to collect goods brought to London – causing tailbacks so acute they reached Hyde Park. *Plus ça change*.

Today, Paddington Basin is quieter: ringed by new homes, it also includes posh offices and eateries offering diners quayside meals. But a reminder of its industrial past can be found a street away, in Junction Mews.

Now a private home, a sign still informs you that the industrial-looking Boatman's Institute was founded here. Built in 1827, it was used as a meeting place and chapel for the men, women and children who plied their trades as longboat operators on the canal. The hard daily grind of canal life would be offset by the solid hot meals served there, the chance for a good wash and a gossip with others on the waterways.

Its design holds clues to the history of canal: strongly influenced by Dutch architecture, it boasts pitched roofs and decorated gable ends. Inside, vaulted ceilings add another Low Countries touch – and were a nod to the close trade with Holland and Belgium, as well as the influence of Dutch barges on the craft that plied the UK's waterways.

From the Boatman Institute in Junction Mews, Tyburnia, we head back to Paddington Basin. Today, its paved and patterned tow path is a very different look compared with its original purpose as a major depot for all manner of goods. Built in 1801, the basin was a hive of activity as boats from the Grand Union and Regent's Canal unloaded produce to then be taken along the New Road into central London.

The basin's current houseboats and floating cafe are, despite the swanky post-industrial look, nothing new. When the basin was built, there had been what historian Julian Dutton describes as 'an extraordinary tectonic shift' on the canals. Between 1780 and 1830, half a million people quit land living for life on the waterways, joining a long-established class of water traders like the Thames boatmen who lived aboard their places of work.

The approaches to the basin were full of bargees and their families pulling up for an overnight stay, and while moored they could buy sustenance from boats converted to provide cuts of meat and fill jugs from barrels of differing-strength ales. Such floating kitchens date from before the canal craze: as early as 1636, the entrepreneurial John Rooke applied for permission to open a floating eaterie on the Thames.

And today's vogue for non-work-related canal life, which features in Sunday supplements with clockwork regularity, is nothing new, either: it came to prominence in the late Victorian period, rising in parallel with the Arts and Crafts movement. This backlash to the grimness of the industrial age saw the houseboat as a refuge to the scolding conditions of city life.

And with this new breed of canal folk, the traditional artwork associated with barges and narrowboats was celebrated: a style associated with Romany culture boasted detailed brushwork that enjoys Louis XVII airs, alongside gentle floral and castle motifs. They remain the bargee's trademark today.

A less-attractive secret lies beneath the waters of this stretch of the Grand Union, which has had volunteers who help dredge the waters scratching their heads. They keep a chronicle of what they find and where.

Recently they noticed a strange, silvery reflection glinting out from beneath the silt. Closer inspection revealed thousands of cylinder containers, used to hold laughing gas. They cleared them up – but much to the volunteers' chagrin, they keep reappearing.

It is believed they are linked with secretive parties held nearby, as laughing gas has become a recreational drug in certain circles. Why those tidying up after such speakeasy shenanigans think it's OK to send the capsules to a watery grave rather than shove them in a bin is an ongoing cause of annoyance.

Moving on, let us consider how the coming of the railways put paid to canals as a primary form of transport, and turn our attention towards Paddington Station.

It was from Paddington that the first ever train to chug undergroundset off on 9 January 1863, along the new Metropolitan line. Built using the cut-and-cover method, it ran beneath the New Road as it headed to Euston and King's Cross.

That first underground passenger train was described by *The Times* as enjoying a 'degree' of comfort. 'The novel introduction of gas into the carriages is calculated to dispel any unpleasant feelings which passengers, especially ladies, might entertain against travelling for so long a distance through tunnel,' a correspondent reported. 'The gas burnt brightly and, in some cases, turned on so strong that when stationary, newspapers might be read with facility; but in motion the draught created so much flickering as to render such a feat extremely difficult ...'

The writer also noted that, despite assurances that travellers would not be engulfed by the engine's polluting vapours, at times the interiors were 'enveloped in steam and subjected to the unpleasantness of smoke'.

FUNK SOUL BROTHERS

Praed Street, where you will find the entrance to the station, is also home to a nice footnote in the history of London's jazz-soul-funk scene.

It was the blistering hot summer of 1976, and the popular funk band Hi Tension were on stage at the Q Club – a club on Praed Street established in 1962 by Count Suckle, sound system proprietor and Jamaican émigré who became a key figure in London's Black music scene.

In the audience was Johnnie Jackson, a cousin of the Jackson family, and he took Hi Tension back to a Mayfair hotel to meet the family singers. According to bassist Camelle Hinds, four of the Jacksons were very amiable over drinks – but Michael would 'only talk to his brothers in this little voice. But can you imagine what this meant to us as a young Black band? This was the biggest young Black band on the planet, and they were talking to us.'

The Q Club was the creation of the famous Count Suckle, and that Suckle should have played a part in such a meeting is par for the course in terms of his career. His influence can still be felt, reverberating through west London streets whenever anyone turns on a car stereo.

Born in 1931 with the name Willbert Augustus Campbell, he grew up in the slums of Kingston. As a youngster, he soaked up the sounds of downtown Kingston and became a figure in the early sound system culture of the city.

He would wait harbourside in Kingston for American sailors to disembark, and buy up whatever rhythm and blues records they had. Later, he would run an import business, providing DJs with the latest music by Black artists in America.

In 1952, Suckle decided his fate lay away from the hardships of Trench Town, and he and a his friend, Vincent Forbes, snuck aboard a ship full of bananas destined for England.

He and Forbes settled in Ladbroke Grove, and were to become pioneers in London sound system culture. Forbes, who would take the stage name Count Vin, was working as a cleaner for British Rail and earning £5 a week. One day, a couple of years after arriving in west London, he saw something for sale at Portobello Market that would prove to be a very wise investment.

As he recalled in an interview before his death in 2014, 'One morning I came down Portobello Road and I see a box with a 10-inch speaker in it. I gave a man

265

£15 for it. I had an amplifier made for £4. Then two guys asked me to use this for a party.'

Vin showed up at a party – he was paid £5 for his troubles – and played music that touched a nerve with his fellow homesick Jamaicans. Before long, Vin was much in demand. 'Sometimes until 12 o'clock the next day – until police came to stop it. But I was just thinking to liven up the place.'

Inspired by Vin, Campbell changed his name to Count Suckle and became a regular DJ at private shebeens and community dances. It wasn't all plain sailing: in 1958, as Teddy Boys stalked Notting Hill streets with violent, racist intentions, Suckle nearly lost his life when a party he was playing at was firebombed.

Suckle had had enough of police busts and far-right aggro. He got a gig in the fully licensed Carnaby Street's Roaring Twenties Club, where he smashed the dance floor to pieces with a mix of never-heard-before R'n'B from Chicago, St Louis and elsewhere, and then 7-inch cuts he had been sent by his friends Prince Buster and Duke Reid, ska pioneers who were at that time rocking the dances he had left behind in Kingston.

Suckle played a part in breaking down barriers. His ten-hour ska DJ marathons prompted the Roaring Twenties owners to welcome Black clubbers, something unheard of at the time. The house band boasted both Georgie Fame on the keyboards and Led Zep bassist John Paul Jones. It soon became a hotspot for 1960s beat groups like the Stones and The Who. It was also here that John Profumo spent evenings dancing suggestively with Christine Keeler and Mandy Rice-Davies.

The central London location, however, meant it became an easy target for the notorious West End vice squad, who would demand adherence to whatever they fancied with menaces (boiling down to lining the coppers' pockets), and fed up with his friends being hassled, Suckle moved to a former snooker hall in Praed Street (hence the original name, Cue Club).

Here, he gradually moved from ska and R'n'B to soul and funk music, with Marvin Gaye, Tina Turner, Stevie Wonder and the Commodores all appearing.

THE ROAD
RUNS STRAIGHT

Now we move north-west along the towpath and peer into Warwick Crescent, once described as the worst slum in west London. Built in 1852 by builder William Buddle, the original houses were eventually demolished by the GLC in 1966.

Yet despite – or perhaps because of – its reputation, it attracted literary types. It was home to poet John Browning for many years, and Katherine Mansfield lived at Beauchamp Lodge, a hotel for musicians, in 1907. Mansfield, who would become friends with DH Lawrence and be a key figure in the Bloomsbury Group, entertained scribes at the lodge. It would later host a boys club in the 1940s and '50s, activities including table tennis, boxing, football, camping and singing.

The area around Warwick Crescent developed slowly, a place of scattered cottages in the 1700s. The number of pubs, a sign of homes being built, went from a single alehouse in 1552 to just three by 1760, when the nicely named Three Jolly Gardeners opened for business.

It was not so jolly for those who found themselves residing at Brindley Street, along the road from the Gardeners – it was home to the Paddington workhouse. Built in 1845, with separate wings for men and women, it developed a reputation that was unenviable even for such a place. Its beadle, who went by the name of MacIntyre, was accused in 1861 of various acts of violence against those under his care. Before he could be questioned, he disappeared, along with the workhouse funds. There were rumours, which were never confirmed nor dismissed, that he had not absconded but been done in by furious workhouse residents, and then his weighted body thrown into the canal and the contents of the cash box divided among those who had felt the lick of his belt.

At the outbreak of the First World War, the building became a military hospital, caring for soldiers who had lost limbs. Eventually, it was taken over by Paddington Hospital and it closed in 1986. The workhouse buildings, pictures of which show it as austere, tall, brick blocks with pitched roofs, gave off a vibe of Victorian sternness. They have since been demolished.

Now, doubling back on ourselves a little, we continue walking the stretch of streets that come off the Edgware Road. Like the decorated branches of a Christmas tree jutting out from the trunk, the bauble and tinsel represent the tales we shall stop and share.

Our journey has meandered and wriggled to and fro – unlike the Edgware Road, which runs straight as an arrow for 10 miles. The reason for its course goes way back to the Roman invasion of these isles in AD 43.

This messy thoroughfare was once a track surrounded on both sides by the great Middlesex Forest. It started in Dover and ended in Wales, cutting through this immense wooded expanse on its way. When the Romans moved in, they named it Watling Street – and it's no-nonsense sense of direction owes a debt to the Ancients, who wished to get from A to B, ASAP.

This forest, which would be enveloping us if we stood on this spot 1,000 years ago, sounds rather marvellous. It spread for 20 miles outside the city walls, and after the Norman invasion, William the Conqueror liked the look of it, and no wonder – it was described in the 1100s as being 'a vast forest, its copses dense with foliage concealing wild animals – stags, does, boars, and wild

William the Conqueror.

bulls'. Its bountifulness was recorded in the *Domesday Book*, where it stated that the woods could support 20,000 herds of swine.

Later, King Henrys I and II granted those living in the City of London the right to hunt there, but Henry III was not such an accidental permaculturalist as his forebears. Under his reign, a period of deforestation and selling off parcels of land marked the beginning of the privatisation of what was once public property, and which is the basis of the yoke of modern ownership we toil under today.

Right – let's stop in St Mary's Churchyard, and gaze at the Georgian church, perched defiantly against the roar of the Westway. Modelled on the shape of a Greek cross, it opened in 1791. It is here we see the tomb of the sculptor Joseph Nollekens, who honed his talent in Rome as a young man. As well as creating his own pieces, he restored works by Michelangelo.

Back in London, he made a living in the tomb and memorial trade, as well as making beautiful busts of all the great and good of the period. As was the vogue, he'd kit them out in classical clothing. It makes for a funny image if transposed to today: politicians having sculptures of themselves in togas. You can imagine this would appeal to some of the current members of the House.

He made a fortune – a bust of William Pitt was copied seventy times and each sold for a pretty penny – but along with his success came a certain reputation. Nollekens was notorious for his eccentric behaviour and grotesque stinginess.

After his death, at which he left an estate of £200,000, a scathingly honest biography was written by his one-time student, John Thomas Smith. Smith, who was a member of that unique club who can claim to have been born in the back of a hackney carriage, had studied under Nollekens for a time. One can only speculate what happened, and why later in life Smith was brutal in his warts-and-all portrait of the artist. In 1828, his book was variously described as full of 'malicious candour and vivid detail', and 'perhaps the most candid biography ever published in the English language', as he laid it on thick about what a miser Nollekens was.

Smith, who would forget his dreams of being a sculptor and turned to the study of antiquities (earning the rather nice nickname of Antiquity Smith), became friendly with a young John Constable and helped him get started. Maybe Smith was also not the easiest to get along with, and the blame for his short and unsuccessful tenure with Nollekens was partly his fault? He would later have a public spat with writer John Hawkins over a book they had hoped to collaborate on. Accusatory letters from both belligerents were published, and show Smith in a rather antagonistic light.

PAY BY THE PANE

Now for an altogether happier art-related halt. We're on the corner of Chapel Street and Edgware Road, and we're going to admire the work of sculptor Allan Sly. Called 'The Window Cleaner', it's a bit of bronze fashioned into the image of a George Formby-esque cheeky chappy.

Completed in 1990, the piece was Allan's first really big public commission, and if you stand on the shoulder of Allan's cleaner and follow his gaze, you'll see he is looking with incredulity at a soaring tower block covered in glass. No wonder he has that grimace on his face.

Let us linger briefly outside The Heron pub, in Sussex Gardens. It's home to what are known by members as 'graspable extremities', a name that refers to the moustaches they boast. As well as getting together for a pint and a laugh, members of the Handlebar Club, formed in 1947, share tips on things like wax brands and trimming techniques.

And you don't have to have a handlebar 'tache to enjoy the fun – they have a special club for Friends to show their support and respect for those who find themselves at a place in life's journey where sporting a 'bar seems the right thing to do.

'The Window Cleaner'.

From the spectacular 'taches of Sussex Gardens, let us cross Edgware Road, and on to Old Marylebone Road. We have no way of verifying the following snippet, but it's too good not to share – apparently, Old Marylebone Road is the only street in Britain to have a completely unique name. There are Foggy Bottom Lanes all over the world, it seems, but only one Old MR.

The Old MR earned its moniker because the new-ish Marylebone Road can be found 50 yards north. It was London's first ever bypass, built in the 1700s to cut congestion and steer through traffic away from the well-heeled town houses of Mayfair. The Old MR once led on to a place called Marylebone Circus – a wheel-jostled junction that in its day was as well known and important as any of the other London circuses – Piccadilly, Ludgate, Oxford, etc. There's no evidence another existed.

It was here that a quiet revolution in road use took place in 1935. A little shed-like box could be found in Marylebone Circus, the intersection of what is now Marylebone Road and Baker Street, and inside sat someone whose title was 'traffic integrator'. Their job was to monitor a set of twenty detectors set into the roads that counted the number of axles that went over them. Mr or Mrs Integrator spent their working day going through the figures minute by minute – and then pressing buttons and pulling cranks to operate traffic lights, giving roads with heavier flow more time to get across or on to Marylebone Road. It is considered the first computer-operated traffic light system of its type in the world and cost a hefty £40,000 to install.

TROUBLED TIMES

Now a hop and skip north, to Balcombe Street, a name that has gone down in history for tragic reasons. It was here that four members of the IRA held a couple, John and Sheila Matthews, hostage for six days in 1975.

The gang – Hugh Doherty, Eddie Butler, Harry Duggan and Martin O'Connell – were part of a Republican active service unit, and had been involved in bombings and shootings on London streets. Their capture came down to their penchant for returning to places they had already attacked to commit a second act of terror. Detectives noticed this pattern – and sent plain-clothes officers to keep an eye out for suspicious activity near previous targets.

The group had thrown a bomb through the window of Scott's Restaurant, in Mount Street, Mayfair, in November 1975. The device killed a diner, and caused serious injuries to others. The gang was spotted returning in a stolen car, pulling up outside and firing guns indiscriminately into the restaurant. A chase entailed – and the Republicans were cornered after breaking into the Matthews's home, hoping to find a place to lie low. It was reported that the poor couple were watching an episode of *Kojak* on the TV, and didn't realise the gun shots they were hearing were coming from outside their flat and not the trademark Saturday night action sequences from the popular detective series.

The IRA unit would receive forty-seven life sentences at their Old Bailey trial – and used their moment in the dock to try and get other crimes added to their charge sheets. O'Connell told the court as he was sentenced that he and his friends were also responsible for bombings in Woolwich and Guildford, crimes for which the Guildford Four had been convicted.

They instructed their lawyers to raise the offences, but no action was taken. The Guildford Four – Carole Richardson, Gerry Conlon, Paul Hill and Paddy Armstrong – spent another fifteen years inside. O'Connell told the court: 'We have instructed our lawyers to draw the attention of the court to the fact that four totally innocent people are serving massive sentences for three bombings, two in Guildford and one in Woolwich, which three of us and another man now imprisoned, have admitted that we did.'

THE SOOTY WICKET

Now we walk one street west and gaze at the terracotta façade and the iron and glass canopy of Marylebone Station. It is the youngest of London's major termini, opening in 1898, long after its steam-choked compatriots.

The plans for another line into town caused controversy. The influential Marylebone Cricket Cub, based at nearby Lord's, argued the train tracks and station were too close to their hallowed ground for comfort. The Great Central Railway Company got embroiled in a costly legal argument, and while they finally won the day, it ate into their budget and delayed things sufficiently to make it an issue for the directors.

It is said Marylebone's rather cute, villagey station feel was due to the man behind the scheme, the great railway entrepreneur, Sir Edward Watkin, running into cash flow problems because of the batters and bowlers of the MCC. Watkin had built railways all around the world by this point in his career, and was getting on a bit. Yet he still had big ideas and schemes he wanted to pursue. He saw his new London terminus, which brought carriages in from the Midlands and north of London Home Counties, as a starting point for another grand project – a rail link down to the south coast and then into a tunnel that would take trains over to France.

He was also responsible for attempting to build a giant, eight-legged iron behemoth on the site of what is now Wembley Stadium. Inspired by the Eiffel Tower, Watkin poured a fortune into his own iron folly, but his chosen location was soggy underfoot and the foundations squelched into the mud.

Eventually, two years after Watkin had died, the iron edifice, which had barely got above 150ft, collapsed. Never mind, Sir Edward – your legacy is a beautiful late Victorian station, whose unimposing branch-line feel has made it much loved by Londoners.

St Marylebone.

THE LIFE OF BRAIN

L ike so many heartbroken lovers, we have said our farewells on the glorious
forecourt of St Marylebone Station, but unlike the star-crossed variety,
we are in good fettle as we head from there gently eastwards to stop briefly at
St Cyprian's, the turn-of-the-twentieth-century church in Glentworth Street.

St Cyprian – which happens to also be the name of the awful prep school
a young George Orwell attended – was an early Christian scholar and bishop
in the city of Carthage, where Hannibal sprang from. He protected Christians
against persecution by Romans in what is now Tunisia.

The church that bears his name was built by a man with a moniker that
tickles surely even the most rigid of face: Sir Ninian Comper. Known as the
last of the great Gothic Revivalists, as well as creating this marvellous little
church, he designed stained glass windows for Westminster Abbey (his ashes
are scattered beneath them).

Comper, who would live till the ripe old age of 96, saw his studio hit by
a bomb in the Second World War. He clambered among the debris, rescuing
draughts and pictures, stamping out smouldering bundles of papers, and
relocated to a small shed in his garden, previously used by his son, Nicholas,
to design aircraft.

From Comper's delicate backstreet masterpiece, we head along the grander
edges of Regent's Park until we reach that hallowed institution, the Royal
Academy of Music, which is the oldest conservatoire in the world and now
found set back off Marylebone Road. Founded in 1822, and originally based
in Hanover Square, Mayfair, it moved to its current premises in 1911. George
IV gave the academy a royal charter in 1830, and its alumni range from Henry
Wood, Harrison Birtwistle and Simon Rattle to John Dankworth, Annie
Lennox and Elton John.

With such a long and celebrated history, it's hardly surprising its library
houses more than 160,000 items, ranging from early music manuscripts to
medieval instruments. Luckily, some of these 160,000-odd items are not
tucked away out of sight, they are on display inside the academy's museum.

While we're here, let's pop inside and gaze at the damaged horn once owned
by the great Dennis Brain. Brain, who descended from a great line of horn
players, had been told by his family not to go near the instrument until he was

into his late teens, as the mouth and diaphragm were still maturing. Instead, he learnt the piano and other musical must-knows to prepare himself.

By the age of 21, he was the first horn in the National Symphony Orchestra, but was then conscripted as war broke out. Like the Boogie Woogie Bugle Boy From Company B, he was drafted but allowed to find time to play – he joined the Central Band of the Royal Air Force and travelled to British bases around the world with the orchestra to remind troops of what they were fighting for. He was lauded by composers – Benjamin Britten wrote *Serenade for Tenor, Horn and Strings* in 1943 in anticipation Brain's return from service.

Brain was known for being wonderfully careless, his horn was bashed and battered as he swung it about during gigs, dumped it roughly on train luggage racks, RAF transport planes and the backs of army lorries, and generally lived the lifestyle of a gigging musician with his horn in tow. Britten would even give him two copies of each score, aware that one may be left on a bus or in the loo.

Known as 'The Genius Who Tamed The Horn', Brain sounds a lot of fun. He became friends with the legendary artist and musician Gerard Hoffnung and the pair got up to musical mischief together, with Hoffnung meeting Brain for strolls around Regent's Park, ending up with a concert at the academy.

Hoffnung had been sent to London by his German Jewish parents in the 1930s, and after attending Highgate School and the Hornsey and Harrow colleges of art, became a much sought-after illustrator and cartoonist. His other love was classical music, and much of his humorous penmanship was based on inventing new instruments out of household bits and bobs.

In 1956 Brain chose to perform at one of Hoffnung's alternative music festivals that celebrated his hilarious designs for musical instruments. Brain took a piece of hosepipe, trimmed it with garden shears to tune it, and performed a rendition of a Leopold Mozart horn concerto.

The horn on display at the academy, however, has an air of tragedy behind it. Brain was not only a skilled musician, but a man with the need for speed. He was a car enthusiast, and would place a copy of *Auto Trader* on his music stand to skim through during rehearsals when the horn parts weren't scored for action. On a wet night in September 1957, Brain was heading home in his Triumph sports car after playing in Edinburgh. As he sped down the A1, he lost control and spun off the road, into a tree. He died from his injuries, aged just 36.

The academy is situated on the corner of Macfarren Place – named after the Victorian composer who joined the academy aged just 16 and would eventually teach there. George Macfarren had a lifelong problem with his eyesight and would eventually become blind, but it did not stop his productivity as a composer. He employed friends to help him with his scores and get down the music in his head onto paper. Macfarren lived – and died – in Hamilton Terrace, St John's Wood. It is said he would walk to work each morning via as many of Westminster's squares as possible, and pause to listen to birdsong.

Sir George would memorise what he heard during the dawn chorus and then over a morning coffee at the academy he would challenge himself to write down the notes from different bird species, before asking a handily placed student, no doubt heading past his office door on their way to a lecture, to play the notes on whatever instrument they had tucked under their arm.

FLYING THE FLAG
AT WINDSOR

L eaving the Royal Academy of Music, just off Marylebone Road, with the stories of brass players ringing in our ears, we'll head north a little, following the curve of John Nash's marvellous Regent's Park terraces, and stop for a quick livener to get the circulation going.

We briefly popped in to say hello to the members of the Handlebar Club at The Windsor Castle in Crawford Place and we shall now stop for refreshment at another Windsor Castle. There are lots of places with this name round and about – too many in the UK for the internet to count accurately, a quick search online suggests.

Anecdotally, there are a few nearby: another WC can found in St John's Wood, another in Kilburn, and then it appears there are more and more as you head out towards west London and up the Thames Valley until you reach Windsor itself. This royal borough, one suspects, has nothing but pubs with that name.

Sadly, a personal favourite, the Windsor Castle in Camden Town, has been turned into a burger joint. Still, there are plenty more to choose from if you like the name.

This Castle, which would offer Winston Churchill a quiet spot by the fire to warm himself after a stroll through Regent's Park, dates from the Georgian period and enjoys a beautiful curved façade. It opened in 1826 and its first publican was Joseph Spicer, whose trade was described as victualler. His name rests in the books of the Sun Fire Office records – an insurance firm that provided a private fire brigade for subscribers. He lasted seven years at the pub before handing on the business to a John Flowers, who in turn, it appears, gave the pub to his daughter, Jane Brooks Flowers, in 1839.

The longest tenant appears to have been a man called B Worth, whose name is prefixed with the word 'German'. The records do not make it clear if this is his first name, or a reference to his country of origin.

German B Worth, as we will call him, took on the place in the 1880s, a period when many people of German origin worked in the London brewing industry. It is telling that his name disappeared from the register in 1915, suggesting he passed the pub on to escape the anti-German feeling directed towards businesses as a result of the Great War. Records show that many other German-named firms and pub owners in Westminster removed their names – or anglicised them – from 1914 onwards.

This lovely building is part of John Nash's vision for Regent's Park, and while we think of his grandiose terraces, his attention to detail was such that the pubs are worthy of attention, too.

It wasn't just buildings that Nash was keen to make as good as possible – a shimmy from the Windsor and we come across his Grade II-listed western entrance into the park, known as Hanover Gate.

One can wonder at what Nash was day-dreaming about as he lazily sketched out the early drawings for this wonderful piece of Baroque folly. It has painted stucco on its frontage, rises two storeys and includes porches for classical statues. It's a rather nice place for the gateman to spend his days, nodding at horses and carriages entering the Regent's dandified open space.

HOW THE WAR WAS WON

Now we duck into the backstreets between Regent's Park and Edgware Road. As we stroll down Hatton Street, we turn to peer at a pretty-looking sign on the side of a wall of a rather outlandish art deco, coloured-tiled building for the neighbourhood.

The plaque reads: 'The Old Aeroworks, 1912–1984. These buildings built in the 1920s were occupied by the Palmer Tyre Company who produced wheels, tyres, brakes and gun turrets that were fitted to wartime Spitfires, Hurricanes, Wellington and Lancaster fighter and bomber aircraft. The company continued aerospace research and development in this building until 1984.' This declaration is surrounded by splendid black and white mosaic tiling depicting the types of aircraft that used the parts made within.

The building was taken over by the architect Sir Terry Farrell in the mid-1980s to create an office for his practice and studios for other creative types. He built a penthouse for himself on the top floor, adding plenty of nods to the building's former life, such as shiny propellers hanging from roof struts.

The building started out as a furniture-making hub for the firm Bovis. The house-building company employed scores of joiners to knock out furniture, cupboards, kitchens and the like for their new developments. But in 1940, when the Palmer Aeroworks in north-east London was hit in a raid during the Blitz, the government took over the building. Instead of interiors for ribbon development housing, engineers moved in.

And the Palmer aero engineers are one of those many groups of unsung war heroes. As well as making lots of bits and pieces for a range of RAF planes, they invented and patented the 'Palmer Cord Aero tyre and wheel rim', which was the first ever pneumatic aircraft tyre not to burst on landing, thus making aviation safer and saving countless lives.

TRADING PLACES

Now for some more refreshment alongside more architectural wonders. We head into Church Street, and swing into The Traders Inn. Opened in 1839, this lovely pub still has echoes of those who have swilled back pints in her, and in a good way.

Once managed by the Watney Combe & Reid firm, it enjoys the company's exquisite, historic branding inside. That means examples of historic mirrors galore – the Watney workers loved a mirror – and if you look around you carefully, you can still spot other features such as original panelling and ornate wooden columns.

Perhaps the nicest of the lot is a stained glass sash window that was installed when the pub first opened. The window features an image of a watermill and another of the miller's cottage – very rustic. Does it perhaps speak of the River Tyburn that flows beneath the ground nearby? To its left is a slightly younger but no less lovely Guinness mirror, representing the other type of liquid flowing in these parts.

On that note, chin up, down the hatch and cheers.

Suitably refreshed by the stained glass windows and the amber glass pint pots of The Traders Inn, we step out on the corner of Church Street, the market stretching out in front of us.

The Traders Inn.

First, a bit of background. Dating from the 1790s, fields to the north were used as a hay market from around 1830, and soon traders selling vegetables and whatnot joined in. Its success was such that developers wanted a piece of the action, and Portman Market was built, named after land owner Sir William Portman, with an eye to rivalling Covent Garden. Its high ambitions never came to fruition, and in 1906 the market was sold off to become a car and lorry depot. But the traders weren't giving up so easily, and the rising population wanted a place to shop – so they set up their stalls in Church Street instead, and there they remain to this day.

As well as food and perishables and household goods, Church Street became home to bric-a-brac and antiques sellers. In the 1960s, a flea market-style air was apparent alongside the spuds, fish and meat. Eventually, the former Jordan's department store was taken over by Alfie's Antiques – offering space for nearly 100 different traders.

It was through this market the writer and illustrator Geoffrey Fletcher wandered, and recorded in his seminal London social history work, *The London Nobody Knows*.

For such a Londonphile, Fletcher was, perhaps surprisingly, born in Bolton in 1923. He moved to the city to study art at the Slade, and after graduating, began illustrating column breaks for the *Manchester Guardian* in 1950, and then moved to the *Telegraph*. Under the pseudonym Peterborough, which is still used today, he wrote and illustrated a diary column for three decades.

The London Nobody Knows.

Church Street Market.

Church Street Market.

Architecture, the townscape and how we interacted with our streets was part of his passion: documenting what he saw with his artist's eye and writer's words gave flesh to this. Fascinated by the rapidly disappearing Georgian and Victorian parts of the city, those buildings not yet deemed worthy enough for preservation, he set about recording them and raising awareness of what was being lost.

In 1962, *The London Nobody Knows* was published and its words and illustrations touched a deep nerve. Many recognised the changes Fletcher highlighted, and it helped kick-start a debate about what progress and the city scape actually meant. It would later be transferred to screen, with a marvellous voiceover provided by James Mason.

Watching Mason recite Fletcher's words – and the footage of the Church Street traders, which you can find online – is a haunting experience. It is so close – within a generation and within living memory – but feels so far off.

'The street markets still have a certain Victorian boisterousness. They are London's free entertainment,' Mason says. 'One of the best of them is here,' he continues, standing in the middle of Church Street while leaning suavely on a brolly. 'A nice quiet street, you may say … but you should see it on a Saturday.'

BREAKER-BREAKER
TEN-FOUR

From the memories of Mason and Fletcher, we leave Church Street behind and now go on to Edgware Road. We shall pause for a moment and see if we can detect the ghostly crackle of static, the hum of an amp, and the whispered codes of 'Romeo Alpha Delta India Oscar' buffs.

Once this stretch was the haunt of radio hams and hi-fi geeks: home to such celebrated stores as Henry's Audio and Lee Electronics, Electro-Tech and the famous HL Smiths, which had towering, tottering shelves packed with dusty old valve amps. Then there was Marshalls, known for its transistors, while Technomatic was forerunner of the computer age: your correspondent's older brother bought a ZX Spectrum over the counter in the early 1980s, while they also sold DIY microprocessors.

Henry's was the place for this writer, an Aladdin's cave of components that you never knew you needed but suddenly became just the thing. It began life in 1948, a little to the west on the Harrow Road, before opening a branch here.

As well as the hi-fi parts and the speaker cones, the woofers, tweeters, amps and valves, the miles of cabling, the disco lights and the CB radio dashes, you'd find those little, everyday things that before the dominance of online retail were heaven-sent to be picked up in a high street shop. One reviewer of Henry's remembered how he found an exact replacement intercom box for a block of flats built decades ago among their shelves.

Lee was mainly aimed at the radio ham, shifting portable personal radios. Those pre-mobile phone days saw the airwaves inhabited by those who enjoyed building radios and gassing away into the ether, but they were also used by minicabs, vets and others.

Sadly these shops are gone, and the reasons behind their demise are interesting. Much of the supplies at places like Henry's or Lee came originally from surplus government stock. In the same way army surplus clothing stores such as Laurence Corner in Euston traded in the gear made during the Second World War and into the Cold War, electronics stores did a good trade taking on both Ministry of Defence cast-offs, manufacturing surpluses and defunct projects.

Edgware Road hi-fi stores.

Edgware Road was also well placed for light industries in London to sell up what they had spare – as we have already seen, an aircraft component factory was based just a block away. Nowadays, factories are more precise with their output, and much has moved to places where wages are low – cutting out a vital supply line for those old electronic bazaars. Added to this, the customer base has dwindled; building things from scratch is not the pastime it once was, while high street rents mean component sellers may as well do it online from a front room.

PLAYS IN THE ROUND
AND THE GENEROSITY
OF OLD MAN MACTAGGART

From nostalgic musings on the cluster of old radio ham and sound system shops that could be found there, we're ducking back off the main fare and walking to Gateforth Street, to marvel at the little cultural gem that is the Cockpit Theatre.

Built by the Inner London Education Authority in 1969 – oh for those progressive days! – it's interesting for a number of reasons. Designed by architect Edward Mendelsohn, it was originally called the Gateforth Street Youth Arts Centre. It's snappier title, adopted a decade after its opening, references the famous West End seventeenth-century theatre that also doubled up as a cock-fighting ring.

Our Cockpit was the first theatre to be built 'in the round' – meaning with an audience forming a circle with the players in the middle – since the Great Fire of London. In the early 1970s, London Weekend Television took over the space to film a music show called – wait for it – *In the Round*, presented by BBC2's first head of music and arts, the pioneering broadcaster Sir Humphrey Burton. Marc Bolan rocked out there in 1972 and today it is a full-time theatre, and remains a hands-on training space.

Now we head a few streets north to pause outside a classic St John's Wood mansion block, Grove End House. This area is interesting for its city-living designs. London had not been big on apartment blocks as other European cities had in the nineteenth century, but the idea started taking root around the turn of the twentieth. Buyers sought modern efficiency – and less need for domestic help – but with a sense of opulence. Design issues were based on Edwardian ideas of behaviour; it wouldn't do to have the dining room too far from the kitchen, but the bathroom must also be accessible without any guests having the uncomfortable experience (apparently) of walking past one's bedroom to wash one's hands.

Once such niceties were dealt with, there was a mansion-block-building boom and St John's Wood was at its centre.

Builder Abraham Davis was a key player. His father, Wolf, had been in the tailoring trade in Whitechapel and he and his six sons started building shops and housing in the East End. Abraham would eventually be responsible for more than 2,000 flats in the immediate vicinity of where we currently stand.

As we gaze at Grove End House, a classic example of this type of project (although GEH dates from the 1930s), there is a lovely story behind its front door, all about 'the man who made Glasgow bathroom conscious', according to a mid-century Whitehall enquiry into living standards.

Glasgow-born John Mactaggart was the son of a coppersmith. After leaving school he got a job in a timber yard and over the next ten years built 1,500 high-quality homes for working people before setting out on his own.

By 1900, his genius at prefabricating units was married with a philanthropist's sense of duty and care. He made sure each home he built was carefully designed, financed and managed to ensure they remained affordable for those on low incomes, but always offered the tenant a sense that they had moved up in the world, epitomised by the inside loos each home boasted.

Like the chocolate industrialists, the Bournville and Cadbury families, Mactaggart wanted everyone to have not just a decent home but decent community. He insisted on playing fields, gardens and communal areas in his estates. Such was his reach in Scotland that his model would be adopted pretty much wholesale by local authorities during the golden years of council housing.

Mactaggart had many strings to his bow – a dedicated political campaigner on issues of world peace, he was a vocal advocate of the League of Nations. He also was fascinated by the film industry and invested in productions. Aged 60, Mactaggart headed to the USA and became friends with FD Roosevelt, who he advised on housing and the New Deal.

In London, he built housing in Westminster and used the income from the flats to finance other philanthropic schemes. On his death, many were surprised at how little he left in his will – the reason being he had disinvested all his assets and poured them into his housing schemes so they had a secure future – and one such canny investment, made by the charity he established, is Grove End House, whose income supports charities decades after John's passing.

Now to Scott Ellis Gardens. The name comes from the fact it was built on land owned by Lord Howard de Walden, who earned the monarch's favour for his derring-do to defeat the Spanish Armada.

The eighth descendent, Thomas Evelyn Ellis, born in 1880, added Scott to his name, which came from his grandmother's side. Called 'Britain's wealthiest bachelor' by the press in 1901 after inheriting land in Marylebone, Scott-Ellis drove a speedboat in the 1908 Olympics.

A Boer War veteran, he also served in the Royal Tank Corps in the Great War. He fell hard for Welsh culture, and used his money to become a patron of Welsh arts, teaching himself the language.

He wrote books under the name TE Ellis, and was also an inspiration to others: in his 20s, Auguste Rodin sculpted a bust of him. He also collected medieval armour, and the painter

Thomas Evelyn Ellis.

Augustus John recalled visiting Scott-Ellis at his castle in Kilmarnock to find him sitting comfortably in an armchair, puffing on a pipe, reading *The Times* and clad head to foot in armour.

THE STORY OF A HERO

From Scott Ellis Gardens it's a gentle stroll northwards to the quiet garden vibes of Alma Square.

The name immediately tells us a bit about when it was built: the Battle of the Alma, spun as a heroic victory for Allied forces against Russia in the Crimean War, was fought in September 1854. Lord Raglan's troops had forced Prince Menshikov's soldiers from the heights above the Alma River, and reports by the first modern war correspondent William Russell brought news of a victory. Patriotic house builders created a raft of streets in honour.

As the Crown sold off parcels of its land in the 1700s, the successful wine merchant Henry Samuel Eyre saw an opportunity, and snaffled up 500 acres of grassland and farms around St John's Wood. It was on his manor that Alma Square was built.

Alma Square.

Work started in the late 1700s but took time to get going. Land use was for growing crops and animal feed – although less idyllic pursuits were also recorded. In 1806, the Earl of Orford, Horatio Walpole, who had land here, fired off a series of increasingly angry letters to the City of Westminster complaining that a neighbour, John Hill, was not caring properly for his land and had created a stench-making 'soil pit' that had become a dumping ground for 'all sorts of London filth and nastiness'. Hill was also accused of building cottages, which broke the terms of his lease. This patch now houses the famous Abbey Road Studios of Beatles fame.

Soon such open space was gobbled up and by the end of the Georgian period the Eyre estate was laid out. Running alongside Eyre's patch was land owned by Harrow School – and its influence echoes down the street names in the neighbourhood, such as the obvious Harrow Road, and then Abercorn Place and Hamilton Terrace (named after the school's governor, James Hamilton, the 1st Duke of Abercorn).

It is outside No. 20 Hamilton Terrace where we stop and recount a tale of tragedy. It was here, on a cold day in 1841, that a member of the Admiralty ascended the front steps bearing news no spouse wants hear.

No. 20 was home to Captain Richard Drew and family. Hhe was a retired naval officer who was an Elder Brother of Trinity House – a board that oversaw the installation and maintenance of lighthouses and buoys.

We know a little of Drew's background from evidence he gave to a Parliamentary Select Committee investigating which port should become a hub for steam packets bringing mail from the colonies in the Caribbean. He told the MPs, 'I was 14 or 15 years sailing out of Bristol as boy and man, and 10 or 12 years out of London. Since I retired from the sea I have been 15 years at Trinity House. A great portion of my time has been devoted to ascertaining the state of the harbours and the pilotage connected with them.'

He said he felt Dartmouth would be best positioned – but added he had not surveyed the Bristol Channel yet, and so was instructed by MPs to head west and do so.

It was this project that would end disastrously. A report published in the *Colonial Magazine* and *Commercial Maritime Journal* in 1843 reads, 'while engaged on a survey of the Bristol Channel on 4 July, as four of the Elder Brethren of the Trinity House were in their steam packet inspecting the buoys in the Channel, they found it necessary to enter a small attendant boat in the course of their investigation. On their return the steamer cut the boat in two, and all of them were immersed in the water. Two saved themselves by swimming, viz Capts Probyn and Madan, but we regret to say the others, viz Capts Drew and Jenkin perished.'

From here, we move on and turn our attentions to the humble sea squirt. This creature, found in the Coral Sea, was studied by the natural philosopher TH Huxley, who lived in the street that is our next stop, the nearby Marlborough Place. Dubbed Darwin's Bulldog, the biologist is responsible for the term 'agnostic', and his work helped the pursuit of science and reasoning.

Huxley, born in a small flat above a butchers, was the son of a schoolmaster at an evangelical institute. In the 1830s, the family settled in Coventry, and it was here Huxley's world view was forged. Falling in with Dissenters, he threw himself into studying science and religion. It would lead to him spending a life challenging traditional orthodoxy.

In 1847, while sailing with the Royal Navy on a research trip in the Pacific, he noted that the larvae of the sea squirt had tail muscles like a tadpole. With this devastating observation, he extrapolated that they were ancestors of vertebrates – creating another link in the evolutionary chain.

Huxley was full of wisdom and a fair amount of spiky wit: when he was awarded the Gold Medal by the Royal Society of London he complained that 'it is all praise and no pudding', referencing the lack of financial rewards. He also delivered a withering put-down to Samuel Wilberforce, the ultra-conservative Bishop of Oxford, in a debate on evolution at a British Association for the Advancement of Science meeting in a 1860. Wilberforce, playing to the crowd, asked Huxley if apes were on his grandmother's or grandfather's side.

Huxley, quick as a flash and illustrating his anti-clerical and anti-privilege beliefs, responded, 'I would rather have an ape as an ancestor than a wealthy bishop who prostituted his gifts.'

And on that philosophical bombshell, we'll decant to the Blenheim Road home of the celebrated Victorian opera singer Sir Charles Santley.

Described by George Bernard Shaw as possessing a singing voice that was 'humanly speaking, perfect … not a scrape on its fine surface, not a break or a weak link in the chain anywhere; the vocal touch was impeccably light and steady, and the florid execution accurate as clockwork', it is no wonder that Santley's successful singing career stretched over six decades. While known for his role in high culture, Santley recognised the cultural importance of music hall, and would amuse friends by mimicking common-sounding stars such as Marie Lloyd, Harry Champion and George Robey, when he wasn't singing fancy stuff in Italian.

From Santley's place, we head on to Carlton Hill and gaze at the house of sculptor Sir George Frampton. The abode was originally built in 1873. Sir George took it on in 1908, and he wasn't happy with his purchase, describing it as a 'Mid-Victorian suburban house of a commonplace and ugly type'. Being an advocate of the William Morris School of Arts and Crafts, he wanted fresh workmanship to knock it into shape.

Lady Frampton had her own artist's studio built, Frampton designed a fireplace for the sitting room and Morris provided inspiration for the wallpaper. Sir George's studio was described as 'perfectly lighted and of great extent, but with no pretence of adornment ... literally a workshop designed by and for the use of a workman'.

Frampton, who lived there until his death in 1928, created perhaps his most famous sculpture, of Peter Pan for Kensington Gardens, while in Carlton Hill. Decades after his death, another sculptor took on his workspace to create renowned pieces. Arthur Fleischmann moved into the studio in 1948 and it inspired his work in bronze and perspex. His success was such that he was commissioned to create pieces of not one but four popes from Carlton Hill.

HIT IT FOR SIX

These impressive streets were once the haunt of another type of craftsmen – the Warsop family, who were the premier makers of cricket bats in the Victorian era. In 1870, Benjamin Warsop had moved from Nottingham to St John's Wood and with the help of his four sons created the renowned brand that bears the family name.

In 1888 Ben and his family travelled to Essex to cut down a willow that soared over 100ft and had a diameter that was nearly 6ft across. The family would make 1,179 cricket bats from this sole specimen, and Benjamin's craftsmanship was such that, in 1893, WG Grace ordered them to make him a version of their famous Conqueror bat.

Their St John's Wood base had a ground-floor area for the sawing up and treating of willow trunks, while upstairs these materials were fashioned and shaped by hand for players to guard their wicket with.

Demand continued to rise as Warsop won contracts to provide Lord's, test match sides and almost every public school in the country with their polished wooden blades. Such was the Warsops' reputation, they had to be careful about making sure they could source enough quality willow.

In 1909, the workshop was looking for new suppliers – and word got round. They were sent letters from estates, councils and farms across the country, all offering wood, and they gathered enough stock to see them through the years of the Great War.

From this classically English pastime to something more murkily internationalist as we head to Grove End Road. It was from a basement flat here that Edith Tudor-Hart would earn the title of Grandmother of the Cambridge Five.

Born into a socialist family in Austria, Edith moved to London to train as a nursery teacher in the 1920s. She was told to leave the country in 1931 after being spotted at a communist rally. Edith then went to the famous German design school, the Bauhaus, and studied photography, before falling in love with English doctor Alex Tudor-Hart. The pair were forced to leave Austria in 1933 due to her Jewish background and communist sympathies – but it was during this period she began working for the Soviet Union's secret police, the NKVD.

In London, Edith set up a photography studio and her subject matter reflected her political interests – she sought out those who had been hit by the Depression, and highlighted the disasters of capitalism. After she and Dr Tudor-Hart divorced, she lived in her small Grove End Place flat – and it was here she began to cause mischief that would reach the top of the Establishment.

She had met Cambridge spy Kim Philby in Vienna and when he returned to London she introduced him to Arnold Deutsch, an academic who was actually a Soviet agent. Philby was recruited on Edith's say-so – and declassified KGB files describe how Edith and Philby walked from her home to a rendezvous in Regent's Park with Deutsch for the first time, taking a zig-zag route to throw off any tails. MI5 rumbled her, and in 1952 they raided her flat and quizzed her for forty-eight hours. They bugged her home and followed her around but the only misdemeanour they could pin on her was not paying a bus fare. Despite being uncovered eventually, Edith was never prosecuted and retired to Brighton to open an antique shop.

And on that slightly Lovejoy-like note, we shall head in a southerly direction. Our first stop is in Lisson Grove, a thoroughfare that has a long and distinguished connection to those with an artistic bent.

Let us stop outside the Gateway Academy, a red-brick, London County Council building that in the 1940s and '50s was known as Regent's Park Central Secondary School, which specialised in teaching typing and shorthand. It sits on the corner of Frampton Street, named after the sculptor George Frampton. And Frampton is not the only arty type recognised by local place names.

After the First World War, when David Lloyd George pledged to build 'Homes fit for heroes', the Lisson Grove area got its fair share. St Marylebone Council built a series of blocks known as the Fisherton Street estate, and all commemorate the area's great and good who made their names with brushes and chisels.

There is Gibbons House, named after Grinling Gibbons, a Dutch wood carver who worked on St Paul's with Sir Christopher Wren. Eastlake House marks the life of Charles Eastlake, a celebrated Victorian furniture maker, while Poynter House is named after the Royal Academy President Sir Edward Poynter, who specialised in grand historical dramas in oil. It was also the haunt of Sir Edwin Landseer, who sculpted Trafalgar Square's lions, so the council plumped for a block with his moniker, too.

From here we head down the road a little and to our left see a more recent social housing project known as the Lilestone Street estate. Let us look past these 1970s blocks and consider the Great Central Railway Company's Marylebone Goods Terminus, which was built on this site in 1899 and, it seems incredible today, in doing so caused the demolition of two Nash terraces. Less celebrated homes were also swept away to clear the 51 acres for the railways: 4,448 houses deemed 'labouring classes' dwellings' were dealt with by the wrecker's ball.

The GCR installed a steam crane for lifting goods from barges on the Regent's Canal and for a few decades it became a major interchange, providing thousands of jobs for railwaymen and stores' clerks. There were sidings and train sheds, goods warehouses and associated industrial gubbins. The yard also once boasted four bridges across the canal – and one still remains for pedestrians, at Paveley Street, and it is to this little bridge we now turn our attention.

At first glance it seems a strange place for such a span, heading from nowhere in particular to nowhere else. But the answer as to why it appears here casts light on the battle for transport custom in the Victorian period.

As the railways made their sooty way across the UK, canal owners were rightly concerned as trade moved from serene waterborne haulage to the noisy, messy and very fast railway tracks. Some operators saw the writing on the towpath, as it were, and sold off their canals for conversion into railway routes. Others decided to switch to rail for their transport businesses. But the firm who owned the Regent's Canal decided a hybrid was the answer. They created a subsidiary, the Regent's Canal, City and Docklands Railway, and designed a scheme that would see them build a 16-mile railway from Royal Oak to Limehouse. They built four bridges to carry sixteen new canalside tracks, but the plans were never finished.

However, our bridge was not going to be totally useless. Instead, up stepped inventor, entrepreneur and monorail pioneer, Fritz Bernard Behr. The son of a German doctor, he had been decorated in the Franco-German War of 1870.

Behr settled in England, became naturalised – and then turned his talent to designing high-speed, electrified monorails. His first project was to build an experimental version through Westminster in 1886 and it impressed industrialists enough for the Thames Ironworks and Shipbuilding Company to make one of their own.

Word spread: Behr built a 3-mile monorail in Belgium for the Brussels International Exhibition of 1897 and then, at the turn of the twentieth century, headed to New York with plans to create a line from Brooklyn's South Ferry terminus out to Coney Island.

He told investors his carriages would reach top speeds of 100mph, with passengers paying a fare of 5 cents for the pleasure. Sadly for Behr – and New Yorkers wanting such a new-fangled way of getting about – the grubby hands of the money men got in the way. The city's transport commissioners demanded a non-refundable $25,000 deposit to consider the scheme, and then caused a scandal by privately investing in firms to which they would then award contracts.

Meanwhile, back on this side of the pond, Behr got an Act of Parliament passed to allow him to build a monorail linking Manchester and Liverpool at speeds of 110mph, while also working smaller, less speedy schemes, such as plans for a funicular rail up a steep slope on the Isle of Wight.

In 1903, Behr's firm, the Listowel and Ballybunion Railway, drew up a route called the North Metropolitan and Regent's Canal Monorail System. It would have seen a monorail run along the waterway, and the Paveley Street bridge now used for walkers was retained as it was due to be the starting point for the scheme.

By 1965, Dr Richard Beeching's sharpened axe hung over the depot and with a wave of his red pen the entire GCR line was scrapped. The depot lay silent for a few years, and then Westminster Council began their plans to use the land for new housing, creating the estates that sit there today.

PUT YOUR DAUGHTER
ON THE STAGE,
MR SIDDONS

O ur next port of call is at the Grove's southern end, where we pause outside the red-brick Gothic façade of the Philological School, originally established in 1792 in Fitzroy Square by Oxford don Thomas Collingwood.

The school aimed to provide education to forty pupils, with its founding statement declaring, 'Education is here afforded, almost free of cost, to a certain number of boys, the sons of professional gentlemen, who have suffered under the blows of fortune.' It offered a career route – ten pupils would be prepared for work in government, another ten earmarked for the navy and twenty given a grounding in mechanics.

After early successes, a series of poor headteachers and financial decisions meant by 1800 they were in debt to the tune of £1,000. One new governor, coming in to help sort the mess out, was the Abolitionist MP William Wilberforce, who also happened to own a farm in St John's Wood.

In the coming decades, the school would move to the corner of Lisson Grove and Marylebone Road on Wilberforce's land, and appoint a headteacher who would catch the eye of both George IV and the Duke of Wellington for his talent and charisma. His name was Edwin Abbott and, remarkably, when appointed, he was 19 years old. A former pupil at the school, he would stay in the role for the next forty-five years.

Now we shimmy slightly east, and duck down a little street called Siddons Lane, which honours the Georgian actor Sarah Siddons. She lived in nearby Upper Baker Street and her home, marked by a plaque, still has remnants of her time there. A stained glass window she installed has images of Shakespeare, Milton, Spenser, Cowley and Dryden.

She was feted and lauded, a true Georgian stage celebrity. Journalist and wine writer Cyrus Redding, who edited a number of renowned regional newspapers and London magazines, wrote, 'My very first sight of

Sarah Siddons.

Mrs Siddons was in Queen Catherine. Never did I behold anything more striking than the acting of that wonderful woman; for, no heroine off the boards, she was the ideal of heroic majesty in her personations. I have seen real kings and queens, for the most part ordinary people, and some not very dignified, but in Siddons there was the poetry of royalty.

'In Lady Macbeth she made the beholders shiver; a thrill of horror seemed to run through the house; the audience – thousands in number, for every seat was filled – the audience was fearstricken.'

Hilariously, she was told by her father she must never marry another actor, but did so all the same: when confronted with this by the head of the theatre company she and her secret husband were part of, the following set-to played out:

'Have I not,' he shrieked, 'dared you to marry a player?'

Mrs Siddons is reported to have replied, with tear-filled eyes, she had not disobeyed her father's wishes.

'What! madam, have you not allied yourself to about the worst performer in my company?'

'Exactly so,' she responded. 'Nobody can call him an actor.'

Ouch.

Let's carefully cross Marylebone Road once more, and opposite the beginning of Lisson Grove we note the house that was once known as a pub called the Yorkshire Stingo. It's noted in London history as being the place the first London bus departed from, on 4 July 1829, run by George Shillibeer.

Shillibeer, who had already tested his public transport idea out successfully in Paris, used six horses to pull the double-decker. He ran a service to Bank, with a ticket costing a shilling with a newspaper thrown in. His first conductors were sons of a naval officer, who he believed had the proper bearing and gait to collect fares.

THE MARYLEBONE CAKE

Now we pause briefly at a place of fun the Shillibeer omnibuses would have trotted past – Marylebone Gardens.

On land that once housed a hunting lodge for Henry VIII, the gardens were situated next door to the Rose of Normandy tavern; inside was a fruit orchard, and at its a centre an oval bowling green. The gardens were a popular place to escape the bustle of the metropolis, for lovers to hold hands under blossoming trees.

Less savoury events were held here, too: gamblers laid wagers on cock-fighting, male and female bare-knuckle bouts, and bull-baiting. Its reputation was such that it becomes the haunt of highwayman Macheath in John Gay's *The Beggar's Opera*, who tells a henchman that big bets would be laid at the gardens, and so he will keep an eye out for those who have laden purses, and mug them as they leave with their winnings.

By 1738 a new landlord, Daniel Gough, took on the Rose and decided to improve its offerings by installing an organ and hosting concerts. He charged six pence on the door to raise the class of attendees and offered silver-plated season tickets. Food was served, his daughter becoming known for what was called the Marylebone Cake.

An advert of 1760, published in a local Westminster newspaper, read, 'Tarts of a Twelve penny size will be made every day from one to three o'clock. The Almond cheesecake will always be hot at one o'clock, as usual ...'

George Frederic Handel and James Hook performed in the gardens, and its musical links continued right up until 2009. The Rose became a music hall in the Victorian period and then the studios for BBC Radio London.

QUACK, QUACK, QUACK

And on that whimsically musical note, we leave Marylebone Gardens, and as we are near Harley Street, let us have a peek at the road synonymous with the medical profession.

We gaze at No. 48, the home to the fragrantly named John St John Long, who earned notoriety as a quack of the highest order. Hailing from Cork, Ireland, he came to London in 1822 to learn the art of landscape painting under the tutelage of the celebrated artist John Martin.

Good looking and charming, Long ingratiated himself into society circles and Georgian London took a shine to him. He was not talented or lucky enough to make a really good living from his paintbrush, although he enjoyed some success with biblical scenes.

In 1827, he used the anatomy lessons gleaned from life-drawing classes to set up shop in Harley Street as a doctor. He soon had a parade of rich clients enjoying his company and cures that included the bold claim he could tackle TB. Using 'vapour treatments' and rubbing home-made tinctures into the skin, Long's lack of scientific knowledge was quickly exposed by doctors. But it didn't stop him duping the naïve – and with deadly consequences.

In 1830, the police were alerted when a well-heeled country gentlewoman, Mrs Cashin, came to them with the tragic news that her daughter had died – and she believed mistreatment at the hands of Long was to blame.

Long was nothing if not imaginative: he treated Miss Cashin by slapping a gooey mess made up of egg yolks, vinegar and turpentine over her body, telling her it would blister the skin and tease the infection in her lungs to the surface. He told her to cover her skin with cold cabbage leaves to soothe the blistering, and after emptying her purse, sent her on her way. Miss Cashin died a few a days later in extreme pain.

Tried at the Old Bailey, and convicted of manslaughter, he was given a £250 fine – which he paid in cash on the spot – and carried on his trickery. Thankfully, the medical profession made sure his behaviour was made public, and *The Lancet* exposed him. One morning, three years later, Long woke up with a tickly cough. It got worse. He discovered blood on a hanky. Aged 36, Long caught tuberculosis and died a few months later.

Buried in Highgate Cemetery, his grandiose resting place was paid for by patients who believed he had cured them, and the following words were etched on the tomb: 'It is the fate of most men to have many enemies, and few friends. This monumental pile is not intended to mark the career but to show how much its inhabitant was respected by those who knew his worth and the benefits derived from his remedial discovery. He is now at rest and far beyond the praises or censures of this world.'

Joseph Lister.

Now, from a Victorian charlatan, to a nineteenth-century medic who changed the world. Eastwards from Harley Street we reach Portman Place, and here we can gaze on the bronze bust of Joseph Lister.

Lister is the father of modern surgery, and his work has saved the lives of millions of people. Born to a Quaker family, his father spent thirty years perfecting a microscope. Joseph inherited his dad's wits. Working as a surgeon at the Glasgow Royal Infirmary, Lister's enquiring mind hit upon a wheeze that revolutionised the discipline.

He had noted how when fields were sprayed with silage, farmers would treat it with carbolic acid. He noted it got rid of the stench of sewage – and that it was obviously safe to ingest, as the farm's livestock suffered no ill effects.

He began using it as an antiseptic on both wounds and equipment, and what do you know, infections and deaths caused by surgery bottomed out. Death rates plummeted and the modern era of medicine began.

FOUR WHEELS GOOD

Now, for our final pub on this long old walk – The Coach Makers Arms in Marylebone Lane. Why the name, you ask, as we wait for our pints.

This neck of the woods was renowned for some of the biggest innovators in coachbuilding down the centuries, and this historic pub had a number of celebrated coach companies all within walking distance.

There were the Peters, a family firm based in George Street, who designed vehicles for the postal network with extra tough wheels to deal with the terrible roads. Coachbuilding innovator David Davies set up shop in nearby Wigmore Street, and it was here in 1834 he came up with a design known as the Pilentum phaeton.

It was the Georgian equivalent of a convertible car, with a soft-top roof that could be tucked away or extended. It had a low-slung passenger section allowing for easy access – previously, carriages would boast a stepladder to get passengers in and out. It came in different lengths, could be driven by one or two horses, and soon its design had spread across Europe. By the 1850s, Davies's designs had been adopted by the hackney carriage builders – making him the great-great-grandfather of today's black cabs.

And it is on that note we cross over to the Wallace Collection, our final stop on our journey. This is where we started our travels, admiring the fact they had more than 800 items with images of dogs on them.

The collection is now open for you to see for yourself, so pop in and have a look.